DIGITAL VS HUMAN

Richard Watson works with the Foresight Practice at Imperial College London and regularly lectures at London Business School. He is the author of *Future Files*, which has been published in 15 languages, and the publisher of *What's Next*, an online report that documents new ideas and trends.

www.nowandnext.com

*For Anne, aged 89, who found herself
swimming against the current*

DIGITAL
VS
HUMAN

how we'll live, love,
and think in the future

RICHARD WATSON

SCRIBE
Melbourne • London

Scribe Publications
18–20 Edward St, Brunswick, Victoria 3056, Australia
2 John Street, London, WC1N 2ES, United Kingdom

First published by Scribe 2016

Typeset in Adobe Caslon Pro 12/16 pt by the publishers

Printed and bound in the UK by CPI Group (UK) Ltd, Croydon CR0 4YY

9781925321173 (Australian edition)
9781925228427 (UK edition)
9781925307283 (e-book)

CiP entries for this title are available from the National Library of Australia and the British Library

scribepublications.com.au
scribepublications.co.uk

The real problem of humanity is the following: we have palaeolithic emotions; medieval institutions; and god-like technology. And it is terrifically dangerous, and it is now approaching a point of crisis overall.

EDWARD O. WILSON

Anything that gets invented after you're thirty is against the natural order of things and the beginning of the end of civilisation as we know it until it's been around for about ten years when it gradually turns out to be alright really.

DOUGLAS ADAMS

Qui vivra verra.
(Who lives will see.)

CONTENTS

TAMING THE FUTURE

Everybody has a plan until they get punched in the face.
Mike Tyson

The future casts a long shadow — in my case, way back to Australia in 2006 when I was asked to write a book called *Future Files* about where I thought the world was heading over the next 50 years. But the future was always an excuse, used more as a distorting mirror than a crystal ball. What I was interested in then, and remain interested in today, is people and how they respond to new ideas and events.

Also, how we relate and respond to *each other*, which is what this book is about. It is people's lives, their deepest dreams, what they believe in, and what they are most afraid of that captivates me, not the latest ephemeral gadget or app, although these things can, and do, influence us, too.

Future Files must have hit a nerve, because the book ended up being published in 15 languages. One reason was timing — there hadn't been a book about the distant future for a very long time. But I was also lucky with my thinking. I wrote then that debt levels were unsustainable and that a systemic shock to the financial system was inevitable. This was 'not a debt mountain; it's an avalanche waiting to descend ... Big banks, in particular, will come under increasing scrutiny about their lending practices, and there will be calls for salary and profit caps ...'

There's nothing like a page of prophecy to sell some books, although I'm still waiting patiently for the European Union to 'splinter and ultimately collapse', and for the day when 'women with facial lines will be highly desirable'. It seems that I made the mistake of thinking we'd tire of forced unions and pixelated perfection, but evidently we haven't. Nor have we grown tired of debt — in which case, I suspect that history will soon repeat itself, in the form of another major financial crash.

But the main reason the book sold well was due to an emerging epidemic of anxiety and insecurity. The world was changing, and readers were seeking a narrative that explained where things were going. The book provided a comforting cloak of reassurance to those grieving the loss of an imagined future.

The distant future had once been hopeful and at times rather fun. It had been a preview of coming attractions. But by late 2007, people had given up hope of seeing flying cars or owning personal jetpacks. All anyone wanted to know was whether everything would turn out alright. Would there be a comforting resolution after the explosive opening sequence? Would computer-generated special effects continue to enthral us, or would the computer move from all-conquering hero to sinister villain lurking behind our flickering screens?

This dystopian discomfort was likely linked to a feeling that things had got out of control. Events were unfolding too fast for most people to comprehend. Gone were the days when you could start a broken-down car by yourself or understand how a camera worked. Even by 2007, it wasn't just credit default swaps or 'additionality' linked to carbon credits that were baffling — you almost needed a degree in complex-systems theory simply to switch on a domestic washing machine. Seriously, do we really need 40-plus washing choices, including the incomprehensible option to wash your clothes later?

Complexity, synonymous in engineering terms with instability, had become a hallmark of the early 21st century, and the world's axis had shifted towards the outskirts of normal. This was unsettling, especially to anyone brought up in an analog, Western-centric world where globalisation had meant Americanisation and *cheap* washing machines.

There have always been generational waves of future fatigue. Permit me to restate in full the observation by Douglas Adams:

> Everything that's already in the world when you're born is just normal; anything that gets invented between then and before you turn thirty is incredibly exciting and creative; anything that gets invented after you're thirty is against the natural order of things and the beginning of the end of civilisation as we know it until it's been around for about ten years when it gradually turns out to be alright really.

Yet this time, the dismay was different. Sometime after the Millennium (probably after the explosive events of 9/11 or, slightly earlier, after the premature death of Douglas Adams), the future became obscured. The dream that we once called 'the future' soured, and its shadow became awkward and indistinct. But even then, this wasn't true for everyone. How one imagines and responds to the future has always depended on who and where you are. The future is always a mental construct generally projected from things that have been recently experienced.

In large parts of Asia and Africa, rapidly rising incomes and opportunities meant that optimism was in the ascendant, while across swathes of the United States and Europe, declining real incomes meant that it was doom and gloom that was often projected forwards. Nevertheless, by 2008 the US financial crisis that had started with people lending and borrowing too much money had become a global problem, creating a vortex into which many age-old certainties were sucked.

If we had been able to better remember the past and not overreact to the present, we might have been alright. If the crisis had occurred much earlier, ignorance may have remained bliss. There was once less information, and both people and money were less connected, which meant fewer systemic risks.

A study conducted by Angelika Dimoka, director of the Centre for Neural Decision Making at Temple University in the US, found that as information is increased, so too is activity in the dorsolateral prefrontal cortex, a region of the brain associated with decision-making and the control of emotions. Yet eventually, activity in this region falls off. The reason for this is that part of our brain has essentially left the building. When incoming information reaches a tipping point, the brain protects itself by shutting down certain functions. Key outcomes include a tendency for anxiety and stress levels to soar and for people to abstain from making important decisions.

Fast-forward a few years, and some e-vangelists started looking at the world through Google Glass and other augmented-reality devices. Meanwhile, others, a majority perhaps, put on rose-tinted spectacles and framed their gaze firmly backwards. On the fringes, some squinted scornfully and aspired toward self-loathing and obliteration. Yet others suggested that the very idea of human progress had become impoverished. Maybe they had a point, but there was no redemptive framework in sight.

What this amounts to is a clash between those racing toward the future and others fleeing from it. A similar tension between faith and scepticism plays out between Islamic fundamentalism and liberal agnosticism. Some fundamentalists would like to reinstate a seventh-century legal framework, while many online libertarians would like to escape legal constraints altogether.

Western self-loathing remains an especially odd development. On most measures that matter — life expectancy, infant mortality, literacy, extreme poverty, hunger, the number of women in education and employment — life has never been better for most people on the planet. If you doubt this, you have clearly not been paying attention.

But despite the good news about the expansion of the global middle class, the electrification of Africa, or survival rates for cancer, we focus instead on doomsday forecasts about rogue asteroids, global pandemics, and employment-eating robots. These — along with climate change, obesity, resource depletion, falling biodiversity, bioterrorism, and pollution — are serious problems, but I'd suggest that they are generally focal points for deeper anxieties and are unlikely to be terminal for the human race.

So why are we feeling so miserable when there's so little to feel miserable about?

Prior to 9/11 (or the fall of the Berlin Wall in 1989 or the financial crisis of 2008 or … take your pick), people believed that they had a clear view of what lay ahead. With 20/20 hindsight, it's clear that such views were delusional. Yet the detail was irrelevant. At least people had a sense of direction, from which they could construct a narrative to make sense of things. For many people, life was hard, but they knew where they stood, which is why countries such as Russia now long to go backwards and reconstruct previous certainties along with territorial borders.

Today, many people feel that the future has evaporated or they are being held hostage by some unknowable and uncontrollable force. This is, however, nonsense. Firstly, certain elements of the future are predetermined. Demographics retain a high degree of certainty, while geography and geology impose a number of constraints. Parts of the future can therefore be found on the flood plains and tributaries of history. Secondly, the collective psychology of nations, influenced again by the past, can suggest a sense of direction.

Thirdly, there's technology. It's true that technology is neutral — but only if you take humans out of the equation. It is the nexus of human history, human nature, and what many regard as increasingly inhuman technologies where I'd expect the largest tensions to bubble up over the years ahead, especially as we struggle to adapt our slowly evolving monkey brains to the rapidly changing technological landscape.

These thoughts were on my radar in 2006 when I wrote that 'to a large degree, the history of the next 50 years will be about the relationship between technology and people', yet I now believe that I underplayed the significance of this statement.

This is odd, because it's a point well made by Alvin and Heidi Toffler in *Future Shock*, published in 1970, of which I have a well-thumbed copy. Their book argued that the *perception* of too much change over too short a period of time would create psychological problems and mental instability at both an individual and a societal level.

You might argue that they were wrong (it didn't happen), or that they were right but that they got their timing very wrong (futurologists often use the line 'give it time' in relation to suspect forecasts). One might also speculate about who gets listened to and what gets believed and why, however this isn't the time or place.

Personally, I think that the Tofflers anticipated something of significance, and if my book has a dramatic chase scene, this is it — our desire for change and renewal crashing up against our need for permanence and stability. Will we be forced to adapt to new technologies and global norms, or will we insist that new technologies adapt to us, deleting, controlling, and escaping from them as necessary?

How, for instance, should technology serve humanity, and

what, ultimately, is its purpose? Should all forms of automation and artificial intelligence (AI) be made to exist within an agreed moral framework, and where, if anywhere, should the line be drawn in relation to what humans and machines are permitted to do? Should humans and machines be allowed to merge, creating augmented, partially synthetic, or cybernetically hybridised humans, and, if so, where would this leave any remaining unchanged homo sapiens?

Whatever happens, we should never lose faith, because the future is always wide open. The future is shaped by the choices that we make, and these choices can always be challenged and changed, even at the last minute.

In one sense, the problem we currently face is not technology, it's humans — but more about us later. One thing we should certainly do is worry less about what might happen over the coming decades and focus far more on what it is that we, as individuals and institutions, want to happen. And it isn't necessarily logic that will help us to shape this. Rather, it will be our deepest hopes and our darkest fears.

The aim of this book is not precise prediction, but rough illustration. It is a critique of how we live now and a discussion about how we might wish to live next. It is about who we are and where we are going and about the need for human beings to remain central to any new digital interests or perspectives.

Hopefully, the shadow cast by the future will henceforth be our own and will provide a degree of comfort rather than bewilderment.

SOCIETY AND CULTURE

how we came to love our machines
more than each other

Computers make it easier to do a lot of things, but most of
the things they make it easier to do don't need to be done.

Andy Rooney

A few years ago, I had a delicious discussion with Lavie Tidhar,
a science fiction writer, about the meaning of the word 'future'.
Was there, for the practical purpose of writing, a point at which
the future was clearly delineated from the present? How far into
the future need a writer travel to separate fragile fantasy from
rigorous reality? For him, the future is when things 'start to get
weird'. For me, it's when fact becomes more fantastic than fiction.

I was living in Australia when news flashed through that Kim
Yoo-chul and Choi Mi-sun, a couple who had met online, had
allowed their baby daughter to starve to death. They had become
obsessed with raising an avatar child in a virtual world called
Prius Online — their virtual baby was apparently more satisfying
than their real-life one. According to police reports, the pair, both
unemployed, left their real daughter at home, alone, while they
spent 12-hour sessions caring for their digital daughter, cutely
named Anima, from a cyber cafe in Seoul.

It's easy to dismiss this story as being about people taking their love of computer games too far. But this reading of the tale as a kind of teary technological fable could be more misleading than we imagine. A more careful reading would see that it's about identity, purpose, and intimacy in an age of super-smart, emotionally programmed machines. It is also about social interaction, addiction, displacement, and how some people can only deal with so much reality. Most of all, it's about how our ancient brains are not well equipped to distinguish between real relationships and para-social, or imagined, ones.

Seoul itself is fascinating because it gives us an indication as to where the rest of the world may be heading. Being the most wired city on Earth, it has a veneer of the future, but deeper down it is stuck in the 1950s. The country has the fastest average broadband speeds in the world, and there are plans for a 5G network that will make things 1,000 times faster. On the other hand, you need a government-issued identity number to use the internet in Starbucks, and censors cut out chunks of content from the internet each week.

It's possible that more governments will seek to limit what people can access online, and that the open, participatory, and libertarian nature of the internet will be tamed via censorship and regulation. But it's equally possible that weakly regulated companies will create virtual experiences so compelling that people withdraw from meaningful relationships with other humans and no longer profitably participate in society.

Some screen-based gambling machines are already designed to monitor how people play and to deliberately attack human vulnerabilities so that users will gamble for as long as possible. The aim, in industry parlance, is to make people play to extinction. In the case of Kim Yoo-chul and Choi Mi-sun, this is exactly what happened.

More or less human

South Korea's neighbour Japan is another country where the past competes head-on with the future. Ancient cherry-blossom festivals exist alongside robots in kindergartens and care homes. This automation fills the gaps where demographics, community, and compassion have fallen short.

One such robot is Paro, a therapeutic care-bot in the form of a furry seal. The aim is companionship, and the seal modifies its behaviour according to the nature of human interaction.

Used alongside human care, Paro is a marvellous idea. There are tug robots that autonomously move heavy hospital trolleys around, too. These save hospital porters from back injuries, but being faceless and limbless they aren't especially charismatic. They don't smile or say hello to patients either, although they could be made to do so. Looked at this way, both are examples of technology reducing our humanity. What's needed is not more efficiency-sparking electronics, but more human kindness and compassion.

Sherry Turkle, a professor of the social studies of science and technology at MIT, believes that it's dangerous to foster relationships with machines. She says there's 'no upside to being socialised by a robot'. Vulnerable groups such as children and the elderly will bond with a robot as if it were human, creating attachment and unreasonable expectations. Her unsettling conclusion is that we 'seem to have embraced a new kind of delusion that accepts the simulation of compassion as sufficient'. The subtitle of her book *Alone Together* says it all: *why we expect more from technology and less from each other*.

In some ways, creating a caring robot is more of an intellectual or scientific challenge than a practical necessity. But if there are people who cannot relate to others, who don't mind or even prefer sharing life with a robot, perhaps there is some benefit, as anyone who has watched the science fiction film *Bicentennial Man* might attest. Maybe physical presence and human contact don't matter, or they matter much less than we currently think.

Eventually, we will create robots and other machines that become our close friends by simulating reciprocity and personality. We will probably program fallibility, too. And perhaps we won't mind that these traits aren't authentic.

We do not currently seem to care that much of what we readily accept about other people online is an edit of reality. The digital identities and narratives we weave rarely include elements of fear, doubt, or vulnerability. We photoshop ourselves to appear happier, prettier, and more successful than we really are, because we favour pixelated perfection, not analog ambiguity. (The daily news is a similar edit of reality, also opposed to ambiguity, but tends to operate in the opposite direction, generally exaggerating human misery and conflict while ignoring humility and happiness.)

But before we build emotional relationships with machines, shouldn't we be asking ourselves what we might be doing this for? Shouldn't we be delving into debates about what it means to be human, and then measure whether new technologies have a positive or negative impact? Technology, after all, is an enabler, not an end in itself. This doesn't mean travelling backwards, however it does mean that technologists should sit alongside philosophers, historians, and ethicists. We need wisdom alongside knowledge, a moral code alongside the computer code.

Looking back at the origins of modern machines, the purpose of technology was either to do something that humans couldn't do or to remove human drudgery. The word 'robot' comes from the Czech word 'robota', meaning 'forced labour'. Using machines to replace people in dull or dangerous jobs is entirely reasonable. Using machines to enhance human interactions and relationships is sensible, too. But I suspect that in many instances, the aim nowadays is simply to reduce human costs, and we accept this because we're told that it's efficient or because we're given no choice.

As to what the human costs might be in a broad societal sense, this isn't accounted for. The dominant narrative of the early 21st century is therefore machine-centric. It is machines — not people — that are revered, when surely it should be the reverse.

I was watching a BBC television programme recently, and there was a report about a study by Oxford University, saying that around half of current occupational categories may be lost to automation over the next 20 years. This won't be a problem if new and better jobs are created, which is what's happened historically. The industrial revolution destroyed many professions, but created others, increased wages, and ushered in a new era of productivity and prosperity. Yet the internet could be doing the total opposite. According to the computer scientist and author Jaron Lanier, the internet is destroying more jobs and prosperity than it's creating. Amazon might be one example of such destruction; others can be found in industries ranging from music and photography to newspapers and hotels.

What's interesting is how fatalistic most people are about this. One person interviewed by the BBC commented: 'It's just progress, I guess.' But progress towards what?

The illusion of progress

Looked at with a long lens, progress does appear to be on a sharp upward curve, yet this is partly an illusion of perspective. Using a magnifying glass, the curve fragments into a series of advances, frantic retreats, and further advances. Robert Gordon, a professor of macro-economics at Northwestern University in America, claims that many of our so-called revolutionary technologies are nothing of the sort. The impact of older technologies such as running water, sewerage, electricity, automobiles, railways, postage stamps, and telephones was far greater than any of the digital technologies we have today. The internet, as technology writer Evgeny Morozov summarises, is 'amazing in the same way a dishwasher is amazing'. One anonymous wag appears to agree, claiming San Francisco–based 'tech culture is focused on solving one problem: what is my mother no longer doing for me?'

By and large, digital technologies represent incremental change. Above all, they are symbolic of our quest for convenience and efficiency.

Nevertheless, there are some who worship at the shrine of such progress. Martha Lane Fox, a founder of lastminute.com, argues that anyone who is against the digital revolution is a heretic. There are no excuses — everyone must be online. Those who resist, regardless of age, must be given a 'gentle nudge' because being offline is 'not good enough'.

Fox appears to equate any digital resistance to that of the Luddites. But what she might be missing — as Andrew Keen, author of *The Internet is Not the Answer*, points out — is that while the internet does indeed liberate, inform, and empower, there's a danger of being fooled again. Our new boss is the same as our old boss: 'The error that evangelists make is to assume that the internet's open, decentralised technology naturally translates into a less hierarchical or unequal society.'

Moreover, what are the consequences if individuals no longer interact with other human beings as much as they once did, and what might happen if people are replaced with unseen machines in a growing number of roles and relationships?

Is it a problem, for instance, that four-year-old children are having therapy for compulsive behaviour concerning iPhones, or that training potties can now be bought with iPad stands? Would it be acceptable for robots to raise children or for a closure avatar to be the last face that an individual sees before they die — and if not, why not? Will we be forced to get used to such things, or will we fight back, redefining progress and dismantling this dystopia with a simple screwdriver?

For me, the relationship and balance of power between humans and machines is a fundamental one for both current and future generations to figure out. So why is there so much silence? Perhaps it's because most of us are tethered to mobile devices that constantly distract us and prevent us from thinking deeply about the impact of these technologies.

Information is now captured and disseminated 24/7, so there's little time to clear one's head. Or perhaps we prefer to be busy, because slowing down and reflecting about who we are and where we're going — or whether we're achieving anything of enduring substance — is too terrifying to think about.

Me, my selfie, and I

I was in a coffee shop recently, although it was more of a temporary workspace and substance-abuse centre than a cafe. Power cables were strewn across the floor, and almost everyone in the cafe was on a mobile device — unable, it seemed, to be alone with their thoughts or without caffeine for more than 60 seconds. People's personal communications appeared to be thwarting personal communication. These people clearly had hundreds of digital friends, but they were absorbed with their own tiny screens in the company of real individuals, all of whom had been abandoned.

The cafe was full, but people were texting, not talking. Consequently, there was no noise. No chatter. No laughter. The atmosphere was both vacuous and urgent, which was an odd combination.

Were these neurotically self-aware people really thinking? Were they feeling the sensation of time slowly pressing against their skin? Not as far as I could tell. They were writing pointless PowerPoint presentations, were glued to Facebook and Twitter, or were sending desolate photographs of their over-sized biscuits to their acquaintances on Snapchat and Instagram. Most seemed set on broadcast rather than receive, and were engaged in what the informed and bewildered writer Christopher Lasch once described as 'transcendental self-attention'.

This was the same month that Russian separatists had shot down a passenger plane, Syria was soaked in blood, and Palestine and Israel were throwing retributions at each other.

A while earlier, articles had appeared questioning the digital revolution that wasn't, especially the way in which the lethargy of productivity growth in the US appeared to coincide with the widespread adoption of personal computing. As the American economist Robert Solow commented, computers were everywhere except in the numbers.

There was clearly much to discuss. I felt like standing up and shouting, 'I'm mad as hell, and I'm not going to take this anymore', but the film reference would have been lost among the ubiquitous network coverage.

Perhaps this inward focus explains how we are outraged by a South Korean couple starving their daughter to death one minute and then forget about them the next. Our memory erased by the mundane minutiae of our daily digital existence.

Another reason we might not be asking deep questions about why we're here and what we're for — and how technology might fit into the equation — could be that many of the people pushing these new communication technologies are on the autistic spectrum and, paradoxically, have problems communicating with and relating to other people. As the novelist Douglas Coupland comments in *Microserfs*: 'I think all tech people are slightly autistic.' The reason that so many silicon dreamers want to lose contact with their physical selves and escape into a shining silver future might be that, due to their meticulous minds, their burdensome bodies have never been wanted. This dichotomy between autistic technologists and everyone else is reminiscent of *The Two Cultures* by C.P. Snow. A scientist and novelist himself, Snow described in 1959 how the split between the exact sciences and the humanities was a major encumbrance to solving many of the world's most pressing problems.

Or perhaps the whole human race is becoming somewhat autistic, preferring to live largely alone, interacting only reluctantly and awkwardly with others. One thing I have certainly observed first-hand is the way in which an increasing number of people are finding real-life interactions onerous — not only in Silicon Valley, Tokyo, and Seoul, but elsewhere, too. Carbon-based bipeds have illogical needs, and our impulses can be a source of irritation to others.

Human beings are therefore best dealt with through digital filters or avoided altogether. If you doubt this, and you have a spare teenager to hand, try phoning them without warning. This doesn't always work — often because they won't answer your call — but if you do get through, the immediacy of a phone call can be unsettling. A phone call is in real time. It demands an instant reaction and cannot be photoshopped or crowdsourced to ensure an optimum result.

Better still, see what happens when the teenager's phone is lost or withdrawn for 24 hours. It's as though their identity has collapsed, which in some ways it has. As British scientist, writer, and broadcaster Susan Greenfield points out, 'Personal identity is increasingly defined by the approbation of a virtual audience.' Staying connected is also about protection: when a teenager isn't online, they are unable to manage what others are saying about them. None of this is a criticism of younger people. It is merely to say that they could be a harbinger of things to come — and according to some observers, the American psychologist Susan Pinker for instance, technology is pushing humanity towards crisis point.

Yet the success of mobiles and social media is no surprise given how difficult we've made it for younger people to get together in the real world. Yes, there are questions around exhibitionism, narcissism, and hatred online, and as George Zarkadakis, a computer scientist and science writer, has shown, 'social networks erode previous social structures and reintroduce tribalism into our post-industrial societies'. But in my experience, social networks also fulfil a basic need for friendship and human contact.

We've convinced ourselves that the real world is full of physical dangers, especially for children. So while we protest about children being addicted to screens, we are reluctant to let them out of our sight outside unless they are tethered to a mobile device or wearing clothing that emits a tracking signal.

How long, one wonders, before parents program drones with cameras to hover above their children's heads when they are outside or on their own. In this context, it's easy to see how social media is a direct reaction to parental paranoia.

Of course, what we don't realise is that incorrect assessments of risk might be destroying the one thing we value above all else. The emotional shorthand of the digital world could be diminishing human relationships, as might our lack of presence, even when someone is sitting right next to us.

I, too, can feel uncomfortable in the presence of others, but a coffee shop full of people who are physically in attendance yet mentally elsewhere is worse. As the philosopher Alain de Botton has said, it's not so much people's absence nowadays that hurts as much as people's indifference to their absence.

With well over a billion people on Facebook, you might think that friendship would be suffering from oversupply. But according to the US General Social Survey, it's not. Between 1985 and 2004, the average number of close friends (people you can really rely on in a crisis) per person fell from 2.94 to 2.08, while the number of people with no such friends increased from 8 per cent to 23 per cent. This finding has been criticised, yet other surveys have similarly linked rising internet use with increasing isolation.

Facebook may even be making people angry and frustrated, according to a 2013 study by Humboldt University's Institute of Information Systems in Germany. Meanwhile, a 2013 University of Michigan study suggests that Facebook might be making people more envious of others and hence less happy.

There are now websites (e.g. rentafriend.com) that will find you a physical friend. Such websites may have more to do with a desire for companionship than loneliness per se. But if you factor in weakening community ties, ageing populations, and the rise of people living alone, one does wonder whether Theodore Zeldin, the provocative Oxford University thinker, might be right in suggesting that loneliness could be the single biggest problem in the 21st century.

According to a recent Relate survey, 4.7 million people in the United Kingdom do not have a close friend. A poll for the BBC found that 33 per cent of Britons, including 27 per cent of 18-to-24-year-olds, felt 'left behind' by digital communications, while 85 per cent said they preferred face-to-face communication with friends and family.

Viktor Mayer-Schonberger, the author of *Delete: the virtue of forgetting in the digital age*, says that our increasing desire to record every aspect of our lives is linked to our declining number of close relationships, caused notably by falling fertility rates and smaller households. Because we no longer have the context of traditional intergenerational sharing, we are relying on digital files to preserve our memory and ensure that we're not forgotten.

The stability of these files is, of course, a problem. Vint Cerf, one of the early pioneers of the internet, recently said that technology was moving so fast that data could fall into a 'black hole' and one day become inaccessible. His advice was that we should literally print out important photographs on paper if we wished to keep them.

Connected to our sense of such digital instability might be recent events ranging from WMD and Enron to GFC and Libor. Such scandals mean that we have lost faith in the ability of our leaders and institutions to tell us the truth or give us moral guidance. A few years ago, US social scientists suggested the collective trauma of 9/11 might create a sense of cooperation, but indications are that what happened was the reverse.

According to a study of 37,000 Americans over the period 1972–2012, trust in others, including trust in government and the media, fell to an all-time low in 2012. A Pew report, meanwhile, says that only 19 per cent of Millennials trust others, compared with 31 per cent of Generation X and 40 per cent of Baby Boomers. The decline in trust means that we no longer know whom or what to believe and end up turning inwards or focusing on matters close to home.

Overall, the effect is that we end up with an atomised society where we crave elements of stability, certainty, and fairness — but where the individual still reigns supreme and is more or less left to their own devices.

Another example of declining real-life interaction is shopping. Many people now try to avoid eye contact with checkout assistants because this requires a level of human connection. Better to shop online, use self-scanning checkouts, or wait until checkouts and cash registers eventually disappear, replaced by sensors on goods that automatically remove money from your digital wallet as you exit the shop.

This could be convenient, but wouldn't it make more sense if we thought of our shopping as being someone else's job, or of shops as being communities? Doing so would mean giving others more recognition and respect.

As Jaron Lanier asks in *Who Owns the Future?*, 'What should the role of "extra" humans be if not everyone is still strictly needed?' What happens to the people that end up being surplus to the requirements of the 21st century? What do we ask of these people who used to work in bookshops, record shops, and supermarkets? What is their purpose?

Current accounting principles mean that such people are primarily seen as costs that can be reduced or removed. But for older people in particular, sales assistants might be the only people that they talk to directly all week. Furthermore, getting rid of such people can cost society far more than their salary if long-term unemployment affects relationships, schooling, and health.

Are friends electric?

Personal relationships can be frustrating, too. In San Francisco, Cameron Yarbrough, a couples therapist, comments that 'People are coming home and getting on their computers instead of having sex with their partners.' This could be an early warning sign of a decline in deep and meaningful relationships, according to Susan Greenfield, who also says that we may be developing an aversion to sex because the act is too intimate: it requires trust, self-confidence, and — above all — conversation.

In Japan, some men have now dispensed with other people

altogether, preferring to have a relationship with a digital girlfriend in games such as Nintendo's LovePlus. A survey by the Japanese Ministry of Health, Labour, and Welfare in 2010 found that 36 per cent of Japanese males aged 16–19 had no interest in sex — a figure that had doubled in the space of 24 months. To what extent this might be due to digital alternatives is unknown, but unless Japanese men face reality and show more of an interest in physical connection, the Japanese population is expected to decline by as much as a third between now and 2060.

Nicholas Eberstadt, a demographer at the American Enterprise Institute, claims that Japan has 'embraced voluntary mass childlessness', with the result that Japan not only has the fastest-ageing population in the world, but also has one of the lowest fertility rates. This is especially the case in Tokyo, the world's largest metropolis. Commentators have linked the rise of digital partners to a sub-culture known as 'otaku', whose members engage in broadly obsessive geek behaviour associated with fantasy themes.

In the opening pages of *Future Files*, I referenced another Japanese phenomenon, called 'hikikomori', which roughly translates as 'withdrawal' and refers to mole-like young men retreating into their bedrooms and rarely coming out. This can't be good for birth rates either, although in the Japanese case another culprit for low fertility and low self-esteem might be economic circumstances: the Japanese economy has been in the doldrums for decades.

In the 1960s, 70s, and 80s, young people in Japan could reasonably expect a better life than their parents. Job prospects were excellent, work was secure, and the future smelt good. I even have a book, buried in a bookshelf, called *Japan, Inc.* (worryingly, perhaps, located next to *China, Inc.*), about the domination of the Japanese economy and the resultant obliteration of US competiveness. But such optimism has gone, and many Japanese feel that they no longer have a future.

You might reasonably expect that the hyper-connected young in Japan and elsewhere would have a strong sense of collective identity, even a level of global synchronicity in emotions. That they would create a vision of a better tomorrow and then fight for it. But instead of a global village, we've just got a village. Social media is facilitating a narrowing, not a broadening, of focus.

Demonstrations and revolts do happen, and online campaigning organisations such as GetUp and Avaaz have an impact, but it remains to be seen whether such protest will change the direction of mainstream politics. Similarly, in the UK, the singer Jason Williamson of the Sleaford Mods belts out intense invectives for the cornered working classes, however most young eyes and ears seem to be elsewhere.

According to *The Economist* magazine, around 290 million 14-to-15-year-olds globally are neither in education nor working — that's around 25 per cent of the world's youth. In Spain, youth unemployment skyrocketed from 2008, spending years at over 50 per cent. But instead of a strong sense of collective action, we have individualism and atomisation. Instead of revolutionary resolve, we have digital distraction. Instead of discontent sparking direct action, it generally appears to be fuelling passivity.

This lethargy is summed up by an image on the internet of a young man sitting in front of a computer in a suburban bedroom looking out of the window. The caption reads: 'Reality. Worst game ever.' It echoes a comment made by Palmer Luckey, the 23-year-old inventor who sold Oculus Rift, a 3D virtual-reality headset, to Facebook for $2.3 billion in 2014. Palmer has said that virtual reality 'is a way to escape the world into something more fantastic'. This is a statement that's both uplifting and terrifying.

Richard Eckersley, an Australian social commentator, describes young people as 'the miners' canaries of society, acutely vulnerable to the peculiar hazards of our times'. He notes that detachment, alcohol, drug abuse, and youth suicide are signs that the felt experience of the modern age lacks cohesion and meaning. Nicholas Carr, the author of *The Glass Cage*, makes a similar point: 'Ours may be a time of material comfort and technological wonder, but it's also a time of aimlessness and gloom.'

Maybe the two are correlated. Most people's lives around the world have improved immeasurably over the last 50 years, but most improvements have been physical or material. As a result, life has become skewed. An imbalance has emerged between work and life, between individuals and community, between liberty and equality, between the economy and the environment, and between physical and mental health — the latter barely captured by traditional economic indicators.

The shock of the old

In the UK, half a million sick days were taken due to mental-health problems in 2009. By 2013, this had risen to a million. Similarly, in 1980, when anxiety disorder became a formally recognised diagnosis, its US incidence was between 2 per cent and 4 per cent. By 2014, this had increased to almost 20 per cent — that's one in five Americans. And the World Health Organisation forecasts that 25 per cent of people around the world will suffer from a mental disorder during their lifetime. Why might this be the case?

One argument is that unhappiness is a result of self-indulgent navel gazing by people who no longer face direct physical threats. There's also the argument that we're increasingly diagnosing a perfectly natural human condition, or that commercial interests have appropriated anxiety to sell us more things we don't need. Why simply sell a smartphone when you can be in the loneliness business, selling enduring bliss to people seeking affirmation, validation, and self-esteem?

Digital fantasy and escape can therefore be seen as logical psychological responses to societal imbalances, and especially to the sense of hopelessness caused by stagnating economies, massive debt burdens, and ageing workforces that are reluctant to retire. While Japan has been pessimistic since the 1990s, there's an argument that Europe is now heading in the same direction as slow economic growth converges with rising government debt, a declining birth rate, and increased longevity.

Even in the US, that cradle of infinite optimism, some members of the Millennial generation are losing faith in the future, believing that decline is inevitable and that living standards enjoyed by their parents are unattainable. This is the polar opposite to the boundless belief in the future that can still be found in enclaves such as Silicon Valley, where there's a zealous faith in the power of technology to change the world, even if all the technology ends up selling us is the same product — convenience.

Yet thoughts of decline aren't the preserve of the young. I was at a dinner organised by a large firm of accountants not so long ago, when one of the partners recounted a conversation he'd had with the mayor of a large coastal town in the UK. The mayor's biggest problem? 'People come to my town to die, but they don't.'

Over the next two decades, the number of people worldwide aged 65 and over will nearly double. This could create economic stagnation and generational angst on a scale we can't comprehend. The author Fred Pearce has suggested that 50 per cent of the people who have ever reached 65 years of age throughout human history could still be alive. This is a dramatic statement, but it might be true, and suggests that every region except parts of Africa, the Middle East, and South Asia might be on course for lower productivity and greater conservatism in the future.

This demographic deluge could stifle innovation, fuel pastoral nostalgia, and exchange society's twin obsessions of youth and sex for a growing interest in ageing and death. It could also wreak havoc with savings and retirement because the longer we live, the more money we need. In a bizarre twist, we'll need life insurance not in case we die, but in case we don't.

Many pessimistic commentators have equated ageing populations with lower productivity and growth rates, although we shouldn't forget that expenditure on healthcare still boosts the economy. Those aged 65 and over also hold most of the world's wealth, and they might be persuaded to part with some of it. Other positive news includes the fact that older populations tend to be more peaceful (more on this later).

Let's also not forget that globalisation, connectivity, and deregulation have lifted several billion people out of poverty worldwide, and according to a report by the accountancy firm Ernst & Young, several billion more will soon follow suit. One billion Chinese alone could be middle class by 2030. These are all positive developments, but the forces that are lifting living standards are also creating risks that are a threat to continuing progress.

If we add to this the uncertainty caused by rapid technological change, political upheaval, environmental damage, and the erosion of rules, roles, and responsibilities, it looks like the Tofflers were right and that the future will just be one damn thing after another. Anxiety will be a defining feature of the years ahead. One psychological response to this is likely to be misty-eyed nostalgia, but there could also be dangerous attempts to go backwards economically or politically.

We are already seeing some right-wing groups, such as Golden Dawn in Greece, favouring extreme solutions. These can be attractive because, as George Orwell reminds us, fascism offers people struggle, danger, and possibly death. Socialism and capitalism, in contrast, merely offer differing degrees of comfort and pleasure. The promotion of localism as a solution to the excesses of globalisation can also be attractive, but while cuddly on the outside, localists have an affinity similar to that of the fascists for closing minds and borders. There's nothing inherently wrong with localism, however taken to extremes it can also lead to nationalism, protectionism, and xenophobia.

In 2014, some commentators drew anxious parallels with 1914. This was a little far-fetched, yet there are curious similarities, not only with 1914, but also with 1939. These include: rising nationalism in politics, the increased printing of money, inflationary pressure, politicised debt, challenges to reserve currencies, the fraying of globalisation, the expansion of armed forces, finger-pointing toward religious minorities, and last but not least widespread complacency.

It might be a logical leap, but I noted in *Future Files* that the top five grossing movies back in 2005 were all escapist fantasies. Was this an early sign that reality was getting too much for people even back then? Fast-forward to the present day, and dystopias and fantasy still dominate the box office, often featuring werewolves, vampires, and zombies. The latter, according to the author Margaret Atwood, are alluring because they have 'no past, no future, no brain, no pain'. At the same time, there's also a new trend for films containing fewer people or almost none at all, including a film called *Her*, set in 2025, about an emotional relationship between a human being and a computer operating system.

We shouldn't read too much into these films, because they are just entertainment. On the other hand, films — especially those set in the future — are usually commentaries on contemporary concerns, particularly regarding technologies we don't understand or can't control. Most monsters are metaphors. *Modern Times,* released in 1936, was about a character trying to come to terms with a rapidly industrialising society where the speed of change and level of automation were unsettling. *Plus ca change, plus c'est la meme chose*, except that the current surfeit of digital wonders and computer-generated imagery could be desensitising us to the wonders of the real world and, counterintuitively, curbing our imaginations.

Our new surveillance culture

So have we invented any new fears of late? Is it the warp speed of geopolitical change that's unsettling us? Is technology creating a new form of digital disorder that's disorientating, or is it something else? Do we still fear our machines, or do we now want to become part of them by welcoming them into our minds and bodies? I will expand on digitalised humans later in the book, but for now I would like to discuss reality, how we experience it, and how we're changing it.

Before computers, globalisation, deregulation, multiculturalism, and postmodernism, we had a reasonably clear view of who we were and what we were not. Now it's more complicated. Increasing migration means that many people, myself included, are not quite sure where they're from, belonging neither to the place they grew up nor the place they ended up. Rising immigration is also challenging our ideas about collective and national identity because some historical majorities are becoming minorities.

Similarly, what was once science fiction has become science fact, although sometimes it's hard to tell the difference. Amazon's much publicised plan for parcel-delivery drones is a good example. Was this just smart PR or could it actually happen? If enough people want it to happen, it probably will.

The smartphone, which started to outsell PCs globally back

in 2012, has been hugely important in changing our external environment, although it now looks as though phones may soon give way to wearable devices. This in turn may usher in the era of augmented reality and the Internet of Things, where most objects of importance will be connected to the internet or have a digital twin. If something can be digitised, it will be.

Wearable computing and smart sensors could also mean datafication, whereby elements of everyday life that were previously hidden, or largely unobservable, are transformed into data, new asset classes, and — in most instances — money.

Embedded sensors and connectivity mean that many physical items will be linked to information, while information will, in some cases, be represented by real objects or even smells. Incoming information such as messages are currently announced via sounds (pings, beeps, music, etc.), but could be represented in the form of glowing objects such as necklaces or even scents emitted from clothes or jewellery. If you are wearing augmented-reality glasses, a message from your boss at work could even be heralded by a small troop of tiny pink elephants charging across your desk.

On the other hand, using an augmented-reality device as a teleprompter in relationships or customer-service roles could render sincerity redundant. Individuals wouldn't know whether you really knew or cared about someone or not. Honesty, authenticity, and even truth, so essential for human communication, could all be in jeopardy. The implication here is that the distinction between the physical and the digital (the real and the virtual worlds of Kim Yoo-chul and Choi Mi-sun) will blur — everything will become a continuum. Similarly, I'd expect spheres of public and private data to become equally confused.

An example of this might be the Twitter stream of one of my son's teachers, who tweeted that she was 'sinking pints and generally getting legless' prior to starting her new job. You might argue that I shouldn't have been following her tweets — but then one might argue that she should have been more careful about what she was saying on a public forum.

But back to how we are changing physical reality. If you're not familiar with augmented reality, it is, broadly, the overlaying of information or data (sounds, videos, images, or text) over the real world to make daily life more convenient or more interesting. Then again, perhaps the word 'augment' is misleading. What we're doing is not augmenting reality, but changing it. Most notably, we are already dissolving the supposedly hard distinction between what's real and what's not real, and in so doing changing ourselves and, possibly, human nature.

Most people would argue that human nature has been fixed for thousands of years. This is probably true. Yet the reason for this could be that our external environment has been fairly constant until now. I'm well aware of the argument that we've used technology to augment reality for millennia — and that once we've shaped our tools, our tools shape us — but the difference this time is surely ubiquity, scale, and impact.

If wearables do become as alluring as smartphones, this may result in many people abandoning real life altogether. It may become increasingly difficult to exist without such technologies. But this is only the beginning, potentially.

We may start by downloading our dreams and move on to attempts to upload experiences. Such things are a long way off, maybe even impossible. Yet we're already close to the prospect of sticking virtual-reality goggles on our heads to trick our minds into thinking something is happening when it's not, and I'm sure implants can't be far off.

The idea of figuring out what human consciousness is, replicating it, and then uploading it (i.e. ourselves) into machines, thereby achieving a kind of immortality, is the stuff of science fiction. But some people believe it could one day become science fact, allowing 'us' to be transmitted into deep space at the speed of light, where we might bump into — travelling as packets of data in the opposite direction — aliens or even God. (Why can't aliens — or God — be digital? Why do we always assume that intelligent aliens would have physical form, usually bipedal?)

In the meantime, don't forget that while corporations may one day anticipate our every need and personalise our experience of reality, governments could be doing something more sinister, such as erasing our memories or implanting false ones, thereby changing reality in another direction.

The things to worry about here are individual freedom, mental privacy, and self-determination, especially what happens to the private self if it is constantly spied upon. It's possible that we'll trade the idea of governments gathering information about us in return for the promise of security, in which case privacy will become collateral damage. But with companies, it could be different. At the moment, we seem happy to trade privacy for convenience or personalisation, yet where is the line legally and ethically? Is it right for Apple, Google, or Facebook to have unhindered access to our personal data or to know more about us than national security agencies?

Is it right, as the digital-security expert Bruce Schneier suggests, that 'The primary business model of the internet is built on mass surveillance'? Or that, if something is free on the internet, you are probably the product?

Flying further into the future, what if companies used remote brain scans to intercept our thinking or predict our actions? Remote brain scanning could be impossible, but Facebook is doing a good job of mind-reading already. No wonder the WikiLeaks co-founder Julian Assange described Facebook as 'the greatest spying machine the world has ever seen'.

CCTV cameras, along with phone intercepts, are largely accepted as a fact of life nowadays, but what if everything you say and do were captured and kept for posterity, too? How might you live your life differently if you knew that everything you did might one day be searchable? Radical transparency could fundamentally change our behaviour. What, for instance, happens to intimacy when there are no secrets and everything is made public? What happens to a person's individual identity?

And forget Big Brother — we're the ones with the cameras. We live in an era of mass surveillance, but the lenses are focused on ourselves, and the trend is towards self-disclosure and selfie-centred activity. In the UK, for example, almost half of the photos taken by 14-to-21-year-olds and uploaded to Instagram are selfies. I'm not saying that Orwell was wrong, however it might turn out that Aldous Huxley was more right.

Ray Bradbury may have been slightly off target, too: you don't need to burn books if nobody reads them any longer. Open discussion in pursuit of truth is irrelevant if it's watered down to the point of invisibility by a deluge of digital trivialities.

Transparency is a force for good. It can expose wrongdoing, promote cooperation, uncover threats, and level the playing field in terms of the distribution of economic power in society. But too much transparency, along with near-infinite storage capacity, could turn us into sheep. Peer pressure could become networked, and conformity and conservatism could result. Hopefully, new rules and rituals will emerge to stop people observing what other people don't want them to see.

We may also come to realise that certain things are best left unsaid — or at least unrecorded.

Perfect remembering

I'd imagine that for some people, wearables and implanted devices would enable a kind of sixth-sense computing. Individuals will record and publish almost everything from birth to death, and the resultant 'life content' will be searchable and used to intuit various needs and to fine-tune efficient living.

It will also enable people to become intimately acquainted with those who died before they were born. For example, gravestones might allow interaction so that family members, friends, and other interested parties would be able to find out details about the lives of the deceased. It may even be possible for algorithms to combine 'life content' with brain data and genetics to create holograms of dead people that would respond to questions.

Of course, some people will choose to turn these recording technologies off or use them with restraint. Such individuals will understand the need for boundaries surrounding the use of technology and will appreciate that not everything in life needs to be measured, augmented, or kept forever for it to be worthwhile.

Their beliefs would probably be an anathema in South Korea, where apps such as Between already allow lovers to record every significant moment in their lives, along with the duration of their relationships. This doesn't currently include the ability to track how many other people your partner has looked at each day, but if eye tracking and facial recognition become commonplace, there's no reason to suppose that it won't be added.

Whether or not a significant 'tech-no' movement will ever emerge, I'm unsure. I can imagine an eventual backlash against Big Tech, as occurred with Big Tobacco, but I think it's rather doubtful — although if you talk privately to people of a certain age, it's surprising how many would find it a relief if the internet was turned off at weekends or disappeared altogether. What we're more likely to see is a rebalancing. Certain places will limit what you can and can't do in them, and Screen-free Sundays at home or Tech-free Tuesdays at work may appear.

We might see cafes or churches using special wallpaper or paint to block mobile signals. There was a case recently of a person who responded to news that a friend had died with the text 'RIP INNIT'. This person may soon be forwarded straight to hell — which for them might be an eternity in Starbucks with no mobile reception.

There's also an emerging trend where people who spend all day looking at screens or communicating with people remotely want to engage physically with other people or use their hands to make things when they're not working. I met an accountant recently who had taken up making fishing flies by hand because this was, in his words, 'an antidote to the world of computer screens and numbers'. There's even a spark of interest in chopping and stacking your own firewood, although I suspect this has more to do with a crisis of masculinity than an attempt at digital detoxing.

But assuming, for a moment, that we don't significantly switch things off, what might a hyper-connected world look like 20 or 30 years hence? More specifically, how might our identities change if we never switch off from the digital realm and are never allowed to escape into a private sphere?

Early indications are that a significant number of people are finding two-dimensional simulations of life more captivating and alluring than five-dimensional reality, and that while collaboration and sharing are on the increase, compassion, humility, and tolerance are not. Why might this be so?

One reason could be chemistry. Sending and receiving messages, manipulating virtual worlds, and gamifying our everyday lives can result in blasts of dopamine, a neurochemical released in measured doses by nerve cells in our brains to make us feel excited, rewarding certain types of behaviour. Online friendship has not been described as the crack cocaine of the digital age for nothing: even the tiniest text message, flirtatious email, or status update results in a small jolt of pleasure — or what animal behaviourists call 'operant conditioning'.

There is some good news on the horizon, however. David Brooks, writing in *The New York Times*, posed the question of whether technological change can cause a fundamental shift in what people value. To date, the industrial economy has meant that people have developed a materialist mindset whereby income and material wellbeing become synonymous with quality of life. But in a post-industrial or knowledge economy, where the marginal cost of digital products and services is practically zero, people are starting to realise that they can improve their quality of life immeasurably without increasing their income. This is a radical thought, not least because many of the new activities that create quality of life or happiness do not directly produce economic activity or jobs in the conventional sense.

It could be argued, for example, that Facebook creates happiness — but Facebook employs very few people. It is in the self-actualisation business, and allows people to express themselves *themselves*.

In the past, great fortunes were made by making things that people wanted. Making people want themselves might make the great fortunes of the future. Moreover, if human happiness is fundamentally derived from helping other people then the new philosophy of online sharing and collaboration could herald the dawn of a new age of fulfilment.

Regardless of material possessions, it seems that what most people want from life is straightforward. They want connection, support, and respect from family and friends. They want purposeful work, enough money, freedom from violence and abuse, and a community that cares for everyone. People also want a shared vision of where society is heading, and to be part of something meaningful that is larger than themselves — this could be family, an organisation, a nation, a belief, or an idea.

In the case of Kim Yoo-chul and Choi Mi-sun, work was absent, but arguably so too was everything else.

Our environment has changed an awful lot since the Stone Age, while our neural hardwiring has not. One major consequence of this is that we still crave the proximity, attention, and love of other human beings. This could change, but currently it's what marks us out as different from our machines. We should never forget this — no matter how convenient, efficient, or alluring our machines become.

Dear LifeStory user # 3,229,665 Daily data for Friday, August 12, 2039 ---

DEVICES CURRENTLY EMBEDDED:	6
DIGITAL DOUBLE STATUS:	OK **(NEXT PAYMENT DUE SEPTEMBER 1, 2039)**
TODAY'S TIME ONLINE:	18.4 HOURS
DATA UPLOADED:	67,207 ITEMS
DATA DOWNLOADED:	11,297 ITEMS
IMAGES SHARED:	1,107 ☺
IMAGES TAKEN WITHOUT CONSENT **(AUTOMATICALLY REMOVED)**:	4,307 ☹
MICRO-CREDITS EARNED:	186 @ $0.00001
NUDGES:	144
GOOD CITIZEN POINTS:	4 ☺ ☺ ☺ ☺
NIKE POINTS:	11
PIZZA PLANET PIZZA POINTS:	18
COKE REWARDS:	4
OUTSTANDING INFRINGEMENT NOTICES:	1
CONTACT WITH PEOPLE OF MODERATE RISK:	1
HOME SECURITY:	FUNCTIONING
ANXIETY ALERT LEVEL:	MODERATE
VITAL SIGNS:	NORMAL
WATER QUALITY:	GOOD **(SUPPLY CONSTRAINTS FORECAST)**
AIR QUALITY LEVEL **(AVERAGE)**:	5
FLAGGED FOODS:	45 ☹ ☹ ☹
CALORIES CONSUMED:	1,899
CALORIES BURNT:	489
TOTAL STEPS TAKEN:	3,349 ☹
ENERGY INPUTTED INTO LOCAL NETWORK:	-112
CO2 EMISSIONS **(12 MONTH AVERAGE)**:	22.8 TONNES
NON-NEUTRAL TRANSPORT:	14 KM
TRAVEL ADVISORY:	RECOMMEND ROUTE B12
AUTOMATIC APPOINTMENTS CONFIRMED:	8
GOODS APPROACHING WEAR OUT DATE:	16
PERSONAL NETWORK SIZE **(AVERAGE)**:	13,406

EYE CONTACT WITH PEOPLE IN
CLOSE NETWORK: 3
EYE CONTACT WITH PEOPLE NOT
IN NETWORK: 2
INDIVIDUALS TO BE DELETED: 4
AUTOMATED GREETINGS SENT: 87
CURRENT RELATIONSHIP STATUS: SINGLE, TIER 4
PEOPLE CURRENTLY ATTRACTED TO YOU: 2

PUPIL DILATION SCORE (**DAYTIME**):   12
PUPIL DILATION SCORE (**EVENING**):   0

LAST COUPLING: 43 DAYS ☹
COUPLING AGREEMENTS SIGNED: 3
ATTENTION LEVEL: 4
LEARNING LEVEL: BRONZE
LESSONS LEARNT: 0
CURRENT LIFE EXPIRY ESTIMATE: JANUARY 11, 2064

....

MEDIA AND COMMUNICATIONS

why instant communication is killing the art of conversation

One of the best protections against disappointment is to have a lot going on.

Alain de Botton

I once heard about a mother who'd been asked by her six-year-old whether bread should be put in a toaster 'landscape or portrait?' I mentioned this to a friend's eight-year-old, who responded, 'Why didn't they just Google it?' To which they added, 'Google knows everything?'

This is one legacy of our digital culture, where the virtual seeps into the real, where Google becomes a fount of knowledge, and where mobile devices have hijacked our everyday existence. A few years earlier, I'd taken one of my young sons to a contemporary dance performance in Sydney — an attempt at broadening his cultural experience, even if I disliked contemporary dance myself (I've never quite got over a school teacher asking me to express my loathing of sprouts in dance). We sat down in the third row, the curtain opened, and he shouted, 'Look, Dad, it's in 3D!' As I write his words now, they still make me laugh, although not as much as a recent incident involving a women in her 30s.

I was on the Gatwick Express from Victoria Station in London, and a woman sat down next to me and put an iPad on the table between us. Another man sat down opposite, and the woman plugged some headphones into the iPad and began to listen to an audio book. As we discovered, the audio book was *Fifty Shades of Grey* and, unfortunately for the women, the headphone cable wasn't properly inserted. Symbolism aside, the result was an audio leak that resulted in a series of steamy lines filling the sweaty carriage. This incident didn't result in any actual conversation, although it did provoke a series of awkward looks between myself and the man opposite concerning which of us was going to say something.

These are just a few examples of how the world is changing and simultaneously isn't. On the one hand, we use media as we've always done: to inform, to entertain, to kill time, to affirm tribal loyalties, or to create conversations. On the other hand, digital technology is distancing us from each other and reality.

Ricky Jackson holds the unpleasant record for being the person that's served the most time in a US prison for a crime he didn't commit. In 1975, he was wrongly convicted of murder, and he didn't see the outside world again until 2014. Asked by a TV reporter about what had changed since he was locked up, he replied: 'Technology — I think that's the biggest thing that I've had to adapt to … the way that people relate to each other now … I'm not saying that I came from a perfect world in 1975, but people were more in touch with each other … it's about a text now.'

The digital shift is hard to ignore. The average Briton spends eight hours a day looking at a screen. That's more time than people spend doing anything else, including sleeping. Texting in particular has become an obsession. In the UK, the average adult sends and receives around 400 texts per month. With teens, it's a whopping 3,700 per month.

Such activity can certainly create addiction. According to Elias Aboujaoude at Stanford University, around one in eight people is addicted to the internet, and authorities in China and South Korea are talking in terms of a national health crisis. California psychologist Larry Rosen goes further than those who compare the internet to a drug, saying it 'encourages and even promotes insanity'. But it's not only the internet that affects our mental health.

Susan Pinker, author of *The Village Effect*, says that toddlers who watch more than 120 minutes of television per day are at risk of behavioural problems and poor examination results later in life — yet digital TV is available 24 hours per day, often without any parental guidance or restriction. Meanwhile, girls aged between eight and 12 who heavily multi-task with screens in general and social media in particular feel more alone and unhappy than those that don't. Furthermore, according to researchers at the Sackler Centre for Consciousness at the University of Sussex, the use of multiple screens at the same time could result in damage to the anterior cingulate cortex: this is part of the brain that regulates decision-making, impulse control, and empathy.

Why has digital media become so infectious? One reason is the ease with which we can create and share digital content. This creates distraction and amplifies herd behaviour. Perhaps one day, expropriating human attention without permission will be seen as a form of theft, but until then the digital deluge is set to continue.

The second reason digital media has become so ubiquitous is that it's generally free. Media once cost a lot of money to create and distribute. Legions of researchers, writers, filmmakers, and editors were employed to craft stories, and their salaries were paid for via cover price, subscriptions, and advertising. Because it cost a lot of money, people were careful with what was created and with what they consumed.

There was a hierarchy of sources, too, with some channels or brands being more trusted than others. Now that media can be created and circulated by consumers, there's a lot of it. This means the non-monetary value of content has also been cheapened. It's more difficult to distinguish between what's worthy and what's not — and because it's constantly available, we never turn the tap off. You can't finish the internet like you can a newspaper or a book.

We've forgotten that just because you can doesn't mean you should. Just because a channel is there doesn't mean we should use it. Not knowing is vastly underrated. If you know everything about someone, they're less interesting than if they hide in the shadows maintaining an aura of mystery. If you don't know everything about someone, there's something to talk about, although there needs to be a certain amount of shared knowledge to create a conversation.

If content is less frequent but of higher quality, it has far greater value. And there's something to be said about discovering things by accident. Quality and value have nothing to do with volume.

Finally, media has become addictive because of personalisation. Thanks to the digitisation of media content, it's now easy for users to filter and select only what they're interested in — and easier for advertisers to hyper-personalise messages for narrow audiences, often just one person. In other words, we have moved from the few publishing to the many, to the many publishing to the few.

But the trend towards personalisation goes beyond content, and includes the devices we own and use, too.

The 'I' in Internet

Back in the day (a popular phrase these days, which may have something to do with a yearning for things lost), most media devices were shared. Televisions, telephones, stereos, and computers were all shared household appliances to be argued over. Their use had to be negotiated, and a level of compromise was often required, especially when a group wanted to watch or listen to something collectively. Nowadays, of course, these technologies are wireless and personal. We can access or watch whatever we want whenever and wherever we want. There's less collective access, less negotiation, and, one imagines, less awareness about the needs of others. It's as though the autistic brilliance often required to design such devices has been imposed on the rest of society.

Andrew Keen has commented on how ironic it is that Mark Zuckerburg 'lacks any experience or knowledge of human nature'. Yishan Wong, a former director of engineering at Facebook, similarly recounts that Zuckerberg had 'zero empathy'. Many other geeks, including Bill Gates, are said to have an autistic aura or a touch of Asperger's about them. Jaron Lanier refers to the tendency of 'incredible technical intelligence [to be] coupled with appalling naïveté about people'.

There's more to this than intuition and insinuation. Simon Baron-Cohen, an expert on Asperger Syndrome at Cambridge University, has run a number of studies demonstrating concentrations of autism among techies. He claims that autistic children are twice as likely as non-autistic children to have fathers or grandfathers who were engineers; has found a higher rate of autistic traits among maths students at Cambridge than in other disciplines; and has argued that in Silicon Valley, geeks intermarry and are more likely to produce autistic offspring. It also turns out that a considerable number of criminal defendants diagnosed with Asperger's are computer hackers.

Juan Enriquez at Harvard Business School thinks that such autism isn't so much a vestige of the past as a glimpse of the future: 'the next evolutionary step' in an increasingly data-driven world. There is certainly something to the idea of an affinity between people with autism and the Information Age.

Likewise, the behavioural economist Tyler Cowen argues that the internet is shaping our behaviour in 'what is broadly a more autistic direction', in that it lets us 'pursue our identities and alliances based around very specific and articulable interests'. He even sees texting, especially on mobiles, as an autistic style of communication. Cowen's vision is of internet culture being on the autism spectrum, of whole corporations missing social cues from customers. It certainly explains how services such as Facebook and Google continually offend people with their actions — whether changing privacy settings without permission or photographing people's private homes for Google Earth. In the case of businesses such as Napster and BitTorrent, it explains how they can be completely indifferent to intellectual property and then seem genuinely, naively surprised about people's reactions.

Prior to 1980, one in every 2,000 children in the US was believed to be autistic. The latest figure is one in 88, although if you look at just boys, the figure is one in 54 (and one in 38 in South Korea). Why this is happening, nobody knows. It could be culture, parenting, or genetics — or it could be technology. Most likely, it's all of these things, although as *New York* magazine astutely points out, it could also be a 'deriding tool to soothe our cultural anxiety about the ongoing power shift from humanists to technologists. As the coders inherit the Earth, saying someone's on the spectrum is how English majors make themselves feel better.'

A life in solitary confinement

Finding a home with four people inside is hard enough these days, thanks to demographic shifts. But if you do manage to find a nuclear family at home one evening, chances are that each individual will be in a separate room using a separate media device. Some individuals will be working, others will be watching videos or doing homework, but almost all will be plagued by FOMO — fear of missing out. If there are teenagers in the house, there's a two in three chance that they will be using several screens simultaneously.

I still have an advertisement torn out of a magazine, promoting the ISP BigPond, in which every member of the family is on a different screen in a different room of a house. The headline reads: 'Entertainment for the whole family'.

The idea of everyone in a family having their own room is a relatively recent invention, as is the idea of people ten metres away sending electronic messages to each other. Even 15 years ago, sending an email to someone in the same house would have been as ridiculous as posting them a letter. Now it's less pathological. I know of family members and co-workers who email or text each other when they're half a metre apart. There's even a builder in the US who is constructing homes with multiple entrances so that individual family members can enter and exit without disturbing each other.

Could our behaviour with mobile devices, especially phones, ever change back? According to Ofcom, the UK telecommunications regulator, 51 per cent of adults and 65 per cent of teens say they will answer a phone while socialising. Twenty-three per cent of adults and 33 per cent of teens will also answer during mealtimes, while 27 per cent of adults and 47 per cent of teens will answer on the toilet. Even texting during funerals, which was once seen as unacceptable, is becoming popular. Thirty-three per cent of Americans admit to online shopping while paying their last respects, and a New Zealand–based company, One Room, has started streaming funerals as a 'cost effective' option for mourners too busy to attend in person.

Perhaps this doesn't sound important. But if more of us are living alone and accessing personalised information through personal devices then what of shared experiences and collective memory? What of the chances of us living harmoniously with each other? More importantly, does the fact that more of us use individual devices to distract ourselves from reality mean that we're exposing ourselves to future problems relating to human connection and identity?

One intriguing aspect of digital culture is that on the one hand, we're altering reality to make it more interesting, some would say inauthentic, yet on the other hand technology is simultaneously making reality more likely to intrude. An example might be how constant exposure to one's own hyper-connected image on social-media sites is making teens more neurotic about how they look. As the Millennial actor Astrid Berges-Frisbey says, 'There is almost an injunction on today's youth to lead fascinating lives. But if we fail, and most of us are doomed to, we'll be considered losers.'

The nature of our on-screen conversations favours showman-ship and extroversion. This means that the connections that do exist are based partly on false information. As a result, lives can become a long and rather exhausting show in which the boundaries between private utterance and public performance dissolve. We are also entering an era where unless something is documented online, it isn't real.

In my view, Facebook was never set up to facilitate meaningful conversations. It was more a platform to escape the suffocating re-strictions of parents and society. Nevertheless, it has morphed from a template for technological escapism into a personal performance platform that cultivates narcissism and illusory lifestyles. A US study by the National Institutes of Health found that individuals in their 20s brought up with digital media are almost 300 per cent more likely to exhibit narcissistic personality disorder than individuals aged over 65 (brought up without, naturally).

Susan Greenfield thinks that Facebook and sites like it create 'ephemeral connections between imaginary identities'. This means that people are becoming increasingly fragile and less able to cope with anything remotely negative. Most status updates on Facebook are positive, which creates an arms race of insipid exhibitionism that doesn't correspond with reality. At the time of writing, Facebook was looking at using filters to improve the appearance of video clips, ultimately leading to a distortion of any online image.

Where this fakery will end up is unclear, although at the moment most of the smart money is heading towards the acceleration of self-absorption. The development of augmented-reality glasses and virtual-reality goggles has the potential to delete life's annoying parts, covering up real spots in real time on a continual basis. But we all grow old eventually, and bad things still happen to people. At some stage, reality will inevitably pop up, which could be devastating.

The solution to this, surely, is to listen to people who tell you the truth — about imperfections, disappointments, and failures alike. As Alain de Botton points out, 'It is in dialogue with pain that many beautiful things acquire their value', and 'People only get really interesting when they start to rattle the bars of their cages.'

Yet rather than connecting us to people, our mobile devices are pushing us further apart, making us feel more alone, vulnerable, and insecure. John Cacioppo, an American psychologist, claims there's a correlation between online activity and isolation, with the most fervent sharers of information being the loneliest. Similar studies have suggested a linkage between emotional instability and what the Swiss psychologist Jean Piaget called 'collective monologues'.

John Henry Clippinger, a senior fellow at the Beckman Centre for Internet and Society at Harvard Law School and the author of *Crowd of One: the future of individual identity*, argues that people only become themselves through their relationship with others, so connection is a good thing. However, he also says that if we become isolated, our growth becomes stunted. Lonely people tend to have elevated levels of the stress hormone cortisol, which can lead to heart problems and a susceptibility to infection. I'm not suggesting that fervent users of Twitter will have heart attacks, but I've already got high blood pressure and I'm not taking any chances.

Sherry Turkle, who studies the interface between technology and psychology, says that the world is more talkative now than at any time in its history. But this is increasingly at the expense of meaningful conversation. We are talking *at* rather than *to* each other and are living in the moment, separated from the context of both past and future. Turkle also comments that 'what people mostly want from public spaces these days is to be left alone with their personal networks'. This chimes with Andrew Keen in *Digital Vertigo*, who says that social media 'is an architecture of human isolation'.

Mobile devices, especially smartphones, have invaded formerly quiet or private spaces, and we now spend more time looking downward (at screens) than outward (at each other and our environment). Friendship and even love are increasingly mediated and filtered through screens, and the real world is being looked at second-hand.

The UK-based photographer Babycakes Romero points out that there's a 'certain symmetry' to individuals on mobile devices, and that individuals are 'locked simultaneously yet separately into the same action'. He also comments on a 'sadness to the proceedings'. This is especially apparent in restaurants, where the 'dining dead' (his phrase) can hardly look at each other such is the pull of potential information. Meanwhile, some individuals remove themselves further with headphones to eliminate auditory distractions, or with virtual-reality headsets to get rid of other people altogether. You really need to see Romero's photographs for the point to hit home, but it's extraordinary how addicted we've become and how most of us don't even realise it.

Some individuals use mobile devices much as they previously used cigarettes — to pass the time or to hide awkwardness. Both illuminate people's faces with glints of guilt. In a sense, what we do online today is merely a software update to what we've always done.

You might argue that in a culture dominated by individuals and personalisation, there's less common culture available to identify with and to talk with others about. Or perhaps we're using our devices to hide our insecurity.

These devices induce quietness, yet we have simultaneously become less able to deal with real silence. We have lost both the ability and the desire to be alone. Hence, mobile devices provide an excuse for people, especially couples, to withdraw rather than engage in conversation — to keep the world and each other at a controllable distance.

We still say 'I like you' and 'I love you'. Yet by our public captivation with our devices, we're openly saying that any person could be trumped at any moment by something or someone else. This can't be good for self-esteem, and in a bizarre twist, we are more likely to turn to mobile devices to satisfy our hunger for connection. A cycle of endlessly unsatisfying connection and disconnection.

But how we behave with our phones will develop. It would be as much of a mistake to regard our phones as fully developed as it would be to think that human evolution is over.

A few years ago, for instance, Apple bought an Israeli start-up called PrimeSense, which partly developed the Kinect sensor used by Microsoft. The idea here is to create a depth-sensing camera that could capture 360-degree images and make a phone aware of its surroundings. Why would anyone want such a technology? Consider: if a phone were placed camera-side up, the phone would notice if you walked away without it and could call to you.

A phone could also interact with a user on a deeper level, aware as it would be of the user's surroundings and even which people were in proximity. In other words, your phone could become a close friend, counselling you about opportunities and risks. Given that 84 per cent of people worldwide can't spend a day without having their mobile device close by, this doesn't bode well.

Confusing familiarity with intimacy

It's been said that the popularity of comedy is evidence of a culture at its wits' end. I once attended a live showing of the British television comedy *Little Britain* in Sydney. It was at a large theatre, and we had terrible seats.

The first odd thing about this show was why anyone would repeat a TV show live on stage. Odder still: because the venue was so large, there were giant screens everywhere so that people could watch the live version of the TV show on TV screens. Even odder: about half the audience was recording what was on the large screens through tiny screens. And don't even get me started on how my evening was largely ruined by my eyes constantly being drawn to the glow of these tiny screens in the darkness.

It's no better in art galleries, where people walk with selfie sticks, taking pictures of *themselves* in front of the art. Apparently, the 'dwell time' — a nasty phrase — in front of the Mona Lisa in the Louvre is a ridiculous 15 seconds.

Again, the focus here is recording and being seen rather than really seeing or experiencing. The emphasis is on documenting life rather than living it, as if experiences are only worthwhile if they're recorded and available for all to see.

Maybe this is another example of a frivolous and asinine culture. Or maybe the fact is that we're being turned into post-apocalyptic zombies. If William Wordsworth were alive today, the words to his famous poem might be:

I wandered, lonely in the cloud
That floats on high o'er virtual hills,
When all at once I saw an online crowd,
A host, of golden narcissists

Maybe the opposite will occur. We'll continue to document everything, but never bother looking at our documentation. We will delete our own history and fade from our own minds. We will fall into a passive collective stupor, blindly following whatever our devices tell us to do or whatever is contemporary or popular. Both depth and context will collapse, and the internet will become our only reality. Humans will then become algorithms to be maximised for efficiency — 'passengers in our own bodies', as Nicholas Carr puts it.

It's a nice thought that Google is digitising the world's libraries so that you and I can broaden our reading, but I suspect that the real reason is to allow machines to do this instead. Apart from questioning what Google is ultimately searching for, this thought raises the question of why people read books, watch films, listen to music, or talk to each other at all. From the way they've restructured these activities, I suspect the digital giants of today have a different answer to your average person.

Interactive e-books offer lots of things that paper books can't

— personalised endings, audio commentaries, and video extras. You can even personalise textbooks so they adapt themselves to individual learning styles. Once a book is online and connected to a publisher, the publisher can in theory look at who reads what, where, and when. This could be a positive development, encouraging authors to write in a way that engages more people to read their work, but it could work against difficult or complex reads. And don't forget that digital books, hosted on our mobile devices, will potentially read you, linking your reading habits to Amazon files or government databases.

There's even the disturbing prospect of newspapers printed on electronic paper that adjust themselves according to your world view. This is unlikely, but *The Guardian* is looking at producing a newspaper with stories selected by algorithms, while the *Los Angeles Times* already uses Quakebot to automatically generate stories about earthquakes. In 2013, another American company, called Wordsmith, used automated natural-language processing to create 300 million news reports for its clients.

In theory, it wouldn't be too hard to marry natural-language generation to image recognition, creating a system to automatically write reviews of restaurants that had never been visited. A program could filter social-media comments, cross-referencing them with current images of the kinds of people who frequent the restaurant. It could also use sound recognition to comment on noise levels or the kind of music being played.

Sit back and relax. There's no need to think. And there's no need for middlemen or human interaction of any kind. So efficient.

Yet sometimes, inefficiency is important. Accidents and illogical actions can be worthwhile, too, especially if you're trying to invent something really new. Following trends is fine, but taken to the extreme, all you ever get is more of the same.

I'm a fan of Shazam, the app that can distinguish and identify any song in the midst of background noise. Shazam is a real-time radar for what people are listening to and, by implication, what they're not. It can predict the music that will sell, replacing expert judgement with the wisdom of crowds. All good, except two downsides are that we are hearing the same music with increased frequency and that hits are sounding more alike. Some argue that when we are feeling anxious, we shift our behaviour towards things that are familiar, but as Holger Hennig, a Harvard physics researcher who has looked at robotic rhythms, explains, 'there is something perfectly imperfect about how humans play rhythms'. It's a bit of a leap to link computer-generated rhythms to the one-dimensional character of contemporary pop, but computers are especially good at giving people what programmers think we want at the expense of giving us what we really do.

Furthermore, creativity and innovation depend on diverse inputs and serendipity. If we are all listening to the same music, watching the same films, and consuming the same information then where are we heading? Surely it is our dissatisfactions, imperfections, and mistakes that make things interesting — and ultimately human. Surely it is the element of chance and not knowing that makes each life unique and life itself worth living.

I imagine that it will eventually be possible for a machine to read every book ever written or watch every movie ever made and discover patterns. These could be referenced against sales data or box-office receipts to reveal a secret formula for success. But, pushed to the limit, the end result would surely be one book and one film endlessly recycled. Do we seriously want to live in such a world?

Similarly, it's the imprint of time that makes paper books interesting, while e-books remain identical and pristine. There's no patina on an e-copy of this book, whereas each paper edition tells a different story.

Attention deficit

I'm fully aware that digital media has brought immense benefits to society, and I could mention a long list of positive developments and outcomes. But in this chapter, my question is whether or not digital media is making us happier, smarter, or more literate.

I'm also aware, of course, that negative concerns about technology have a long history: 2,500 years ago, Socrates worried that writing, instead of remembering, would erode knowledge. Even today, some commentators argue that the shift from speech, especially face-to-face speech, to written, remote communications means that we are losing our oratory and persuasive powers.

I'm not worried that physical books, newspapers, or even libraries will completely die. They won't. Even so, long arguments about complex issues are being drowned out by superficiality and popularity. There's social pressure to be informed, but there's also too much information, largely because the people who designed the systems didn't appreciate the difference between information quantity and quality. Add too much access to information and this results in too many instant opinions.

What matters now is not knowledge itself, but knowledge of the fact that something exists. Consuming information first-hand, which takes time, is less important than being aware of the right information feeds.

Equally, having access to too much information can be as bad as having access to too little, because it's difficult to distinguish what's important from what's not. According to an American Press Institute study, almost 60 per cent of Americans admit they only read news headlines. Online commentators write the abbreviation 'tl;dr' (too long; didn't read) before they offer an opinion on the things they haven't read.

Tony Haile, CEO of web-traffic research company Chartbeat, has admitted that there's 'effectively no correlation between social shares and people actually reading'. Furthermore, having any debate about quality nowadays flies in the face of postmodernism, where everyone and everything is of equal merit.

This is especially true in some educational circles. Many schools have simultaneously taken strong positions on digital technology and learning despite a number of studies suggesting that paper and pixels are different. Old and new technologies each have their own strengths, and we need to work out the best technology — pens and paper or Kindles and iPads — for the task at hand.

Screens can dull our attention and work against deep, sustained reading, which in turn affects thinking and understanding. One study of students who took notes by hand versus students who typed notes on a screen found that the handwriters usually understood the content of lectures better. This could be partly because the screens were connected and there's the temptation to do something else. It could also be because it's difficult to listen to someone and type notes at the same time (listening then writing by hand is easier, and tends to highlight key points). The physical architecture of books, magazines, and newspapers also seems to give readers physical clues as to where they are in a story or argument, which aids recall later.

If we follow the lead of digitally progressive schools, will we become less sharp and more shallow?

Aren't we getting smarter?

We know human intelligence has been increasing, thanks largely to higher standards of public health, public education, and social support. In Denmark, a standard IQ test, used from the 1950s to the 1980s to assess the intelligence of potential military recruits, clearly shows IQ levels have risen. Other data confirm this effect.

However, since 1998, something strange has been observed in developed countries such as Denmark, the UK, and Australia. IQ levels haven't just levelled off — they are actually declining.

Evidence to date is thin. It's possibly a blip. But it could be real and caused by cultural or even nutritional factors. An artificial diet of processed foods, the gluttonous consumption of television and computers, or a dubious banquet of educational reforms might not be helping. One might even argue that humans are reaching the limit of natural genetic gains, much as human height has now plateaued.

A controversial view is that since the most intelligent people tend to have the least children, we might be slowly breeding out intelligence and, as a species, evolving to be more stupid. This could be true, but we've had these arguments before, and the outcome last time (eugenics and forced sterilisation) wasn't pleasant. Perhaps, as a species, we are still becoming more intelligent, only in ways that traditional IQ tests don't measure — or ignore completely.

So what's next? Given our limited understanding of the genetic basis of intelligence, it will be a long time before we can tell what is going on, and probably longer before we hack our own genes to improve our intelligence. In the meantime, there's a straightforward solution: better education.

I won't discuss education just yet. For now, let's look at a phenomenon we've likely all encountered at school, and increasingly outside it, too: a dark confluence of distraction, interaction, ignorance, and intelligence.

Deleting empathy

Humans have always been nasty, and some individuals have always excelled at this. To some extent, digital media merely amplifies. Nevertheless, the globally networked nature of digital media does seem to have its own special brand of nastiness. Why does the internet present such a playground for cyberbullying, trolling, and misogyny? One reason is that people think they can behave any way they like and not get caught — either because they think they're hiding behind an invisibility shield or because they believe that certain laws don't apply online. The perceived ability to remain anonymous online is surely unparalleled historically and has no major offline equivalent.

But a better reason is detachment. Because people can't generally see the person they are being nasty about online, they're able to delete empathy and compassion. Because people are physically removed from their target, there are no physical clues as to how the person might be reacting to what they're saying.

If an exchange or confrontation exists purely as lines of text then body language and tone of voice cannot convey how the other person is feeling. You cannot modify your own behaviour as a result. As for the victim, a critical problem is the difficulty of turning any torrent of abuse off. Before ubiquitous connectivity, bullying was confined to in-person encounters. These days, it follows you home and even enters your safest, most intimate spaces — and potentially exists on a website forever. But the problem is as much cultural as technological.

Fifty years ago, we celebrated humility, self-restraint, and discretion. Public and private spheres and the utterances made therein were separate, too. In another 50 years, perhaps, the aggregated and synchronous nature of connected devices could highlight what unites us rather than what divides us, ushering in a new era of altruistic understanding. In the shorter term, this seems unlikely, as one suspects that money and trivial convenience will trump civility and cooperation. But these forces, along with equality and freedom of expression, which have given us our present day of individual self-absorption and self-promotion, illustrate that things do change.

Famous for being famous

Getting back to the question of why people engage with and through culture, I suggest that the answer is to make us feel human. Books in particular guard our aloneness and in so doing allow us to consider the lives of other people relative to our own. Books make us think about the potential for good and evil. During complex and uncertain times, books also allow us to personalise our understanding of events.

When I asked my father, a retired physicist, about the last book he'd read, his reply was 'the Toyota Corolla workshop manual'. Apparently, he only reads when he feels the need to find something out. Fair enough. We read for many reasons. I've read manuals for things I don't even own — the desire to find things out is strong. Putting aside the inner workings of Toyotas, I'm curious about our apparent addiction to another form of information, namely celebrity gossip.

Celebrity is nothing new. Media has always involved gossip. But our new information age is tailor-made for the instant propagation of such heroes — kings and queens known more for their image than their achievement.

This suits a global media distinguished by its relentless pursuit of style over substance. Celebrities are illusory characters that, according to clinical psychologist John Lucas, are 'symptomatic of a rootless culture in which many people feel a sense of isolation'. A similar point is made by Adam Galinsky, an expert in ethics and social psychology, when he comments that 'Humans at the core are social beings, and research has shown that the less connected people feel, the more they turn to celebrities.'

The socialite Paris Hilton, who exists in what appears to be an ongoing soap opera that blurs reality and fantasy, can therefore be seen as both a reaction to our growing sense of impermanence and our increasing ambivalence towards each other. The illusion, courtesy of the media in general and messaging sites such as Twitter and Instagram in particular, is thinking that we know these people. Celebrities appear to be just like us, and tap into an infantile wish that we — like them — will be plucked from our everyday lives into a parallel high-status universe.

Sometimes we genuinely believe that we know these people, that they are our friends even, so when something bad happens to them the pain is almost personal. Spreading the dirt on celebrities, or dishing the dirt on people we know, is a primal way of establishing truth and trust. The vicarious pleasure we gain from famous faces has been shown to make us feel better about ourselves, as we assimilate some of their better characteristics with our own. On the other hand, too much obsession can erode our self-esteem and increase feelings of inadequacy.

At a subconscious level, we may view celebrities as potential mates — in the biological sense. This is partly because celebrities tend to be good-looking, the perception of which gives us a chemical high in a way that's similar to the pleasure we receive when we send or receive a text message. Thus, sending or posting an image of a famous face makes us feel doubly good. But there's also a psychological effect known as the exposure effect. This is a pleasurable biochemical cascade that results from familiarity, which, in brain science terms, means that we find familiar faces easier to process. However, there's a problem — for celebrities at least. After a while, ubiquity tips into tedium, and we go off certain people's faces. This is why clever celebrities such as David Bowie and Lady Gaga have constantly changed the way they look.

You might argue that celebrity worship has replaced ritualised worship. There's the all-powerful presence, shared community values and rituals, and even immortality. I don't buy into this argument, although it's interesting to note psychologist James Houran's claim that 'non-religious people tend to be more interested in celebrity culture'. Nevertheless, I do believe that for many people, celebrities offer a way to transcend lives of quiet desperation and conformity.

So where does this leave us? In 1969, we landed two men on the moon. Forty-seven years later, we've got 140-character status updates, Netflix in every room, 'Break the Internet', and *The X Factor*. Progress? I'll let you be the judge of that.

Minutes of the board of governors of the Ned Ludd Elementary School, held on 27th April 2022

Present: Carole Grant, David Patel, Richard Leggit
Apologies: Malcolm Talot, Sue Yoo
Minutes: Minutes of the previous meeting were approved.

Finance
An offer by Vodafone to sponsor outdoor play equipment for Years 3–6 was noted but unanimously turned down.

Publicity
A study by NYU looking at information retention by students across analog and digital formats would like to feature the Ludd academy as a best in class example of paper-based learning. The approach follows our much publicised Y6 summer average of 96.8 per cent. This was approved.

Health and safety
Following the Lloyd's of London decision to withdraw all liability for health claims relating to wi-fi networks and mobile devices used on school premises, it has been decided to terminate the remaining network and replace all whiteboards with chalk-boards.

Appointments
Matt Watson, father of Ant (Year 4) and vice president of paper learning systems, has been appointed as our new headmaster. Matt will replace Julian Golhard, who is returning to San Francisco to head up the Slow University. Other new appointments include Sam Chen, head of ethics, Jenny Choo, head of handwriting, and Mike Smart, deputy director of drawing.

Computer museum
It was agreed that the Y3 trip to the computer museum would be co-sponsored by Kathmandu outdoor play centres, bonkers for conkers, and Vinyl Junkie.

SCIENCE AND TECHNOLOGY

*is it safe to build a parallel universe
in your spare bedroom?*

If you have something that you don't want anyone to know,
maybe you shouldn't be doing it in the first place.

Eric Schmidt

In 1926, the inaugural issue of *Amazing Stories* magazine wildly proclaimed 'Extravagant Fiction Today … Cold Fact Tomorrow'. They weren't far wrong. By 1928, the *Daily Mail* newspaper was looking ahead to the year 2000 and correctly forecasting giant screens in public spaces. Historically speaking, chunks of the future have already arrived, which gives rise to the prickly problem of forecasting what on Earth is next.

Andy Sawyer, the science fiction collections librarian at the University of Liverpool, has pointed out that the get-out-of-jail-free card here is to say, as sci-fi writers Vernor Vinge and Damien Broderick have done, that it's increasingly impossible to predict the future. Developments are now happening so fast that by the time you've thought of something, it's already happened.

The idea of terrorists hacking self-driving cars or taking control of aeroplanes with mobile phones is a case in point. Neither has happened just yet, but wild speculation about both has. This not only brings the future closer, but also helps create self-fulfilling prophecies. If enough people predict something, it can happen.

Now is the past

A couple of years ago, I was writing another book and was looking for examples of weirdness. Pretty quickly, I stumbled across the 'fact' that particles had been found travelling faster than the speed of light, which fundamentally challenges Einstein's theory of relativity. Turns out, this wasn't true — but for a while, most people, caught up in the hectic hurly-burly of modern living, accepted it anyway. The only difference now between reality and fiction is that fiction has to be believable.

One way of dealing with this problem might be to travel further into an imagined future, but if we go too far we can end up with an even bigger problem, which is part philosophy, part relativity, and part quantum physics. Here goes ...

The sci-fi writer Philip K. Dick has suggested that reality is something that, if you stop believing in it, doesn't disappear. Mountains exist whether we want them to or not. Yet think about money. If enough people stopped believing that a $50 bill had real value — or stopped believing that a company or government had legitimacy — it would effectively vanish. They are all myths.

Better still: imagine a planet with no people. We think of language, ideas, or history as real, but without humans they all disappear. As Max Planck, the originator of quantum theory, observed, 'I regard consciousness as fundamental. I regard matter as derivative from consciousness.'

Such solipsism might be getting too much like the movie *The Matrix*, but it gets better. Think again of Kim Yoo-chul and Choi Mi-sun, the couple that allowed their daughter to starve to death. We regard their daughter as real and their digital daughter as not, which is a binary distinction. Putting to one side the problem of human versus animal rights (scientists have shown that some apes and birds can be more intelligent than three-year-old children, yet it's the children that get the legal rights), there's the question of avatar and robot rights once technology develops to the point of blurring digital versus human further.

For example, the European Union parliament is considering giving robotic companions legal personhood in a move that could allow them to carry out financial transactions or collect prescriptions on our behalf. One of the implications of this is that robots could be made liable for damage to property or injury to people, with the very real consequence that the owners of the robots — individuals, corporations, or governments — might be shielded from any responsibility. That's a serious get-out-of-jail-free card.

Blurred lines

Fortunately, the above situation is some way off. The robot most likely to succeed — or for the average person to encounter at the moment — is possibly Jibo, the world's first family robot. Jibo is part 'bot, part au pair, and can be optimised for sociability via its digital eye and two-section twisting body, designed to express emotional states. Quite how Jibo ended up looking like Kenny from the TV series *South Park* is beyond me, but perhaps this will add to its quirky attraction. Or maybe its cartoon-like character will offset any spooky behaviour.

Another robot, called SociBot-Mini, has a talking head, with eyes that can recognise you and follow you around a room. This is another personal assistant or chatbot that's able to hold conversations. For added character and authenticity, its makers are thinking of incorporating features such as animated, telepresence

3D faces. Whether users will add the faces of friends or film stars is unclear, although one can imagine a scenario where every robot ends up with the same face — George Clooney, perhaps?

Thus one spooky future is where instead of robots looking like robots, they start looking like us, partly because robots would more easily assimilate themselves into human society if they moved around like us. It's hard to convey how humanoid robots with squishy bodies or skin might bring to life the link between science fiction and science fact. Suffice to say that working robots that look identical to their creators — such as Hiroshi Ishiguro in Japan and Zou Renti in China — already exist in laboratories.

And if you think that's weird, how about robots designed for empathy or deception, or machines modelled on biology, such as robotic bees that interact with real insects? And who's to say that flying robots need to be tiny? Perhaps the future of fighter aircraft is closer to the movie *Transformers* than *Top Gun*.

Or there's a future where instead of trying to scale robots up, we create microscopic robots, possibly at a nanoscale, and ingest them. Or allow larger versions to form colonies to do useful work, much like ants and bees.

My point here is to question where the line between human and non-human will be drawn, and to ask to what extent humans will be happy to use machines in place of people and in what roles. Is there an obvious limit? Robots in place of au pairs is one thing, but how about in place of a doctor, teacher … or child? The trajectory for robot bodies seems fairly clear. Robots will need bodies akin to our own if they are to move freely in our environment — it's only through sensory inputs from bodies that their brains will ever emulate being alive.

Machine learning isn't a new area, but it is becoming more sophisticated as software is developed that allows machines not only to capture and observe events, but also to find patterns and transfer understanding into rules or even wisdom. In other words, machines that can sense their environment, analyse it, and make judgements about how to respond based on a set of logical rules or desired goals.

Again, you might think that such machines are a long way off, but they already exist inside research establishments, and judging by the rapid acceptance of robotic cars, autonomous robots walking along shopping strips carrying our bags might not be far away. And if that's acceptable, why not robots as friends and companions? Friendship is often regarded as a fundamentally human trait, yet we have relationships with pets, so why not with machines so convincingly human that we fall for them over and above human or animal alternatives?

The future belongs to children

It has been said that Rene Descartes, the Enlightenment mathematician and philosopher, once told his pupil Queen Christina of Sweden that the human body could be thought of as a machine — at which point, the Queen turned her head to a mechanical clock on the wall and ordered Descartes to 'See that it produces offspring.' This was a joke, but in the world of technology, it may no longer be funny.

The ultimate dystopian scenario is where machines not only develop consciousness, but also self-replicate. In 1964, Stanislaw Lem published a novel called *The Invincible*, about a mission to a distant planet that discovered a form of mechanical life millions of years in the making. But the idea of non-biological replication goes back much further. In 1802, William Paley published a teleological book called *Natural Theology*, in which religion, not surprisingly, got top billing. Paley argued that something as complex at the time as a watch could only exist if there were an ultimate watchmaker — or God. Yet Paley admitted that this argument would vanish if a clock could assemble itself.

This brings us to Darwin and whether technology is subject to the same evolutionary imperatives as biology. Like living species, technologies develop by error, accident, and mutation, partly as a result of changing external conditions. Perhaps machines that make themselves or factories that build other factories are where we're heading. After all, we've already built a 3D printer that can print many of its own parts.

Taken to extremes, such developments could eventually mean that the human species is relegated to a support species, nudged aside or thrown out of the way by highly adaptable machines with superior strength and intelligence. Or maybe, as humans are still the designers of such machines, we will deem robotics, artificial intelligence, biotech, nanotech, and neurotech too dangerous, and will either destroy the machines or banish them to another planet.

Such thoughts don't appear to concern many ten-year-olds, who seem perfectly happy to design parallel universes, complete with new planets, three-gendered aliens, and mechanical plants in their bedrooms. Perhaps this is because robots are currently incapable of doing most tasks that a five-year-old, let alone a ten-year-old, takes for granted.

If you're interested in technological doomsday scenarios, I suggest you read an essay written by Bill Joy, former chief scientist at Sun Microsystems, called 'Why the Future Doesn't Need Us'. If you're more optimistically inclined then try *Erewhon* by Samuel Butler. Or, for a combination of the two, read *The Machine Stops* by E.M. Forster. But is there a middle ground between digital and human?

Love in the age of spiritual machines

If a robot were to glance into the distance when you asked it a question, or displayed random head movements or hand gestures while talking, we might feel comfortable to the point of confiding in it or even falling in love with it. We might do this in the physical world or we might replicate the physical inside the virtual. At this point, what really exists and what doesn't? Could love for a machine ever compete with human love? If we can one day accept robots as companions, why not lovers?

There's an offshoot of robotics called teledildonics, where hobbyists turn parts of industrial machinery into mechanical sex machines and remotely controlled sex toys. In such instances, where would *you* draw the line?

Some experts believe that we'll never be able to create machines capable of being true companions because to do this would require machines to be conscious, and this in turn would require the total integration of memory or experience. For example, there's a huge difference between a computer containing digital photographs of everything that's ever happened to you and one that can make connections between each photograph to create memory or identity, or edit the images to tell meaningful stories.

On the other hand, how do we know that what we experience is real whereas that which a machine experiences is merely a simulation? Surely both could be simulations? How do you know, for instance, that you are not dreaming about reading this? Or what if VR (virtual reality) becomes so compelling that RL (real life!) lacks lustre? Could withdrawing from daily existence one day be so complete that people give up on the real world altogether?

Maybe that's what we're already seeing in places such as South Korea and Japan, and maybe that's where we're all eventually heading, although if that's true, how do we know that our future ancestors haven't simulated reality already? With enough computing power and enough neural understanding, surely anything is possible, and why should consciousness be limited to biological neural networks?

This mind-bending idea belongs to, among others, Nick Bostrom, a philosophy professor at Oxford University, and tips us back not only into *The Matrix*, but also into juicy questions about the nature of reality, religion, and the universe. What if, for example, life — along with heaven, hell, and indulgences — existed as simulations or games, and we progressed between levels over time?

There are plenty of objections to this idea, as there are to any discussion regarding the nature of time and space, which obviously intersects with any discussion of where we've been, where we are, and where we're going. For most physicists, time is not real. Taking a long-enough view, the past, present, and future are all indistinguishable and any sense of now is nonsensical. 'Now', in galactic terms, is as silly as 'Here' or 'Me' on a timeline of the universe from inception to end. 'Now' happens at different times and depends upon what speed anything, or anyone, is travelling. 'Here' depends upon your vantage point. Many of the stars we see no longer exist — it's just their 'historical' light that's reaching us. Time does not flow any more than space or identity does. That's the theory, at least.

But surely the flow of time is essential to how we on Earth perceive ourselves. Time flowing is one of the primary human experiences. Machines, in contrast, know nothing of 'Me', 'Here', or 'Now'.

If you throw out relativity theory and look at quantum theory instead, the picture is rather different. In quantum physics, future events are determined by present possibilities, much as human reality exists in more than one state depending on who is experiencing or viewing it. The practical and rather energising outcome of this thought is clearly that the future does not exist until we create it. It shimmers into existence one small decision, or outcome, at a time. Or perhaps multiple futures and realities coexist, but only one ever becomes available when we decide to pursue one path versus another.

Because you're worth it

But perhaps this is getting too far away from the question at hand, which is how the historically hard distinction between reality and fantasy might change in the future. How might science and technology alter our generally perceived experience of reality, especially how we experience and relate to other human beings?

Let's take a more concrete, everyday focus. One of the biggest social transformations of late has been hyper-connectivity created by the internet, which in turn has created a radical increase in transparency, corresponding declines in privacy, and the development of collaborative communities that co-create and share everything from healthcare data to product reviews. What if these trends were to reverse? We might decide that some things still work best in private. We may become fed up with Apple's new iBeacon micro-location technology that informs Apple devices of their position and further invades our locational privacy. We may become disillusioned with too much choice, fractured attention spans, cybercrime, or corporate control. Governments may become frustrated by security leaks or the aggregation of leaderless protests.

Or the cost of using our devices might become too high environmentally. In 2010, the internet was responsible for 5 per cent of global power use. The expansion of connected cars, digital mirror-worlds, and virtual realities could increase this number substantially. Which means that while futuristic technologies may become possible, it could become too expensive to use them.

Don't panic. More likely than not, the internet will continue in a recognisable form, although with increasing connectivity to the world around us. A while ago, it was possible to make jokes about connecting trees, toothbrushes, and cows to the internet, but you can't do this any longer because all of these links now exist. This is the Internet of Things that I mentioned in Chapter 1: hyperlinked to wearable computing, smart sensors, self-tracking, Big Data, data analytics, and gamification.

Once you connect humans to things, all kinds of other things become possible, too, especially if you add near-infinite digital recording and storage capacity. Friendship, for instance, used to be a relatively private and unquantifiable thing, but is now an asset class against which you can target advertising and make money, although directly making money out of your friends doesn't win you very many.

Another example: once your stuff is connected to the internet via computers the size of pinheads, it's possible to see what gets used and what doesn't. Your outdoor hiking boots could start to record their mileage in the same way as a car does. Amazon might then contact you saying that you aren't using them, and asking if you wish to consider selling them in exchange for some more running shoes, which clearly are being used. Suddenly, shoe companies could be in the information business.

Conversely, if you're a keen cyclist, your bike might alert you to the fact that components have clocked up a certain number of hours and are approaching typical failure times. In other words, once we place more of our possessions in cyberspace we'll start to manipulate them. And once we do this, the data — the digital record — will become valuable in itself, and we'll probably start to insure the data, lock it away in secure storage vaults, and even trade the data for things we want. Even something as mundane as home insurance could be transformed, because you'd have digital records of buildings, building repairs, and building contents, some of which might be used as proof of value or collateral against loans. Suddenly, insurance companies are offering something more valuable than loss protection.

Having said this, some people believe that algorithms and automated online loans were partly responsible for the subprime mortgage crash. Automated systems scraped the data to find high-risk borrowers that could be charged high interest rates and then deliberately targeted them, much in the same way that online search results can be skewed based on location.

There's also the problem that algorithms can accentuate existing biases in the data, so perhaps human oversight is still needed.

Relating risk to individual behaviour and real-time conditions instead of using aggregations and averages could also transform the insurance industry. Of course, a key issue here is whether people think that the goods and services — or level of personalisation — they receive in return for sharing such information is worth it. Currently they do, but as Jaron Lanier points out, if data is worth money then people should be paid for any data they produce.

The future will be recorded

One consequence of people wearing internet-connected glasses or contact lenses that constantly record video is that it would be possible to revisit memories. One day, we might say, 'Show me November 2015.' Or if physical objects such as museum exhibits or trees are similarly connected, we might be able to view November not only from our own experience, but also from the perspective of a tree or a museum exhibit. You might argue that such developments will make us more aware of other people, although I suspect the opposite could be true: we may focus even more on ourselves and be even less aware of what occurs outside our immediate line of sight.

Science fiction? In 1998, a Microsoft scientist, Gordon Bell, started wearing a camera to record as much of his daily life as possible. The result was a series of huge digital files and a book called *Total Recall*. At the time, recording almost everything wasn't easy or cheap, but both bandwidth and storage cost have fallen dramatically since then. You can now buy life-logging cameras such as Autographer or Narrative Clip for less than $400. You might argue that this is a lot of money to watch yourself staring at screens all day, yet it would at least allow people to record reality rather than having to rely on their fickle memories.

Cathal Gurrin, a lecturer in computing and a 'lifelogger' at Dublin City University, has conducted a similar experiment to Bell's. Since 2006, Gurrin has been recording his field of view every minute, indexing the recordings, and making them publicly available. So far, Gurrin has built up an archive of 12 million images and produced a terabyte of data every year. A terabyte is more memory than was available in the whole world in 1982.

Yet what if such ubiquitous recording wasn't captured by individuals, but by corporations? Google has been granted a patent for a camera that tracks eye movements reacting to adverts and then links this with emotional responses to individual ads. Google banned facial recognition in Google Glass, however an app that recognises gender could easily be used to determine how many women a man looks at each day and to target him with ads accordingly. Or governments could use similar technology to ascertain who had negative feelings toward their policies or politicians. They could even monitor how individuals reacted to certain genders or racial groups.

Police already use cameras to identify individuals in political demonstrations, and lip-reading CCTV should arrive shortly, so how long before this results in fully masked demonstrations? If cameras and recording devices make their presence felt (as in South Korea and Japan, where cameras that make a shutter-click noise are mandatory), this may be acceptable, but what if stealth technology was widely used by governments? Equally, is it OK for technology to allow every stranger to instantly know exactly who you are?

Maybe personal data recorders and black boxes are the way forward, and Mark Zuckerberg is right that privacy is no longer a social norm. But the freedom that a technology gives one person or group can often reduce it for another — surely freedom must include some right to privacy? What happens in a world of total recall?

Dementia patients would find memory aids invaluable, but for the rest of us, it's questionable whether capturing every element of our daily existence is a good idea. This isn't how our brains work. As with information overload and the glut of digital photography, we shouldn't confuse quantity with quality. Forgetting is often more useful than remembering.

It might seem fine to recall happy events, although recording every one would make each less special. Yet what about unpleasant memories? You might argue that you could deal with this by hitting the delete button, but even then you'd need to witness the memory by recalling the file name to delete it.

Of course, in a rush to record the new, we often destroy the old. Tim Berners-Lee's seminal first ever webpage is long lost, as are virtually all of my own first webpages and early family photographs. Moreover, if connectivity allows us to control or access large parts of our environment with no more than a hand gesture, this might give rise to narcissistic thoughts about superpowers, leading us to wave away our backups on a whim.

Power dressing

Gesture technology that allows people to control anything from computers to UAVs by simply moving the muscles in their forearms already exists and should enter into mainstream use soon. We've already experienced Microsoft Kinect, so how about wristbands that intuitively allow us to turn on and control taps, lights, or appliances? Combined with something like Google Glass, the possibilities are endless.

Goodbye keyboards and computer mice; hello human–machine symbiosis. Of course, wearable computing could be merely the beginning. It's likely that implanting control mechanisms *inside* the human body would result in greater command accuracy, and might be useful from a security point of view. We already implant devices inside our family pets, so why not ourselves? Perhaps the logical conclusion to this will be using brain prosthetics to make the human brain into the control interface. Or perhaps we'll invent ways to allow communication between individuals that bypass our sensory mechanisms.

Direct brain-to-brain communication — what used to be called, rather disparagingly, telepathy — could open up a whole new world. At the moment, human communication is primarily written or verbal. This is fine most of the time, but can be inadequate for human emotion. If emotion could be expressed without the need for external signals or symbols, we might create a new hierarchy of ideas and intelligence. Imagine, for instance, if one day we could send emotional feelings as email attachments. Or imagine if such technology could be used to communicate with animals.

Chatting with your pets could be some way off, so in the meantime, how about clothes that can diagnose disease before you feel ill, socks with electronic sensors in the fabric that measure physical activity, shirts that record heart rate, hats that measure brain activity, gym clothing that manages exercise regimes, and smart underwear to monitor soldiers' vital signs (and protect against bomb damage to psychologically important organs)?

At the moment, most wearable computers are actually pseudo-watches, headbands, or wristbands, i.e. accessories, but surely the most universal form of human augmentation is clothing, so ultimately I'd expect most external devices to disappear and then reappear, invisibly, in no-longer-quite-so-ordinary items of clothing. Similarly, at the moment, most wearable devices are bought for performance-enhancement purposes, but I'd expect this to change as the overall aim shifts towards health.

It could be more important than ever to wear the right clothes, think the right thoughts, and own the latest piece of technology. Perhaps those 40-plus washing-machine options mentioned earlier might become 400-plus, including 'whites with embedded heart monitor and GPS'.

The robots *are* coming

Last night, I watched a 2012 movie called *Robot and Frank,* which seemed like a reasonable collage of what the future might hold. Most things are familiar. Some things, telephones for instance, don't work, yet there's a robot that does. At first, you want the central character to lift the robot's darkened visor and look inside, but you eventually accept that there's nothing conscious in there.

Household robots won't become commonplace overnight, but I believe they are coming, and that we may be more accepting of them than many of us imagine. That's assuming, of course, that they don't steal our jobs — or our souls — in which case, we might start to treat them as illegal immigrants and campaign to banish them. Or maybe they'll be welcome in some areas, where they work dirty and low-paid jobs for instance, but ostracised in others. Or perhaps we'll practise silicon separatism, whereby certain towns and cities will be robot-friendly while others will fight to keep robots and any non-organic humans out.

If this is starting to sound a little like science fiction again, that's not a wholly bad thing. What we softly dream of in science fiction can be useful in revealing potential trajectories.

What we imagine, we often invent; but we should nevertheless embrace and discuss stories about potential technologies. They are a way of revealing what we might ultimately want, and what it is that we fear. In this sense, all stories of the future are lies that set our minds free.

Status Update, Lifedate 71166.9

It's a normal Saturday evening. I'm at home uncorking a bottle of 'Back in the Day', an especially buttery chardonnay from the Mornington Peninsula.

I've swept the garden of leaves with a rake and cleaned the car by hand, which has been deeply satisfying. The dishwasher on the other hand has been playing up again. The human personality program has overridden my instructions and it's refusing to wash anything until I apologize for calling it 'a dumb piece of landfill'.

My eldest is out in his car and I'm receiving a series of feeds that will alert me if he exceeds the speed limit or turns away from our pre-agreed route. If he's involved in an accident I can access video footage and telemetry from two hours either side of the event via camera footage covering all sides of the car and there's an audio feed available too.

If I feel he's driving irresponsibly I can click on a link and have the car safely brought to a standstill. I also have the option of the car driving itself back home automatically. Of course he might simply have disconnected the driver recognition technology, given the car to a friend and taken out the 1973 T, which doesn't have anything computerized in it at all.

I worry about that boy, although his wilfulness and ingenuity impress me.

— 4 —
ECONOMY AND MONEY
is digital cash making us careless?

The idea of the future being different from the present is
so repugnant to our conventional modes of thought and
behaviour that we, most of us, offer a great resistance to
acting on it in practice.

John Maynard Keynes

A few years ago, I was walking down a street in West London
when a white van glided to a halt opposite. Four men stepped out
and slowly slid what looked like a giant glass coffin from the rear.
Inside it was a large shark.

The sight of a live shark in London was slightly surreal, so
I sauntered over to ask what was going on. It transpired that
the creature in question was being installed in an underground
aquarium in the basement of a house in Notting Hill. This secret
subterranean lair should, I suppose, have belonged to Dr Evil.
To local residents opposing deep basement developments, it
probably did. A more likely candidate might have been someone
benefiting from the digitally networked nature of global finance.
A partner at Goldman Sachs, perhaps, the investment bank
immortalised by Matt Taibbi in *Rolling Stone* magazine as 'a great

vampire squid wrapped around the face of humanity'. Or possibly the owner was the trader known as the London Whale, who lost close to six billion dollars in 2012 for his employer, JP Morgan, by electronically betting on a series of highly risky and somewhat shady derivatives called credit default swaps.

London real estate had fast become a serious place to stash funny money, so maybe the house belonged to a slippery individual dipping their fingers into the bank accounts of a corrupt foreign government or international institution. In the words of William Gibson, the feted sci-fi prophet and writer, London is now 'where you go if you successfully rip off your Third World nation'. (Not that the nation necessarily has to be Third World.)

Whichever ruthless predator the house belonged to, something fishy was underfoot. My suspicion was that it had something to do with unchecked financial liberalisation, but also how the digital revolution is turning the economy into a winner-takes-all online casino.

The shift of power away from locally organised labour to globally organised capital has been occurring for a while, but recent developments have accelerated and accentuated this. Digitalisation hasn't directly enabled globalisation, however it certainly hasn't restrained it either, and one of its negative side effects has been a tendency towards polarisation, both in terms of individual incomes and market monopolies.

Throughout most of modern history, around two-thirds of the money made in developed countries was typically paid as wages. The remaining third was paid as interest, dividends, or other forms of rent to the owners of capital. Yet since 2000, the amount paid to capital has increased substantially while that paid to labour has declined, meaning that real wages have remained flat or fallen for large numbers of people.

The shift towards capital could have an innocent analog explanation. China, home to an abundant supply of low-cost labour, has pushed wages down globally. This situation could soon reverse, as China runs out of people to move to the cities, their pool of labour shrinks due to ageing, and Chinese wages increase. Alternatively, low-cost labour may shift somewhere else — possibly Africa.

Another explanation for the weakened position of labour is that humans are no longer competing against each other, but against a range of largely unseen digital systems. It is humans that are losing out. Given that automated systems will take on an increasing number of roles and responsibilities, a future challenge for governments worldwide will therefore be the allocation of resources (and perhaps taxes) between people and machines.

Same as it ever was?

Ever since the invention of the wheel, we've used our creations to supplement our natural abilities. This has always displaced certain skills. And for every increase in productivity and living standards, there have been downsides. Just to take one example: fire cooks our food and keeps us warm, but it can burn down our houses and fuel our enemy's weapons.

During the industrial revolution, machines enhanced human muscle and we outsourced as many dirty and dangerous jobs to machines as we could. More recently, we've used machines to supplement our thinking by using them for tedious or repetitive tasks. What's different now is that digital technologies, ranging from advanced robotics and sensor networks to basic forms of artificial intelligence and autonomous systems, are threatening areas where human activity or input was previously thought essential or unassailable.

In particular, software and algorithms with near-zero marginal cost are now being used for higher-order cognitive tasks. This is not digital technology being used alongside humans, but as an alternative to them. This is not digital *and* human. This is digital *instead of* human.

Losing an unskilled job to an expensive machine is one thing, but if highly skilled jobs are lost to cheap software, where does that leave us? What skills do the majority of people have left to sell if machines and automated systems start to think? You might be feeling pretty smug about this because you believe that your job is somehow special or terribly difficult to do, yet the chances are that you are wrong, especially when you take into account what's happening to the cost and processing power of computers. It's not so much what computers are capable of now, but what they could be capable of in ten or 20 years time that you should be worried about.

I remember ten or so years ago reading that if you index the cost of robots to humans with the year 1990 as the base (where all labour is equally worth 100), the cost of robots had fallen to 18.5. In contrast, the cost of people had risen to 151. More recently, *Der Spiegel* magazine reported that the cost of factory automation relative to human labour has fallen by 50 per cent since 1990.

Over the shorter term, it's unlikely that there will be much to worry about. Even over the longer term, it's probable that there will still be jobs that idiot-savant software won't be able to do very well — or do at all. But unless we wake up to the fact that we're training people to compete head-on with machine intelligence, there's going to be trouble eventually. This is because we're filling people's heads with knowledge that's applied according to sets of rules, which is exactly what computers do. We should be teaching people to do things that machines cannot. We should be teaching people to constantly ask questions, find fluid problems, think creatively, and act empathetically. We should be teaching high abstract reasoning, lateral thinking, and interpersonal skills.

If we don't, a robot may one day come along with the same cognitive skills as us, but with a price tag of just $999. That's not $999 a month, that's $999 in total. Forever. No lunch breaks, holidays, childcare, sick pay, or strike actions, either. How would you compete with that?

If you think that's far-fetched, Foxconn, a Chinese electronics company, is designing a factory in Chengdu that's totally automated — no human workers involved whatsoever. I'm fairly sure we'll eventually have factories and machines that can replicate themselves, too, including software that writes its own code and 3D printers that can print other 3D printers.

Once we've invented machines that are smarter than us, these machines may go on to invent their own machines — which we then may not be able to understand — and so on ad infinitum. Let's hope these machines are nice to us.

It's funny that our addiction to machines today, especially mobile devices, is undermining our interpersonal skills and eroding our abstract reasoning and creativity when these skills are exactly what we'll need to compete against the machines tomorrow. Who ever said that the future couldn't be deeply ironic?

There are more optimistic outcomes, of course. Perhaps the productivity gains created by these new technologies will eventually show up, and the resulting wealth will be more fairly shared, offsetting our ageing populations and shrinking workforces. Perhaps there'll be huge cost savings made in healthcare or education. It's highly unlikely that humans will stop having interpersonal and social needs, and even more unlikely that the delivery of all these needs will be within the reach of robots. In the shorter term, it's also worth recalling an insightful comment attributed to NASA in 1965: 'Man is the lowest-cost ... all-purpose computer system which can be mass-produced by unskilled labour.'

But if the rewards of digitalisation are not equitable, or designers decide that human agency is dispensable or unprofitable, then a bleaker future may emerge, one characterised by polarisation, alienation, and discomfort.

Money for nothing

Tim Cook, the CEO of Apple, who recently announced the largest annual profit in corporate history ($53.4 billion), once responded to demands that Apple raise its return to shareholders by saying that his aim was not to make more profit. His aim was to make better products, from which greater financial returns would flow. This makes perfect sense to anyone except speculators carelessly seeking short-term financial gains at the expense of broader measures of benefit or value. As Jack Welch, the former CEO of General Electric, once said, 'shareholder value is the dumbest idea in the world'.

It was Plato who pointed out that an appetite for more could be directly linked with bad behaviour. This led Aristotle to draw a black-and-white distinction between the making of things and the making of money. Both philosophers would no doubt have been disillusioned with high-frequency trading. In 2013, algorithms traded $28 million worth of shares in 15 milliseconds after Reuters released manufacturing data milliseconds early. Doubtless money was made here, but for doing what?

Charles Handy, the contemporary philosopher, makes a similar point in his book *The Second Curve*: when money becomes the point of an activity then something is wrong. Money is merely a secure way to hold or transmit value (or 'frozen desire', as James Buchan more poetically put it). Money is inherently valueless unless exchanged for something else.

Yet the aim of many digital companies appears to be to make money by selling themselves to someone else. Beyond this, their ambition seems to be market disruption by delivering something faster or more conveniently than before. But to what end ultimately? What is their great purpose? What are they for, beyond saving time and delivering customers to advertisers?

In this context, high-frequency trading is certainly clever, but it's socially useless. It doesn't make anything other than money for a small number of individuals. Moreover, while the risks to the owners of the algorithms are almost non-existent, this is not generally the case for society as a whole. Huge profits are privatised, but huge losses tend to be socialised.

Connectivity has multiple benefits, but linking things together means that any risks are linked, with the result that systemic failure is a distinct possibility. So far, we've been lucky. 'Flash Crashes' such as the one that occurred on 6 May 2010 have been isolated events. On that date, high-speed-trading algorithms decided to sell billions of dollars worth of stocks in seconds, causing momentary panic. Our blind faith in the power and infallibility of algorithms makes such failures more likely to happen and more severe when they do. As Christopher Steiner, author of *Automate This: how algorithms came to rule our world*, writes, 'We're already halfway towards a world where algorithms run nearly everything. As their power intensifies, wealth will concentrate towards them.'

Similarly, Nicholas Carr has written that 'Miscalculations of risk, exacerbated by high-speed computerized trading programs, played a major role in the near meltdown of the world's financial system in 2008.' Digitalisation helped to create the subprime mortgage market, and expanded it at a reckless rate. But negative network effects meant that the market imploded with astonishing speed, partly because financial networks were able to spread panic as easily as they had been able to transmit debt.

Network effects can create communities and markets very quickly, but they can destroy them with velocity and ferocity, too. Given that the world's financial markets, which influence our savings and pensions, are increasingly influenced by algorithms, this is a major cause for concern. After all, who's analysing the algorithms that are doing all of the analysing?

Out of sight and out of mind

Interestingly, it's been shown that individuals spend more money when they use digital or electronic money rather than physical cash. Because digital money is somehow invisible or out of sight, our spending is less careful. And when money belongs to someone else — a remote institution rather than a known individual, for instance — any recklessness and impulsiveness is amplified.

Susan Greenfield claims that digitalisation creates a mindset of disposability, and has linked this to modern financial problems. If, as a trader, you have grown up playing rapid-fire computer games in digital environments, you may decide that similar thrills can be achieved via trading screens without any direct real-world consequences. You can become desensitised.

Looking at numbers on a screen, it's easy to forget that these numbers represent money and ultimately people. Having no contact with either can be consequential. Worse, we tend to take less notice of information when it's delivered on a screen amid a deluge of other digital distractions.

Carelessness can have other consequences, too. Large basement developments such as the one I stumbled upon represent more than additional living space. They are symbolic of a gap that's opening up between narcissistic individuals who believe they can do anything they want if they can afford it and others who are attempting to hang on to some semblance of physical community. A wealthy few even take pleasure seeing how many local residents they can upset, as though this were some kind of glorious computer game. Of course, in the midst of endless downward drilling and horizontal hammering, the many have one thing that the few will never have: enough.

Across central London, where a large house can easily cost ten million pounds, it's not unusual for basement developments to include underground car parks, gyms, swimming pools, and staff quarters, although the latter are technically illegal. It's fine to stick one of nature's most evolved killing creatures 15 metres underground, but local councils draw a line in the sand with Filipino nannies.

The argument for downward development is centred on the primacy of the individual in modern society. It's their money (digital or otherwise), and they should be allowed to do whatever they like with it. There isn't even a need to apologise to neighbours about the extended noise, dirt, and inconvenience. The argument against such developments is that it's everyone else's sanity and that neighbourhoods and social cohesion rely on shared interests and some level of civility and cooperation.

If people start to build private cinemas with giant digital screens in basements, this means they aren't frequenting public spaces such as local cinemas, which in turn affects the vitality of the area. In other words, an absence of reasonable restraint and humility by a handful of self-centred vulgarians limits the choices enjoyed by the broader community.

This isn't totally the fault of digitalisation, far from it, but the idea that an individual can and should be left alone to do or say what they like is being amplified by digital technology. This is similar, in some respects, to the way in which being seated securely inside a car seems to bring out the worst in some drivers' behaviour towards other road users.

Access to technology, especially technology that's personal and mobile, facilitates remoteness, which in turn reduces the need to interact physically or consider the feelings of other human beings. Remote access in particular can destroy human intimacy and connection, although on the plus side such technology can be used to expose or shame individuals who do wrong in the eyes of the broader community.

In ancient Rome, there was a law called Lex Sumptuaria that restrained public displays of wealth and curbed the purchasing of luxury goods. Similar sumptuary laws aimed at superficiality and excess have existed in ancient Greece, China, Japan, and Britain. Perhaps it's time to bring these laws back — or at least to levy different rates of tax or opprobrium on immodest or socially divisive consumption, or on digital products that damage the cohesiveness of the broader physical community.

What's especially worrying is that studies suggest that wealth beyond a certain level erodes empathy for other human beings. Maybe the shift from physical to digital interaction and exchange is doing much the same thing.

It's not just the wealthy who are withdrawing physically. Various apps are leading to what some commentators are calling the 'shut-in economy'. This is a spin-off from the on-demand economy, whereby busy people, including those that work from home, are not burdened by household chores. They can use an app to order not only groceries or fast food, but also just about any item they would have traditionally gone shopping for, laundry services, and even housemaids and cleaners. As one food-delivery service, DoorDash, says: 'NEVER LEAVE HOME AGAIN.'

Where have all the jobs gone?

I'd like to dig a little deeper into the question of whether computers and automated systems are creating or destroying wealth, and what happens to anyone who becomes irrelevant to the needs of the digital economy.

The digitally networked nature of markets is making some people rich, but also spreading wealth around far more than you might think. Globally, the level of inequality between nations is lessening and so is extreme poverty. In 1990, for example, 43 per cent of people in emerging markets lived in extreme poverty, defined as existing on less than one dollar per day. By 2010, this figure had shrunk to 21 per cent.

Or consider China. In 2000, around 4 per cent of Chinese households were considered to be middle class. By 2012, this had increased to two-thirds, and by 2022 it's predicted that almost half of the Chinese population will be middle class, defined as having annual household incomes of between US $9,000 and $16,000. This has more to do with demographics and deregulation than digitalisation, but, by accident or design, global poverty has been reduced by half in 20 years.

Nevertheless, the gap between the highest- and lowest-earning members of society is growing and is set to continue with the onward march of digital networks. The novelist Jonathan Franzen says it well: 'The internet itself is in an incredibly elitist concentrator of wealth in the hands of the few while giving the appearance of voice and the appearance of democracy to people who are in fact being exploited by the technologies.'

These days, if you have something that the world feels it needs *right now*, it's possible to make an awful lot of money very quickly, especially if the needed thing can be transmitted digitally. However, the spoils of regulatory and technological change are largely being accrued by people who are highly educated and internationally minded. If you are neither of these things then you are potentially destined for low-paid, insecure work, although at least you'll have instant access to free music, movie downloads, and computer games to pass the time until you die.

There's been much discussion about new jobs being invented, including jobs we can't currently comprehend, but most current jobs are fairly routine and repetitive and therefore ripe for automation. Furthermore, it's unrealistic to expect that millions of people can be quickly retrained and reassigned to do jobs that are beyond the reach of robots, virtualisation, and automation. Losing a few thousand jobs in car manufacturing to industrial robots is one thing, yet what happens if automation removes vast swathes of employment across the globe? What if half of all jobs were to disappear?

In theory, the internet should be creating jobs. In the US between 1996 and 2005, it looked like it might. Productivity increased by around 3 per cent and unemployment fell. But by 2005 (i.e. *before* the global recession), this development started to reverse. Why might this be so? According to consulting firm McKinsey, manufacturing, computers and related electronics, and information industries contributed about half of US productivity increases since 2000, 'but reduced (US) employment by 4,500,000 jobs'.

It could be that our new technology, for all its power, can't compete with simple demographics and sovereign debt. Perhaps, for all its glitz, computing just isn't as transformative as we think. Yes, we've got Facebook, Snapchat, and *Rich Cats of Instagram*, but we still haven't got moon hotels or roast dinner in a pill, and traffic in many cities moves no faster today than it did a century ago. Yet it's certainly difficult to argue that nothing's changing. Between 1988 and 2003, for example, the effectiveness of computers increased a staggering 43-million-fold. Exponential growth of this nature must be creating tectonic shifts somewhere — but where exactly?

In its heyday, in 1955, General Motors employed 600,000 people. Today, Google, a similarly iconic American company, employs around 50,000. Facebook employs only 6,000. More dramatically, when Facebook bought Instagram for one billion dollars in 2012, Instagram had 30 million users, but employed just 13 people full-time. When Facebook bought Whatsapp in 2014, the start-up had just 55 employees, but a market value exceeding that of the entire Sony Corporation. This forced Robert Reich, a former US secretary of labour, to describe Whatsapp as 'everything that's wrong with the US economy'. This isn't because the company is bad — it's because it doesn't create jobs.

Another example is Amazon. For each million dollars of revenue that Amazon makes, it employs roughly one person. This is undoubtedly efficient, but is it desirable? Is it progress?

These are all examples of the dematerialisation of the global economy, where we don't need as many people to produce things, especially when customers can be co-opted as free workers who don't appear on any balance sheet.

A handful of people are making lots of money from this, and when regulatory frameworks are weak or almost non-existent these sums tend to multiply. For multinational firms, making money is becoming easier, too, not only because markets are growing, but also because huge amounts of money can be saved by using information technology to coordinate production and people across geographies.

Technology vs psychology

If a society can be judged by how it treats those with the least then things are not looking good. Five minutes walk from the solitary shark and winner-takes-all mentality, you can find families that haven't worked in three generations. Many of them have given up hope of ever doing so. They are irrelevant to a digital economy, or more specifically, to what Manuel Castells, a professor of sociology at Berkeley, calls 'informational capitalism'.

Similarly, Japan is not far off a situation where some people will retire without ever having worked and without having moved out of the parental home. In some ways, Japan is unique — for instance, its resistance to immigration. But in other ways, Japan offers a glimpse of what can happen when a demographic double-whammy of rapid ageing and falling fertility means that workforces shrink, pensions become unaffordable, and younger generations don't enjoy the same dreams or disposable incomes as their parents.

Economic uncertainty and geopolitical volatility, caused partly by a shift from analog to digital platforms, can mean that careers are delayed, which delays marriage, which feeds through to low birth rates, which lowers GDP, which fuels more economic uncertainty. This is all deeply theoretical, but the results can be hugely human.

If people don't enjoy secure employment, housing, or relationships, what does this do to their physical and, especially, psychological state? I expect that a negative psychological shift could be the next big thing we experience, unless a coherent 'we' emerges to challenge some of the more negative aspects of not only income inequality, but also the lack of secure and meaningful work for the less talented, the less skilled, and the less fortunate.

A few decades ago, people worked in a wide range of manufacturing and service industries and collected a secure salary and benefits. But now, according to Yochai Benkler, a professor at Harvard Law School, the on-demand economy is efficiently connecting people selling certain skills to others looking to buy.

This sounds good. It sounds entrepreneurial. It sounds efficient and flexible and is perhaps an example of labour starting to develop its own capital. Yet it's also, potentially, an example of mass consumption decoupling from large-scale employment and of the fact that unrestrained free-markets can be savagely uncompromising.

Of course, unlike machines, people can vote, and they can revolt, too, although I think that passive disaffection and disenfranchisement are more likely. One of the great benefits of the internet has been the ease with which ideas can be transmitted across the globe, yet ideas don't always turn into actions. The transmission of too much data or what might be termed 'too much truth' is also resulting in what Castells describes as 'informed bewilderment'. This may sound mild, but if bewilderment turns into despair and isolation, there's a chance this could feed into radicalisation, especially when the internet is so efficient at hosting communities of anger and transmitting hatred.

There's also evidence emerging that enduring physical hardship and mental anguish not only creates premature ageing, which compromises the immune and cardiovascular systems, but also produces a lasting legacy for those people having children. This is partly because of their own reduced capacity to care for their children, and partly because many of the subsequent diseases can be passed on genetically. A study, co-led by George Slavich at UCLA, says that there is historical evidence for such claims and cites the fact that generations born during recessions tend to have unusually short lifespans. Research with monkeys also suggests that if animals perceive they have a lower social rank, their pro-inflammatory genes become more active. This may be applicable to humans perceiving that they are becoming digital serfs.

Poorer individuals are certainly more attuned to injustice, especially when they've never known anything else. Yet perhaps it's neither the absolute wealth nor relative income levels of the rich that so offend, but the fact that it's now so easy to see what you haven't got. Social media spreads images of excess abundantly and exuberantly.

A narrowing of focus

In the Victorian era, when wealth was polarised, there was at least a shared moral code, a broad sense of civic duty, and collective responsibility. People, you might say, remained human. Nowadays, increasingly, individuals are purely looking out for themselves.

Individualism has created a culture that's becoming increasingly venal, vindictive, and avaricious. This isn't just true in the West. In China, there is anguished discussion about individual callousness and an emergent culture of compensation. The debate was initiated back in 2011 when a toddler, Wang Yue, was hit by several vehicles in Foshan, a rapidly growing city in Guangdong province, and a video of the event was posted online. Despite the fact she was clearly hurt, no vehicles stopped and nobody bothered to help, until a rubbish collector picked the two-year-old girl up. She later died in hospital.

Another incident, also in China, saw two boys attempting to save two girls from drowning. The boys failed and were each made to pay compensation of around 50,000 yuan (nearly double the average annual salary) to the parents for not saving their children.

Such incidents are rare, but they aren't unknown and do perhaps point toward a world that's becoming more interested in money than humankind — a world that is grasping and litigious, where trust and the principle of moral reciprocity are under threat. You can argue that we are only aware of such events due to digital connectivity, which is probably true, and that both sharing and volunteering are in good health. Yet you can also argue that the transparency conjured up by connectivity and social media is making people more nervous about sticking their necks out. In a world with no secrets, ubiquitous monitoring, and perfect memory, people have a tendency to conform.

Hence we click on petitions online rather than actually doing anything. I was innocently eating my breakfast recently when I noticed that Kellogg's were in partnership with Chime for Change, an organisation committed to raise funds and awareness for girls' education and empowerment through projects promoting education, health, and justice. How were Kellogg's supporting this? By asking people to share a selfie 'to show your support'. To me, this is an example of internet impatience and faux familiarity. It personifies the way that the internet encourages ephemeral acts of empathy and belonging that are actually nothing of the sort.

As for philanthropy, there's a lot of it around, yet much of it has become, as one wag rather succinctly put it, 'money laundering for the soul'. Philanthropy is becoming an offshoot of personal branding. It's buildings as giant selfies, rather than the selfless or anonymous love of humanity. One pleasing development that may offset this trend is crowdfunding, whereby individuals fund specific ideas with micro-donations. At the moment, this is largely confined to inventions and the odd artistic endeavour, but there's no reason why crowds of people with small donations can't fund altruistic ideas, or even interesting individuals with a promising future.

I sometimes wonder why we haven't seen a new round of uprisings in the West. Thanks to digital media, we all know all about the haves and the have-yachts. It's even easy to find out where the yachts are moored, thanks to free tracking apps. Then again, we barely know our own neighbours these days, living, as we increasingly do, in digital bubbles where friends and news stories are filtered according to preselected criteria. The result is that we know more and more about the people and things we like, but less and less about anything or anyone outside of our existing preferences and prejudices.

Putting aside cognitive biases such as inattentional blindness — which means we're often blissfully unaware of what's happening in front of our own eyes — there's also the thought that we've become so focused on ourselves that focusing anger on a stranger five minutes up the road is a bit of stretch. This is especially true if you're addicted to status updates of your daily existence or looking at photographs of cute animals online.

Mugged by reality

Are many people out there thinking about how Marx's theory of alienation might be linked to social stratification and an erosion of humanity? I doubt it, but the fall of communism can be connected with the dominance of individualism and the emergence of self-obsession.

This is because before the fall of the Berlin Wall in 1989, there was an alternative ideology and economic system that acted as a counterweight to the excesses of capitalism and individualism. Similarly, in many countries, unions and an agile and attentive left took the sting out of any political right hooks. Then in the 1990s, there was a dream called the internet. But the internet is fast becoming another ad-riddled venue for capitalism, where, according to Jeff Hammerbacher, an early Facebook engineer, 'The best minds of my generation are thinking about how to make people click ads.' The early dream of digital democracy has also soured, because it turns out that a complete democracy of expression attracts voices that are 'stupid, angry, and have a lot of time on their hands'. This is Jonathan Franzen again, although he reminds me of another writer, Terry Prachett, who pointed out that 'Real stupidity beats artificial intelligence every time.'

To get back to the story at hand, the point here is that if you take away any balancing forces, you end up not only with tax-shy billionaires, but also with income polarisation and casino banking — not to mention systemic financial crashes, another of which will undoubtedly be along shortly, thanks to our stratospheric levels of debt, the globally connected nature of risk, and the corruption and the villainy endemic in emerging markets. It's possible that connectivity will create calm rather than continued volatility, but I doubt it. More likely, a relatively insignificant event, such as a further rise in US interest rates, will spread panic and emotional contagion — at which point, anyone still living in a digital bubble will get mugged by reality.

Coming back to some good news, a significant economic trend is the growth of global incomes. This sounds at odds with declining real wages, but I'm talking about emerging, not developed, markets. According to the accountancy firm Ernst & Young, an additional three billion individuals are being added to the global middle class. That's three billion more smartphone-using, Fitbit-wearing, LinkedIn-profiled, hybrid-driving, Instagram obsessives. In China, living standards have risen by an astonishing 10,000 per cent in a single generation. Per capita GDP in China and India has doubled in 16 and 12 years respectively. In the UK, such growth took 153 years.

This development is pleasing, although Ernst & Young's definition of 'middle class' includes people earning as little as ten dollars a day. Many of these people also live behind the Great Firewall of China, so we shouldn't get too carried away with trickle-down economics or the opening up of democracy. Also, what globalisation giveth, automation may soon taketh away — and many may find themselves sinking downward toward working-class or neo-feudal status rather than effervescently rising upward.

According to Pew Research, the percentage of people in the US who think of themselves as middle class fell from 53 per cent in 2008 to 44 per cent in 2014, with 40 per cent now defining themselves as lower class compared to 25 per cent in 2008. Teachers, for example, who have studied hard, worked relentlessly, and benefit society as a whole find themselves priced out of real estate and various socio-economic classifications by the relentless rise of financial speculators.

Even if the newfound global wealth isn't temporary, it simply means the newly better-off can join the developed world in focusing more attention on their own needs at the expense of others.

Of course, it's not numbers that matter. What counts are feelings, especially feelings related to the direction of social mobility. The perception in the West generally is that we are mostly moving in the wrong direction. This can be seen in areas such as health, and it's not too hard to imagine a future world split into two halves: a thin, rich, well-educated, mobile elite and an overweight, uneducated, anchored underclass. This is reminiscent of H.G. Wells' intellectual, surface-dwelling Eloi and downtrodden, subterranean Morlocks in *The Time Machine*. The only difference in our new future might be that it's the global rich that end up living underground, cocooned from the outside world in deep basement developments.

An upside to the downside

It's obviously possible that this outcome could be re-written. It's entirely possible that we will experience a reversal — where honour, courage, or service before self are valued far above commerce, perhaps. This is a situation that existed in Britain and elsewhere not that long ago. It's possible that grace, humility, public spirit, and contempt for vulgar displays of wealth could become dominant social values. Or perhaps a modest desire to leave as small a footprint as possible could become a key driving force.

On the other hand, perhaps a dark dose of gloom and doom is exactly what the world needs. Perhaps the era of cheap money is coming to an end, and an extended period of slow growth will do us all a world of good. A study led by Heejung Park at UCLA found that the trend towards greater materialism and reduced empathy had been partly reversed due to the 2008–2010 economic downturn. In comparison with a similar study looking at the period 2004–2006, US adolescents were less concerned with owning expensive items, while the importance of having a job that's 'worthwhile to society' rose. Whether this is just cyclical or part of a permanent shift is currently impossible to say.

These studies partly link with previous research suggesting that a decline in economic wealth promotes collectivism, and perhaps with the idea that we only truly appreciate things when we are faced with their loss. There aren't too many upsides to global pandemics, rogue asteroids, and financial meltdowns, but the threat of impending death or disaster does focus the long lens of perspective. Perhaps it is only when we're faced with our own extinction that we truly start to live as human beings.

Digital vs physical trust

How else might the digitalisation of money affect our everyday behaviour in the future? I think it's still too early to make any definitive statements about particular technologies or applications, but I do believe that the extinction of cash is inevitable because digital transactions are faster and more convenient, especially for companies. Cash can be cumbersome, too. And, of course, governments and bureaucracies would like to reduce illegal economic activity and collect the largest amount of tax as quickly as possible, thereby increasing their power.

In the US, for instance, it's been estimated that cash costs the American economy $200 billion a year, not only due to tax evasion and theft, but also due to time-wasting. A study by Tufts University says that the average American spends 28 minutes per month travelling to ATMs — to which my reaction is 'So what?' What are people not doing by 'wasting' 28 minutes going to an ATM? Writing sonnets? Inventing a cure for cancer?

But a wholly cashless society or global e-currency won't happen for a long time, partly because physical money, especially banknotes, is so tied up with notions of national identity (just look at the euro to see how that can go wrong!). Physical money tells a rich story. It symbolises a nation's heritage in a way that digital payments cannot. People in recent years have also tended to trust cash more. The physical presence of cash is deeply reassuring, especially in times of economic turmoil.

In the UK in 2012, more than half of all transactions were cash, and the use of banknotes and coins rose slightly from the previous year. Why? The answer is probably that in 2012 the UK was still belt-tightening, and people felt they could control their spending more easily using cash. Or perhaps people didn't trust the banks or each other. Similarly, in most rich countries, more than 90 per cent of all retail is still in physical rather than digital stores.

We should also be careful not to assume that everyone is like ourselves. The people most likely to use cash are elderly, poor, or vulnerable, so it would be a huge error, in my view, if everyone stopped accepting physical money. It's also a useful Plan B to have a stash of cash in case the economy melts down or your phone battery dies, leaving you with no way to pay for dinner. Espousing such a view is probably swimming against the tide though, and I suspect there's huge pent-up demand for mobile and automated payments.

Globally, cash is still king (85 per cent of all transactions still involve cash, according to one recent study), but in developed economies this tends not to be the case. In the US, about 60 per cent of transactions are now digital, while in the UK there are now more non-cash payments than those using physical cash.

Money will clearly be made trying to get rid of physical money. According to the UK Payments Council, the use of cash is expected to fall by a third by 2022. Nevertheless, circumstances do change, and I suspect that any uptake of new payment technologies is scenario-dependent.

I was on the Greek island of Hydra in 2014 and, much to my surprise, the entire economy had reverted to physical money. This was slightly annoying, because I had just written a blog post about the death of cash based on my experience of visiting the island two years earlier. On that previous visit, almost everywhere accepted electronic payments, yet things had changed dramatically. Again, why?

I initially thought the reason was Greek attempts to avoid tax: cash is anonymous. But it transpired that the real reason was trust. If you run a small business supplying meat to a taverna and you're worried about getting paid, you ask for cash. This is one reason why cash might endure longer than some e-vangelists tell us. Cash is a hugely convenient method to store and exchange value and has the distinct advantage of keeping our purchasing private. If we exchange physical cash for digital currency, this makes it easier for companies and governments to spy on what we're doing.

Countless types of cashless transactions

There are many varieties of digital money. We've had credit cards for a very long time. Transactions using cards have been digital for ages and contactless for a while. We've grown used to private currencies, virtual currencies, micropayments, loyalty points, and prepaid cards. We've also learnt to trust PayPal and various peer-to-peer lending sites, such as Zopa and Prosper, although one suspects that, as with ATMs, we are happier taking money out than putting money in.

We're also slowly getting used to the idea of payments using mobile phones. There are even a few e-exhibitionists with currency chips embedded in their own bodies, and while this might take some time to catch on I can see the value in carrying around money in our bodies. A chip inserted in your jaw or arm is a bit extreme, yet how about a tiny e-pill loaded with digital cash that, once swallowed, is good for $500 or about a week? There's even digital gold, but, to be honest, I can't get my head around that at all.

The key point here is that all of these methods of transaction are more or less unseen. They are also fast and convenient, which, I would suggest, means that spending will be more impulsive. We will have regular statements detailing our digital transactions, of course, but these will also be digital, delivered to our screens amid a deluge of other digital distractions and therefore widely ignored or not properly read.

Really thinking or mindlessly consuming?

What interests me most here is whether or not attitudes and behaviours change in the presence of invisible money. There is surprisingly little research on this subject, but what does exist, along with my own experience, suggests that once we shift from physical to digital money, things do change.

With physical money (paper money, metal coins, and cheques), we are more likely to buy into the illusion that money has inherent value. We are therefore more vigilant. In many cases, certainly my own, we are more careful. In short: we think. Physical money feels real, so our purchasing (and debt) is more considered. Moreover, our spending is restricted by how much we can carry. And any money in our pockets is usually ours. Digital money and our behaviour with it have no such limitations.

Perhaps the unseen nature of quantitative easing (QE) is similar. What if — instead of pressing a key on a computer and sending digital money to a secondary market to buy financial assets including bonds — we saw fleets of trucks outside central banks being loaded with piles of real money to do the same? I suspect that our reaction would be wholly different. We might even question whether a government buying its own debt is a sensible idea given that the 2008 financial meltdown was caused by the transmission and obfuscation of debt.

Of course, pumping money into assets via QE circles back to create inequality. If you own hard assets, such as real estate, then any price increases created by QE can be a good thing because it increases the value of your assets (often bought with debt, which is reduced via inflation). In contrast, savers holding cash or people without assets are penalised.

It's a bit of a stretch to suggest QE triggered the Arab Spring, but some people have, pointing out that food-price inflation was a contributory factor, which can be indirectly linked to QE's effects on commodities. If one was a conspiracy theorist, one might even suggest that QE's real aim was to drive down the value of the US dollar, the pound sterling, and the euro at the expense of spiralling hard-currency debt and emerging-economy currencies.

I'm getting back into macro-economics, which I don't want

to do, yet it's worth pointing out that in *The Downfall of Money*, the author Frederick Taylor notes that Germany's hyperinflation destroyed not only the middle class, but also democracy itself. As he writes, by the time inflation reached its zenith, 'Everyone wanted a dictatorship.' The cause of Germany's hyperinflation, initially, was Germany failing to keep up with payments due to France after World War I. But it was also caused by too much money chasing too few goods, which has shades of asset bubbles created by QE.

It was economic depression, not inflation per se, that pushed voters toward Hitler, but this, too, has a familiar ring. Across Europe, we are seeing a significant rightwards shift — and one of the main reasons why Germany is reluctant to boost the EU economy is because of the lasting trauma caused by inflation 90 years ago.

If a lasting legacy of QE, debt, networked risk, and a lack of financial restraint by individuals and institutions — all accentuated by digitalisation — is either high inflation or continued depression, things could get nasty, in which case we might all long for the return of cash as a relatively safe and private way to endure the storm.

Crypto-currency accounts

The idea of a global digital economy that's free from dishonest banks, avaricious speculators, and regulation-fixated governments is becoming increasingly popular, especially, as you'd expect, online.

Currencies around the world are still largely anchored to the idea of geographical boundaries and economies in which physical goods and services are exchanged. But what if someone invented a decentralised digital currency that operated independently of central banks? And what if that currency were to use encryption techniques, not only to ensure security and avoid confiscation or taxation, but also to control the production of the currency? A crypto-currency such as Bitcoin perhaps?

In one scenario, Bitcoin could become an alternative payments infrastructure, competing against the likes of Apple Pay and PayPal as well as against alternative currencies such as frequent-flyer points. But there's a more radical possibility.

What if a country got into trouble (Greece? Italy? Argentina?), and trust in the national currency collapsed? People might seek alternative ways to make payments or keep their money safe. If enough people flocked to something like Bitcoin, a government might be forced to follow suit, and we'd end up with a crypto-currency being used for exports, with its value tied to a particular economy or set of economies.

More radically, how about a currency that rewarded certain kinds of behaviour? We have this already, in a sense, with loyalty cards, but I'm thinking of something more consequential. What if the underlying infrastructure of Bitcoin was used to create a currency that was distributed to people behaving in a virtuous manner? What if, for instance, money could be earned by putting more energy or water into a local network than was taken out? Or how about earning money by abstaining from the development of triple sub-basements or by visiting an elderly person that lives alone and asking them how they are? We could even pay people who smiled at strangers, using eye-tracking and facial-recognition technology on Apple smart glasses or Google contact lenses.

Given what governments would potentially be able to see and do if cash does disappear, such alternative currencies — along with old-fashioned bartering — could prove popular. At the moment, central banks use interest rates as the main weapon to control or stimulate the economy. But this doesn't work if people hoard cash because interest rates are low — or because they don't trust banks.

With a cashless society, however, the government has another weapon in its arsenal. What if, in addition to banks charging people for holding money (negative interest rates), governments imposed an additional levy for not spending it?

This is making my head spin, so we should move on to explore the brave new world of healthcare and medicine, of which money is an enabler. But before we do, I'd like to take a brief look at pensions and taxation and then end the chapter by considering whether the likes of Mark Zuckerberg might actually be OK really.

If economic conditions are good, I'd imagine that money and payments will continue to migrate toward digital formats. Alternatives to banks will spring up, and governments will loosen their tax take. However, if austerity persists or returns then governments will do everything they can to get hold of more of your money — yet they will be less inclined to spend it, especially on what used to be termed essential services. Taxation based on income and expenditure will continue, but I expect that it could also shift towards assets and wealth and, to a very real extent, individual behaviour.

One of the effects of moving towards digital payments and connectivity is transparency. Governments will, in theory, be able to see what you're spending your money on, as well as how you're living in a broader sense, and relieve you of tax in real time (goodbye annual tax returns). Hence stealth taxation. Have you put the wrong type of plastic in the recycling bin again? That's a fine (tax). Kids late for school again? Fine (tax). Burger and large fries again? You get the idea ...

Governments will seek not only to maximise revenue, but also to nudge people towards certain allegedly virtuous behaviours, so people might be forced to pay for the tiniest transgressions. This, no doubt, will spark rage and resistance, but there could be a tax for that, too.

As for pensions, there are several plausible scenarios, but business as usual doesn't appear to be one of them. The system is a pyramid-selling scheme that's largely bust and needs to be reinvented in many countries. One in seven people in the UK has no retirement savings whatsoever, for instance, and the culture of instant digital gratification would suggest that trying to get people to save a little for later won't meet with much success.

What comes next largely depends on whether the culture of now persists and whether or not responsibility for the future is shared individually or collectively. If the culture of individualism and instant rewards holds firm, we'll end up with a very low safety net or a situation where people never fully retire. If we are able to delay gratification, we'll end up either with a return to a savings culture or one where the state provides significant support in exchange for significant contributions.

The bottom line here is that pensions are set firmly in the future, and while we like thinking about the future we don't like paying for it. So what might happen that could change the world for the better and make things slightly more sustainable?

An economy as if people still matter

In 1973, the economist E.F. Schumacher's book *Small is Beautiful: a study of economics as if people mattered* warned against the dangers of 'gigantism'. On the one hand, the book was a pessimistic polemic about modernity in general and globalisation in particular. On the other hand, it was prescient and predictive. Schumacher foresaw the problem of resource constraints and foreshadowed the issue of human happiness, which he believed could not be sated by material possessions. He also argued for human satisfaction and pleasure to be central to all work, mirroring the thoughts of William Morris and the Arts and Crafts Movement. They argued that since consumer demand was such a central driver of the economy, one way to change the world for the better would be to change what the majority of people want.

Looked at unkindly, Schumacher's book is an idealistic hippy homily. Looked at more generously, it manages to describe our enduring desire for human scale, human relationships, and technology that is appropriate, controllable, and — above all — understandable. Physical money encourages physical interaction, whereas digital money is hands-off and remote. There's also an environmental consideration: digital transactions require energy, and while any desire for green computing won't exactly stop the idea of a cashless society in its tracks, it may yet restrain it.

There are already some weak signs of a recognition that people matter, which Schumacher may have approved of. Our desire for steampunk fashion and stories; the rise of craft sites such as Etsy; the popularity of live music, vinyl records, and literary festivals; and our attempts at digital detoxing all point to a wish for balance and a world where humans are allowed to focus on what they do best. A world where machines bring us together, not drive us apart. Of course, digital has its part to play here, too: the partly generational shift towards temporary digital access rather than full physical ownership is an encouraging development against what James Wallman terms 'stuffocation'.

Schumacher also warned against the concentration of economic and political power, which he believed would lead to dehumanisation. Decisions should therefore be made on the basis of human needs rather than the revenue requirements of distantly accountable corporations and governments. In this respect, the internet could go either way. It could bring people together and enable a more locally focused and sustainable way of living or it could facilitate the growth of autocratic governments and monopolistic transnational corporations. But remember that the dematerialisation of the global economy — the analog-to-digital switch, if you will — is largely unseen and therefore mostly out of mind, so very few people are discussing this at the moment.

To some extent, digital payments are a technology in search of a problem. Cash is easy to carry, easy to use, and doesn't require a power source — except to retrieve it from an ATM. Meanwhile, credit and debit cards are widely accepted worldwide and online, so why do we need additional channels or formats? Maybe we don't. Maybe we don't even need money as much as we think.

One of the problems with the digital economy from an economics standpoint is that, as we've seen, digital companies don't produce many jobs. Yet maybe this isn't a problem. Once we've achieved shelter and security and managed to feed ourselves, the things that make us happy tend to be invisible to economists. The things that fulfil our deepest human needs aren't physical, but nebulous notions such as love, belonging, and compassion. This is reminiscent of Abraham Maslow's hierarchy of needs, but — unfortunately — self-esteem, altruism, purpose, and spirituality don't directly contribute to GDP or mass employment. Perhaps they should.

It pains me to say it, but maybe Mark Zuckerberg and the other digital dreamers are onto something after all. Maybe the digital economy will change our frame of reference and focus our attention on non-monetary value and human exchange, even if this goes a little crazy at times.

What would Schumacher make of our current economic situation? Maybe he'd see the present day as the start of something terrible. Maybe he'd see it as the start of something beautiful. The future, as always, will be what we make it. As for what Schumacher might make of the shark, I have no idea, although I recently heard that it's now on medication.

Santa Fe, New Mexico
December 24, 2018.

Dear A,

I can no longer go to bed with you knowing that someone else might join us
at any moment, even in the middle of the night. Even when we are making
love, someone inevitably interrupts.

You give priority to being online over and above anything or anyone else at
all times. Why? What's so urgent or important? Even the children are getting
fed up with it.

I'm leaving you to your own devices.

Goodluck.

D.

HEALTHCARE AND MEDICINE

can we ever acquire immunity against loneliness?

What if the cost of machines that think is people who don't?
George Dyson

Shane Warne with contact lenses or elbow surgery is accepted as human and is allowed to play professional cricket. But how about Shane with bionic eyes, a prosthetic arm, video tattoos (showing advertisements for Bundaberg rum), and augmented-reality sunglasses? Given what's happened to Warne's external appearance lately, the mind truly boggles as to what might have happened if he and Liz Hurley had decided on having genetically modified children.

Human enhancement is not unusual. We've been doing it for centuries. Our methods for enhancing ourselves have just become more sophisticated, whether it's tattoos, piercings, plastic surgery, botox, or hearing aids. It is also a matter of opinion whether enhancement has improved the human body or not. Hearing implants can not only restore hearing, but amplify sounds.

People with disabilities are using prosthetics to replace parts that are missing or that don't work, but now prosthetic designers are creating parts that are better than normal human ones. For example, Oscar Pistorius's 'Cheetah' legs were seen to give him an unfair advantage in the Paralympics. Similar controversy occurred when Ian Thorpe wore a 'sharkskin' swimsuit. Such augmentation, especially when physically part of the human body, will have huge implications, and the ethical debate has barely begun.

Nobody can fail to be moved one way or another by the audacity of enhancement, nor the promise it holds for future generations to be healthier. The question is whether it's interfering with what's natural, although this is an equally subjective question. Moreover, the devices that we constantly carry with us could be regarded as forms of enhancement.

Silicon dreaming

With improvements to our health, our population is ageing, and with this comes an increased fear of Alzheimer's. Memory is a hot issue for the elderly, but research in this area could have pervasive effects.

Fans of the movie *The Matrix* may recall the scene where the character Neo downloads the skills of a kung-fu master. Connecting a digital system to your human brain might sound impossible, yet only ten years after seeing that movie, I bought a toy called a *Star Wars* Force Trainer: this was a headset that allowed its wearer to control a simple machine with their thoughts. A modest connection, perhaps, but suggestive. A few years later, my brain brimming with machine-interface enthusiasm, I found myself working with the Foresight Practice at Imperial College London, where I had a discussion about whether it might one day be possible to interface with a machine and directly download skills or experience into the human brain — foreign-language mastery or kung-fu skills, perhaps. The academic view was that this would not be possible, although they did concede that the downloading and remote viewing of dreams could be commonplace by 2040.

I mention this because things are afoot that are equally weird. In December 2013, a scientist called Sam Deadwyler published a paper documenting a series of experiments that involved transplanting memories into the brains of rats. We have, or soon will have, thought-controlled wheelchairs, robotic limbs, and cochlear and retinal implants, all of which depend on some level of direct brain–machine communication. So why can't we treat the memory loss associated with human ageing by replacing or bypassing damaged parts of the brain?

Conversely, if you could turn off or remove memories, this might also be useful for soldiers or civilians suffering from post-traumatic stress disorder. The US Defence Advanced Research Projects Agency aims to conduct human trials on precisely such technology by 2020. But developments such as these raise a host of dilemmas.

Some of the most interesting implications of the digital era concern transformations of power, community, allegiance, and identity. With identity, memories are critical. They define us as unique human beings and allow us to reflect on who we are. Some people say that if your memory is lost, as it is in some forms of dementia, you become someone else and to some extent can't be held legally responsible for your actions.

Replicating a person's memory isn't easy. Human memory works on numerous levels, but if we could crack the code then all kinds of things would be possible. There's no reason why one day it won't be possible to buy electronic memory implants or e-pills that polish a perfectly normal brain. A student study chip, perhaps? Yet we shouldn't think of such ideas in isolation.

I'm sure we'll invent technologies that allow older people to remember events, although in the shorter term it might be far easier to record everything that happens to us and then to rewind to find whatever we need.

I've already mentioned the problem of never being allowed to digitally forget things: embarrassing images and hastily composed tweets never really go away. Viktor Mayer-Schonberger points out that, in 1950, the storage cost for digital data was $70,000 per megabyte, whereas by 1980 this had fallen to $500, by 2000 was around one cent, and by 2008 had plummeted to 1/100th of a cent. This might be useful for older people wishing to remember everything, but perhaps not so good for younger people wishing to forget things.

Mayer-Schonberger has one intriguing solution to this problem, in the form of digital data with automatic decay dates. This would save us from social awkwardness as well as suffocating amounts of digital garbage. Google has voiced a similar idea regarding clean-slate digital identities once people reach adulthood.

Again, don't think of these ideas in isolation, but always in combination. It may not be what implantable memory or the recording of your entire life means per se, but what they mean in conjunction with other technologies, such as gesture control armbands, mood enhancers, mood recognition, digital drugs, or highly immersive virtual reality.

If this is starting to sound a little like a plot for another science fiction movie, buckle up, because it gets better. If our memories (i.e. our memory of events) define us then what happens if you modify someone's memories? Are they still them? At the extreme, would they still be human — and if not, why not?

Data exhibitionism

In my view, the ability to control information about oneself, especially information we ourselves create, is vital. For instance, I can foresee a future situation where a major pharmaceuticals company is subject to a legal class action for using aggregated, anonymised personal data to develop profit-making drugs, the argument being that at least part of the profits belong to the people who generated the data.

One estimate is that we already give away up to £5,000 worth of personal data every year. The film *Terms and Conditions May Apply* reckons that 'The greatest heist in history wasn't about taking money; it was about taking your information — and you agreed to all of it.'

If you are a member of the quantified-self, or 'lifelogging', movement, you may be proud of the fact that you can optimise your cardiovascular activity or sleep hours using wearable devices. Apps such as Timehop even allow you to view your activity on the same day weeks, months, or even years previously. Rather than keeping such personal data to yourself, you might choose to share it with others, which may facilitate social interaction, which is in turn vital for mental and physical health.

But what if, for one reason or another, you went through a period of prolonged inactivity — or activity that is best kept private — and this data were shared or hacked? You might be subject to networked humiliation or you might receive a letter from your health insurer downgrading your insurance cover. You could almost certainly expect pop-up ads from heart surgeons and sleep doctors offering discount services if your data suggests they may be of interest.

Once information is digitised, it longs to wander. As the writer Stewart Brand famously declared, 'Information wants to be free', although nowadays it also wants to multiply like a plague of locusts and obliterate any surrounding ecosystems.

When information is placed on a sharing network like the internet, you have immediately lost control of it, forever. Others may copy it, forward it, or strip it of its original context. And don't forget that if you entrust your data to third-party services, these can be hacked, too. Indeed, there's nothing about the word 'cloud' that implies permanence or security. I'm sure the many thousands of people who have already had their credit-card details stolen might agree.

Clearly, sharing certain types of information is a force for good. If individual health data is collected, it can change behaviour for the better. User-generated data ranging from wellness wikis to bulimia blogs do change lives. Using millions of patients to report on treatments via websites such as patientslikeme.com is an excellent example of how the medical establishment is being challenged by digitally empowered patients, and I'm sure we've only scratched the surface in terms of open medicine's potential. Increasing aggregation of self-recorded data will likely lead to better and often less expensive treatments and care.

Watch yourself

Where most tracking devices can only track one thing, a Google app called PACO (Personal Analytics Companion) can be set up to track any kind of behaviour or event. You might want to track how drinking coffee makes you more productive or what brings on headaches. Your data may be private or you can share it with somebody, depending on your need or mood.

The value of self-tracking regularly is it doesn't rely on memory, it can be used over time, and it's easy to do. In the medical world, trials are expensive, hard to administer, and generally short. Data tracking could help monitor cognitive impairment, clinical depression, or the onset of infectious disease — and reassure people who falsely represent their own symptoms or habits. Social workers might be able to find out the triggers for feeling negative towards their clients, or teachers might want to monitor how exercise and food affect the behaviour of classes.

Google is also working on a contact lens with sensors that measure the amount of glucose present in the tears of a person with diabetes. For a wide variety of physical tests, there are already numerous medical devices, such as wireless scales, electrocardiograms on smartphones, and the new otoscope, a device that looks inside the ear and sends its results via an iPhone app.

There's also a computer the size of this full stop. If you are suspected of suffering from glaucoma, you can put this tiny machine in your eye to measure the pressure of liquid against your eyeball. Data is sent wirelessly to your doctor.

One company is even testing a sensor that can assess stomach fluids to find out whether patients have taken their medicine or not.

Wait a little longer and we'll see wearable medical devices disguised as jewellery and watches. Also: analytical e-skins. This would be clothing, especially underwear, made from conductive fibres containing gyroscopes, GPS, transmitters, and kinetic-energy batteries to monitor vital signs, detect medical emergencies, and call an ambulance when necessary.

There could also be bio-sensor toilets, digital sticking plasters, e-pills, wireless medical monitoring patches, ingestible robots that dissolve once their task is done, and wirelessly powered sensors embedded in the human body producing full-body telemetry, at which point the body gradually transforms into a technology platform, possibly controlled by Google.

If the thought of all this does not enthuse, you grasp the reticence and conservatism of the healthcare industry, as opposed to the tech head's fascination for novel gadgets. Moreover, doctors are often paid per consultation, and they may be less enamoured with less-frequent visits. On the other hand, insurers are worried such devices may lead to hypochondria — the worried well might fuss over anomalous readings and so make even more visits to the doctor.

Keeping this in mind, we should always assess new medical devices in the same way that we assess new drugs.

The power of networking

Ultimately, healthcare data could be stored within our bodies and we might become nodes on a network. More people means more tracking means more data to feed into Google Flu trends, which identifies flu outbreaks up to seven times faster than conventional methods.

Google Flu Trends is an example of Big Data, which is the name given to the huge sets of data generated in our increasingly digital world, for instance records relating to consumer behaviour or data collected from smartphone sensors and geotags. Simply by looking at internet search terms, Google can predict flu outbreaks. This worked for a while, although some of the forecasts of late have predicted things that didn't happen. This is a big problem with Big Data.

Unless you have *all* the data, big isn't necessarily better, as the economist Tim Harford has pointed out. It's usually better to have a fully representative sample than a big dataset. There's also the problem of becoming over-reliant on historical patterns to predict future behaviour. Nevertheless, assuming we continue to refine our use of Big Data, a key problem remains: what should companies and governments in the 21st century do with all the data they collect, and who ultimately owns or controls this data?

One very interesting development in healthcare is the arrival of Google and Apple on the scene, so it's not too far-fetched to suggest that, some day, doctors may prescribe apps. Unlike Nike or Garmin, these consumer technology brands are not usually associated with wellness, but they are perfectly positioned to offer advice either via mobile devices or by their knowledge of who we are and what we do.

One indication of how things may progress is an app called StudentLife, which was initially designed to find out how students cope at university. Researchers found that flourishing students were generally among other people more often and had longer conversations, while struggling students spent more time alone, often indoors, and had disrupted or extended sleep patterns. The results of StudentLife suggest that phones can be used for continuous mental-health tracking, and should be more reliable than self-completion questionnaires. Questions of privacy emerge, as they always do, but in this case the user has complete control.

Another favourite development of mine is a tooth from Taiwan that watches what your mouth is doing. Developed at National Taiwan University, this 'oral activity recognition' device can monitor when you eat, how much you eat, how fast you chew, whether you cough, and even how often you talk. The artificial tooth would work best fitted into a set of false teeth, but could be a single implant or, potentially, a cap (equipped with Bluetooth?) to send data to your dentist or doctor.

If an e-tooth were connected to a wearable device — a contact lens, for instance — a camera could recognise what pills people take. Or what they are eating, and offer dietary suggestions. It could even photograph food packaging and have the wisdom of online crowds suggest recipes.

Virtual tertiary specialists and virtual hospital wards could follow. Medical cards linked to retail loyalty cards could provide further personalised recommendations or might flag unhealthy purchasing behaviour. Perhaps one end result might be individual health ratings, similar to that of credit ratings. People with good health scores would be offered health-insurance discounts and premium healthcare choices, such as access to top-rated surgeons or to the latest medicines.

Digital me

How about having a medically accurate digital body double? Why? Because, as we are continually being told, we are not all the same, and a physiological simulation of every person on Earth would flip healthcare as we know it upside-down.

We could all have real-time personal healthcare forecasts, which might include projected expiry (i.e. death) dates. This would change daily depending on diet, exercise, and lifestyle.

Looking at our genetic makeup via sites such as 23andme.com is useful because it offers a glimpse as to what we might suffer from in the future, allowing us to personalise our medicine. But genetics won't tell you everything, because it doesn't consider how we live on a daily basis and doesn't look at the complex linkages between different diseases or treatments.

Having a digital double that continually updates itself with healthcare data, including vital signs, would mean you could run virtual tests and even treatment scenarios. If you die, your virtual double could even be virtually dissected.

In theory, developments such as these would make patients pay more attention to the consequences of their own actions and allow doctors to further personalise treatments, but again it could turn people into hypochondriacs and, once more, raises numerous legal and ethical questions. For example, who would own your virtual twin and the data it collects? What if failure to maintain monthly payments meant withdrawal of service, which in turn meant you failed to receive life-saving information? And how about privacy, equality, or autonomy?

Possibly the biggest question is a concern over whether patients

would trust the advice of a machine over human experience —
something of a recurring theme in speculations about the future.
We already delegate authority to all kinds of machines, but
under what conditions would individuals trust fully autonomous
machines, and how could such trust be verified?

Mobile risks

Apart from the ethical questions, staring at screens can have
other downsides, too.

In many countries, such as America, Britain, and Australia,
sedentary lifestyles mean that physical activity levels have fallen
by 20 per cent over the past 50 years, and are forecast to fall
an additional 15 per cent by 2030. Similarly, too much screen-
based entertainment and an almost allergic reaction to being
outdoors in the fresh air and sunlight means that children today
are considerably less fit than their parents and grandparents at
the same age. With this thought in mind, a reversal of long-
established longevity trends isn't completely impossible.

Of course, there's already an app for this problem. But what
about problems caused directly by the devices themselves?

A Swedish study of 1,200 people diagnosed with malignant
brain tumours between 1997 and 2003 analysed their mobile-
and cordless-phone use and found that those who started
using mobiles as teenagers and continued to use them for ten
years were 4.9 times more likely to develop malignant brain
tumours. For cordless-phone users over ten years, the risk
was 3.9 times. There's also evidence emerging that prolonged
exposure to wi-fi signals could be having a serious impact
on health. In 2015, France banned wi-fi in nursery schools
and restricted availability in primary schools, while a Lloyd's
insurance underwriter, CFC Underwriting, has told British

schools that it was excluding liability for claims 'relating from or contributed to by electromagnetic fields, electromagnetic radiation, electromagnetism, radio waves or noise'. This means all wi-fi, smartphones, iPads, and other mobile devices. Because of the possible links to cancer, experts such as Olle Johansson at the Karolinska Institute forecast a 'paradigm shift' in attitudes towards the radiation emitted by such devices.

Mobile phones have been called the 'new cuddly toys' for kids. Some countries take the risks seriously. In France, it's illegal to market mobiles to children under 12, and they can't use them in primary schools. Other countries, such as the UK, Israel, and Germany, merely discourage such use.

Disconnect by Devra Davis claims that children are more susceptible to radiation because their skulls are thinner and their brains are still developing. This leaves parents in a difficult position. Nobody is saying for sure that mobile phones cause cancer in children, but there's enough evidence gathering to make parents nervous.

This begs the question of how much mobile-phone use is safe for adults, given their ubiquity. It may turn out that the risk from radiation is negligible, partly because phones are now better designed to shield against radiation and partly because we are now less inclined to clamp phones to our heads. But there's also evidence emerging that reading using a phone or iPad at night has an 'extremely powerful effect' on sleep length and quality.

How sleep became the new sex

A decade or two ago, taking an electronic device to bed meant only one thing. Nowadays, reading or playing computer games while in bed is fairly normal. Bedrooms are turning into media rooms and workplaces, symbolic and symptomatic of a restless,

116

globalised, ubiquitously connected world. But all at the expense of a good night's sleep.

It's common, especially among alpha males, to brag about how little sleep one has had or needs. Some day, someone might wake up to the idea that an alternative way to extend human lifespans would be to spend less time sleeping. Perhaps it will be someone that remembers reading *Beggars in Spain* in bed — this is a science fiction novella where genetic advances have made it possible to live without sleep. But the fact is that until someone comes up with nightcaps that use transcranial magnetic stimulation to trigger on-demand deep sleep, a proper night's sleep is essential. A continual lack of sleep can affect alertness, attention, judgement, problem-solving, and ideas. It can even affect ageing and our ability to combat infection.

Sleep isn't only restorative, it's where we make sense of things. The phrase 'sleep on it' has been around for a while, yet it wasn't until 1953 that people realised that the brain doesn't switch off when we sleep. Instead, our brains are busy processing information. More specifically, when we sleep the brain takes recent experiences and stabilises them as memories. Our brains do this all the time, but it's only when we're sleeping that we actively filter this information, sorting out what's useful and what's not and linking information together to extract meaning, solve problems, and dream up new ideas. When people try to survive on less than six hours sleep per night, aspects of memory stabilisation and learning do not work as well — or in extreme cases, do not work at all.

Using phones and other mobile devices in bed or anywhere else is, like most things, a matter of common sense. Putting to one side marital risks, health concerns are an issue, but only when devices are used to excess.

Goodbye to the family doctor

Marriage isn't the only relationship that could be harmed through digital interaction.

Doctors' notes and prescriptions may soon exist only as digital files. This is good news on a number of levels. For example, doctors' illegible handwriting can result in misdiagnosis and drug-delivery errors, while, in theory, e-notes mean that patients and doctors will be able to access medical histories anywhere in the world. On the other hand, my own doctor insists that he can talk to me and make handwritten notes at the same time, whereas with notes on a screen he can't. This reminds me of a policeman I once spoke to who said that with handwritten notes he could look a suspect in the eye to glean the truth while writing, something that isn't possible with a tablet computer. If he paid attention to any digital device, he couldn't pay close attention to any potential offender or eyewitness.

Electronic prescribing and dispensing will come, and will be linked with the widespread use of mobile health and telemedicine, although one suspects that a lack of common standards and platforms will create havoc in the early days. Despite this, I'm sure it won't be too long before we'll walk into a chemist with a QR-code prescription on our mobile device rather than handing over a crumpled piece of paper.

Generally speaking, there are two types of mobile health or telemedicine: one to monitor a wearer's physical fitness, such as Jawbone wristbands, and one to link patients to the healthcare system via sensors or other forms of digital monitoring. The second category appears to have the most potential, especially for people that live alone or in remote locations.

A US study in 2008 found chronically ill patients enrolled in a home telehealth programme in the US experienced a 25 per cent drop in bed days of care and a 19 per cent fall in hospital admissions, with an average cost of $1,600 each, compared to $13,121 for conventional care.

Looking at overall health spending in the US from 1970 to 2009, spending increased by around 9 per cent per annum. This is what you might expect with an ageing population, although the US isn't ageing as fast as some. But here's the thing: in 2009, 2010, and 2011, the average increase was less than 4 per cent. How come? The dire economic situation would have something to do with this, but a Harvard study suggests that structural changes — one of the most important of which is keeping people at home rather than in hospital — were a key component, and this is where digital monitoring and diagnosis comes in.

The end of modern medicine

Wait a little longer, and a visit to the doctor could be to use sensors more powerful than what can be embedded about your person — such as handheld medical tricorders that scan and sense illness (a *Star Trek* favourite).

As for surgery, the shift will be away from invasive procedures apart from childbirth. Before this happens, robotic surgery could become commonplace, and we may see automated robotic surgery without human oversight.

There will also be laboratory-made body parts — skin, kidneys, blood vessels, bladders, and even windpipes — all potentially 3D-printed at your local hospital from personalised specifications.

3D printing has certainly caught the imagination of many, including Lee Cronin at the University of Glasgow, who has fabricated simple chemicals such as ibuprofen using a digital blueprint and a 3D printer. While currently intended for chemists, there's no reason why printers like this can't be used by anybody, as long as the software prevents them from making unsafe or illegal drugs. Lee's team is working on a mass-produced kit to make ibuprofen so that the developing world has access to it via their mobile phones. This sounds crazy, but most drugs are just combinations of carbon, hydrogen, and oxygen, helped with a little corn syrup, glycerol, and paraffin.

OMG, we're all going to live!

Some people are worried. They think that there are too many people on our supposedly small planet. We've been breeding like rabbits for too long, and logic would suggest that any ever-increasing population that consumes a finite supply of resources is heading for trouble.

This argument is as old as the hills, going back to the Club of Rome and the publication of *The Limits to Growth* in the 1970s — and further, to Malthus and his doomsday forecasts of mass starvation in the 1800s. Yet to say there are too many humans is nonsense.

The reason there are over seven billion people on our planet is not because we've been breeding like rabbits, but because we no longer drop dead like flies. We've experienced a healthcare revolution during the last century, and average human lifespans have almost doubled. To my mind, this is far more a blessing than a curse.

Having more humans does indeed have serious implications for resources, but these can be made secure through careful conservation, proper pricing, regulation, and behavioural change. We can also switch resources. More importantly, the human species is imaginative — that's why we're still here, and more people also means more brains to fix more problems and invent things.

When it comes to food, water, energy, climate change, and other concerns, I'm fairly certain that we will invent our way out of trouble — possibly at the last minute in many instances. We are on the cusp of a series of inventions, especially around energy and agriculture, and these could be transformational.

In the case of healthcare, we will cure many common conditions and extend longevity still further, although the equitable distribution of such gains is in doubt.

As for the future of medicine itself, the overall prognosis is excellent, although we should be careful not to blindly turn to technology as a cure-all. An article in the *British Medical Journal* has made the point that the supply of technology drives demand. The more technology exists, the more we'll rely on it, and there is already a problem with the over-diagnosis and over-treatment of perfectly normal human conditions.

Around 50 per cent of the increased cost of healthcare is believed to arise from technology, far outweighing the impacts of ageing populations, rising prices, or increased demand. Tech push is a particularly pernicious problem, which, alongside myths such as 'new ideas are always better than old ideas' and 'advanced medicine is always better than simple solutions', causes us to over-prescribe technological cures.

A healthy dose of scepticism

Another major concern is what happens if future medical marvels aren't equally shared. Gordon Moore, the father of Moore's Law, has commented that we now live in two societies divided by education. What if society is further divided by health? What happens if the rich have access to treatments that the poor don't? This happens already, but I suspect that affordability of care will become a greater issue as societies age and rely more on healthcare. For example, at the moment around 35 million people suffer from Alzheimer's, and older patients need expensive care. In the US, more than 25 per cent of Medicare is spent on people in the last 365 days of their life.

By 2050, the number of Alzheimer's patents is forecast to triple. Some observers predict 114 million cases worldwide by 2050, largely due to ageing. Worrying as this is, a scarier thought is that Alzheimer's is a late stage of type 2 diabetes, of which around 270 million people currently suffer. Hopefully, since type 2 diabetes is largely a dietary and lifestyle problem, this can be fixed, especially with some of the new tracking technologies and gamification techniques.

As I've mentioned, rising social inequality can lead to more rapid ageing as immune systems are compromised. In one sense, regenerative medicine — finding ways to repair worn-out old bodies — is a terrific idea, but taken to extremes it will cause problems. At the moment, nobody has had much success extending the human body beyond the current upper limit of around 120 years. Yet if we do, and fertility rates continue to fall, we will inherit societies that are bursting at the seams with older people, with fewer younger people to provide care. Perhaps robotics, for instance exoskeletons (mechanical skeletons wrapped around the human body), will allow ageing populations to remain mobile and independent. But again, who's paying? Maybe it's Google.

It's rather unclear at the moment what Google is searching for, but if recent acquisitions are anything to go by then we are in for interesting times. A few years ago, Google became involved with the longevity business via a biotech start-up called Calico. Google have been buying roughly one company per week since 2010, largely in the areas of search, autonomous devices, robotics, and artificial intelligence. In 2013 alone, Google purchased eight robotics start-ups. Perhaps they are buying these companies to acquire the minds behind them. Or maybe we'll get these technologies for free, but the price we'll pay could be Google knowing everything about us inside and out.

Death as software error

But what of the fortunes resulting from such clever ideas?

One idea is to do away with death. There's a tendency found in high-tech hot spots of people, mainly financially successful men, trying to avoid what's been called the death problem. PayPal co-founder Peter Thiel, for example, says, 'Basically, I'm against it.' Personally, I think death is a good idea. Death has advantages, ranging from generational renewal and wealth transfer to avoiding boredom. If life were unlimited, it would become meaningless.

However, this seems to be a point lost on many digital dreamers. Their longing for the disappearance of death appears to grow from the same philosophy that favours radical transparency and the total removal of regulatory frameworks. A way of achieving the latter could be building floating countries out of reach of legal jurisdictions — what Andrew Keen calls the 'fantasy of secession from the real world'.

One possible future is therefore a world where, if you can afford the payments, your life will be extended even to the point of not dying at all. Aubrey de Grey, a gerontologist who is partly funded by Peter Thiel, thinks this is possible and has even suggested that the first person to reach the ripe old age of 1,000 has already been born. Or maybe not: dying might eventually become a choice we all make, although, if not, we'd presumably have to instead choose not to have children, to avoid overcrowding and resource problems.

Brains in boxes

Yet silicon dreamers' minds stretch further than this. They would like not only to solve immortality, but also to have the chance to crack the most difficult coding problem in the world, namely human consciousness.

To put this into perspective — we cannot currently describe consciousness, so we are a long way off replicating it outside the human body. Some scientists think that consciousness is the drawing together of data: it kicks in when data is networked and becomes more than the sum of its parts.

At the moment, consciousness (the ability to reflect and to think deeply about our own thinking and existential condition) is one way in which humans are different from machines. Consciousness, along with intuition, is not computable.

On the other hand, it may not be essential for consciousness to be located inside carbon-based biochemical neural networks. (God and aliens again?)

I suspect that consciousness is a spectrum and that all animals, even plants, have a level of awareness. However, whether matter is capable of having consciousness, or whether levels of self-awareness could ever be added to machines, is hugely unclear, although some human brains, desperate to turn creator, are trying to do the latter.

The Human Brain Project in Geneva is an attempt, with one billion euros of EU taxpayers' money, to build a silicon brain simulation deep inside a supercomputer. They haven't got very far so far, possibly because they're focused on how humans think as opposed to how humans feel.

Demis Hassabis, the founder of DeepMind, a company bought by Google for $400 million in 2014, is on a similar mission to create artificial-intelligence systems and general-purpose learning algorithms to make machines 'smart'. DeepMind isn't, as far as I'm aware, trying to replicate human consciousness, but is attempting to copy the human brain in a number of ways in order to solve many of the world's most serious problems, including disease.

Hassabis started life as a chess prodigy and became a computer-games designer and neuroscientist, studying parts of the brain associated with memory, navigation, and imagining future events. He is undoubtedly exceedingly smart, and genuinely seems motivated by the idea of making the world a better place. Nevertheless, he seems most at home with logic and efficiency, seeing consciousness and creativity as potential software programs. As he says, 'It's quite possible there are unique things about humans. But, in terms of intelligence, it doesn't seem likely.' In other words, the human mind is a computer.

Peter Thiel and Elon Musk have both put money into DeepMind's AI technologies, which Hassabis refers to as 'neutral in themselves'. This is true, but I'd argue that once any technology comes into contact with humans, they (that is, we) always become something else. Please don't get me wrong — I'm not suggesting that Hassabis is anything other than a nice person. It's just that anyone who's spent from the age of four playing chess, often against adults, might have missed out on something about the human condition. A telling comment he made is that eating, with the exception of eating out, is wasted time and that he'd be happy if he could just swallow tubes of paste: 'It would be good if there was something more efficient.' (There's that word again.)

Clearly Hassabis has a laser-like focus. Like many in Silicon Valley, he has missionary zeal. But I fear that his key interest concerns efficiency rather than humanity. This seems cold and calculating — I prefer the term 'effectiveness', which can be highly illogical. 'Efficiency' reminds me of a primary-school teacher in Norfolk, England, who closed classroom blinds so that the small children wouldn't be distracted by snowflakes falling outside. As the poet W.H. Davies wrote:

What is this life if, full of care,
We have no time to stop and stare.

Teaching a machine to deal with a logical problem such as playing chess is relatively easy. Teaching a robot kung-fu could be a maths problem. But getting a machine to think about snow slowly falling or wind on the Welsh hills, or to be moved by poetry, is different.

Humans have always adapted. In fact, adaptation is what our species does best. As Susan Greenfield points out, we inhabit more environmental niches than any other species. We have survived ice ages, pandemics, revolutions, wars, and Paris Hilton. We've also augmented our bodies and tools in the face of change. We've created clothing, glasses, guns, and some semblance of security. Our survival will depend on us continuing to do all this and more, and we shouldn't assume that human evolution is over. It isn't. We will continue to evolve, most probably by merging with our machines using bio-electronics. As John Rogers, a materials scientist at the University of Illinois, says, 'Bit by bit, our cells and tissues are becoming just another brand of hardware to be upgraded.'

Gaining digital immortality by putting our brains inside boxes may indeed negate the need to eat and would bypass the awkward and inconvenient need to deal directly with other human beings or to inhabit a physical body. Floating digital minds would be free to blast off toward distant galaxies, far beyond any government red tape, where they might spend eternity inventing new forms of Facebook. Given a long enough timeframe, this is a very real risk, so we should focus now on where we're heading as humans and whether or not this is the road we wish to follow.

A thoroughly modern malady

Allow me to end this chapter with a brief discussion of what I see as an emerging epidemic. This epidemic has many causes

— demographic, technological, and cultural among them. How we choose to treat it will likely involve technology, although I suspect that using people might be more appropriate.

My fear for healthcare is that we may be going down a slippery slope where we are forgetting the human touch. But this is not the epidemic of which I speak.

The National Health Service in Britain paid for seven million tranquilliser prescriptions in a single year recently to meet growing demand for drugs to ease the debilitating effects of anxiety. Over one five-year period, the number of outpatients treated in hospitals for anxiety quadrupled. This is a tragic state of affairs for a wealthy country.

The clinical psychologist Linda Blair says that technology is exacerbating economic worries because it causes people to be on a permanent state of alert. Digital media especially means that we are constantly threatened by an endless procession of risks ranging from terrorism and automation to impending economic collapse.

Furthermore, rather than technology allowing us to escape into a world of leisure and relaxation, as was widely predicted in the 1960s, it has done the opposite. The idea of the idle rich has been flipped on its head. Nowadays, it tends to be the moderately wealthy that work all hours. Too much leisure now symbolises idleness and unemployment. This is partly because of something called the substitution effect, whereby high wages make leisure expensive.

Digital communications in particular rob us of the opportunity to switch off. When we are always available and constantly sent messages from the time we wake to the time we fall asleep, we cannot relax or switch off. This can lead to chronic anxiety about what might happen next. Being constantly bombarded with images of what we ought to achieve also creates constant low-level exhaustion. We fear losing control, especially after we wake up one day to discover that the ideal life we once thought we'd lead won't come true.

We also seem to have become less tolerant of adversity, real or imagined, and need a little something to help us deal with our worries. Thus the use of alcohol, food, or recreational drugs to enforce or compress relaxation.

Frank Furedi, a sociologist, takes a contrary view. He says that our culture feeds anxiety and encourages sufferers to wear it with pride. It has become fashionable to discuss anxiety at dinner parties. If you are not anxious then there is something wrong with you. He says even children 'medicalise the everyday' and learn how to speak the jargon of anxiety.

Anxiety is a modern problem, a medical definition of which only appeared in 1980, when the authors of the *Diagnostic and Statistical Manual* (DSM) suggested that between 2 per cent and 4 per cent of a population would typically suffer from an anxiety-related condition. Thirty years on and a US report called *America's State of Mind* said that this number had risen to one in six of the population. A more recent study puts the number of people who are severely anxious or deeply insecure at 20 per cent.

One explanation for this is that the pharmaceutical industry is inventing problems to which only it can supply an answer. Another is that, in countries such as the US, anxious people need to be diagnosed with a disease so that insurance companies can pick up the bill for any treatment.

On many levels, anxiety is perfectly normal. Back in the 17th and 18th centuries, anxiety — or 'nervous disorder', as it was known then — was seen as a badge of upper-class sensitivity. Thus poets were allowed to be anxious whereas coalminers were not. There are certainly links between severe anxiety and high levels of creativity. Equally, some people think that some level of anxiety is good because it means that people are more sensitive to the needs of others.

One thing we should be clear about is that anxiety and depression are often assumed to be the same thing, when they are not. Anxiety is usually linked with worry, whereas depression is linked with loss of interest and pleasure. Both could be linked with low moods, especially loneliness, or they could both be caused, one way or another, by uncertainty.

All forms of anxiety can also be linked to wealth, yet not in the way you might expect. For example, a World Health Organisation study in 2002 suggested that 18.2 per cent of US citizens report anxiety in a typical year, but in Mexico the figure is less than half this. The pattern continues, with some of the poorest countries reporting the lowest levels of incidence.

Nigeria, where almost 85 per cent of people lived on less than US$2 per day in 2002, reported anxiety levels of 3.3 per cent. This suggests that anxiety disorders might be the curse of wealth, freedom, and security, or that we worry when we don't have anything to worry about. Some observers, the psychiatrist Vikram Patel for example, dispute this, suggesting instead that anxiety levels are much the same the world over. Nevertheless, I imagine that there is some correlation between anxiety and a world that feels overwhelming or out of control.

Stop the world, I want to get off

One small story I can't forget, and that I almost started this book with, concerns a retired 89-year-old art teacher and former Royal Navy engineer called Anne, from Sussex. A keen environmentalist, Anne decided to end her life in 2014 because she felt that computers had taken the humanity out of human interaction.

People, she thought, were becoming 'robots' addicted to their gadgets, and she couldn't understand why so many people spent so many hours sitting in front of screens. As she put it, 'They say adapt or die. At my age, I feel I can't adapt, because the new age is not an age that I grew up to understand. I see everything as cutting corners.'

Suicide, alongside anxiety, is reaching epidemic proportions.

In the developed world, self-harm has become the main cause of death for people aged 15 to 49. It surpasses heart disease and cancer. In 2010, self-harm killed more people than war, murder, and natural disasters combined and, for middle-aged Americans, rose in incidence by 30 per cent during the first decade of this century.

According to the World Health Organisation, suicide rates have risen by 60 per cent since World War II. Any simple explanation for this will be wrong. It is likely to be caused by a combination of economic, social, and cultural factors. But this epidemic is still not the one I've got in mind.

As I stated earlier: many years ago, Theodore Zeldin told me that loneliness could be the single biggest problem facing humanity in the 21st century. I think he's right.

Forgotten, but not yet gone

If feelings of anxiety can sometimes be normal, what then of loneliness? I suppose the answer to this depends on whether or not you feel human beings are born social or whether you think being social is thrust upon us. Historically, sociability has been the norm, but perhaps this was because there wasn't much alternative. Nowadays, in contrast, it's relatively easy to be alone, either due to demographics or technology.

Declining fertility, shrinking households, and smaller direct and extended families mean that more people will be living alone in the future. Older people, in particular, can expect to live for extended periods without a partner, and even where there is family, it's either becoming more difficult to physically stay in touch or families are choosing not to. Work, too, is fragmenting, with more people working from home or away from shared office spaces. This means less meaningful contact with colleagues. And with medicine and elderly care, as we've seen, the shift seems to be away from human contact.

What the question here really boils down to, and it is a question that is at the heart of this book, is whether or not humans need to be around other people to be happy and healthy. To what degree do humans need physical connection? Some people say that it's non-negotiable, a must-have; it's in our nature, and human nature is invariable. I'm not so sure. I think that human nature has been fixed for a long time, but this could be changing due to changes in our external environment, especially technology. I hope I'm wrong.

Dear new Dinner Printer ® owner,

WELCOME TO THE FUTURE OF FOOD! SIMPLY PLACE YOUR DEVICE
WITHIN RANGE OF A CORDLESS CHARGING PLATE AND YOU'LL HAVE
ACCESS TO OVER 200,000 DIGITALLY PRINTED DINNER OPTIONS.
YOUR DINNER PRINTER ® COMES WITH 45 DIFFERENT FOOD INKS
AND 900 INSTANTLY DOWNLOADABLE RECIPES, BUT YOU CAN ORDER
THOUSANDS MORE FROM THE DINNER PRINTER ® STORE AT WWW.
DINNERPRINTER.FOOD

MOST MEALS CAN BE PRINTED IN JUST 60-SECONDS AND THERE'S NO
MORE SHOPPING IF YOU PRINT YOUR OWN PERSONALISED PLATES
AND UTENSILS WITH OUR HOME MAKER ® KITCHEN SUPPLIES
PRINTER. YOU CAN EVEN GET RID OF THE WASHING UP IF YOU ADD
OUR REVERSE PRINTER ® KITCHEN DISPOSAL UNIT. JUST MAKE SURE
THOSE PESKY KIDS DON'T STICK THEIR FINGERS IN IT! ONLY KIDDING
FOLKS, IT IS TOTALLY 'ARMLESS FOR CHILDREN.

Please note that all Dinner Printer ® recipes and ingredients are owned by the
Protein Corporation and use of open source inks or recipes will invalidate your
statutory rights. If printers are not used in accordance with the manufacturers
instructions this also invalidates all liabilities.

AUTOMOTIVE AND TRANSPORT

*where might self-driving cars
eventually take us?*

Logic will get you from A to B. Imagination will take you
everywhere.

Attributed to Albert Einstein

One of the concerns relating to an increasingly elderly population is how people will move around, especially if you are
trying to encourage physical interaction and avoid loneliness.
Exoskeletons are one solution. Self-driving personal mobility
pods are another.

Google's self-driving cars have driven 2.9 million kilometres,
with only 14 minor incidents, all of which were the fault of
humans. It seems driverless cars run into a problem: humans that
don't follow rules.

I can sympathise with the humans. I have a fondness for older
cars. I wouldn't go as far as to say that I've ever fallen in love
with one, but I've come close. Like avatar children, cars can be
designed to appeal to a set of very primitive emotions. How some
curved sheets of steel from the 1970s can inspire joyous feelings
is illogical. Perhaps it's Freudian. Perhaps it's my mother. Maybe
it's those womb-like curves. More likely though, it's a designer

working in an era before computer-aided design, which, according to Nicholas Carr, 'bypasses much of the reflective and exploratory playfulness'. Modern automobiles are safer and in some ways more efficient, yet they've lost much of their soul. Contrast a sensual 1966 Lamborghini Miura (designed by a 22-year-old with no computer) or a hypnotic 1973 Ferrari Daytona (designed on paper in seven days) to their modern equivalents (and don't even get me started on a Dino 246 GT).

Modern cars fill me with frustration in other ways, too. Freeman Thomas, a designer at Ford, says that technology is ruining the driving experience. I'd agree. I have a friend, David, who owns a 1958 Alfa Romeo Giulietta, but also a modern Porsche 911. He says he gets more fun out of the Alfa at 60 km/h than the 911 at full throttle.

But I have better examples of how rapid movement isn't necessarily synonymous with progress. The first was when I lost a spare electronic key to a modern Land Rover. The key eventually showed up, yet not before I'd visited a sales representative who informed me that a new computerised key would cost £110, plus tax, plus a further £60 to program it. Surely this is intermediate technology? It's not as good as a metal key, which is almost impossible to damage and can be cut for next to nothing, nor as good as an i-key, which you can locate with your phone, tablet, or laptop when it gets lost.

Or there was the time the Land Rover broke down and I got a loan car for a few days. I spent a frustrating 15 minutes sitting in the driver's seat trying to work out how to start the car. The problem was there wasn't a slot to put the computerised key into as there was on my older Land Rover. Apparently, the key merely needed to be in the car, but the car had to be in park and my foot needed to be on the brake, too.

An even better example of how complexity can be synonymous

with stupidity concerns a Subaru. A friend of my wife drove over not so long ago to drop her child off. She didn't want to stop, but she was persuaded to turn the engine off and have a quick cup of tea. Little did she know, there wasn't a key in the car. It turns out that you can start some cars if the key is near enough to the car — and you can even drive away. The only thing you mustn't do is switch the engine off, because then you can't start it again. Has the automotive world gone completely mad? Back in the day, I could start any car if it broke down. Now if a car won't start, it's me that breaks down.

Is this the end of the road?

The number of cars on the world's roads is set to double in the near future. This has consequences for natural resources and climate — and human safety.

In an average month, 108,000 people around the world die in car accidents, and this figure is forecast to rise to 150,000 by 2020. In 90 per cent of cases, car accidents are caused by human error rather than machine failure, and with ageing populations this could become worse.

A US study, for instance, found that while over-70s were 9 per cent of the US population, they were at fault in 14 per cent of all traffic accidents and were responsible for 17 per cent of pedestrian deaths. Clearly, removing humans, especially older ones, from the driving seat would, in theory, be a good idea. It could make traffic flows more efficient and reduce pollution, too. We already accept the idea of traffic being managed remotely, so why not send data to the cars themselves and have the cars work out what to do?

Yet there are ethical problems surrounding such automation. As Nicholas Carr observes, 'At some point, automation reaches a critical mass. It begins to shape societies norms, assumptions, and ethics.' For example, would it be right to outsource life-and-death decisions away from drivers and place them in the hands of proprietary algorithms? Could you, should you, program a machine to make moral judgements? How would you feel about a car that calculated that it was worth driving into a tree and killing you in order to save the lives of two drunken strangers running across the road?

We've had machines making judgements about drivers for years, although we rarely notice. Automatic license-plate recognition systems have been operating since the mid-1970s and have become common since the 1980s. Cameras monitoring bus lanes and speeding are equally ubiquitous. In the Netherlands and Australia, fines are even regularly sent out with no human oversight or intervention whatsoever. Developments such as these bring the ability to monitor and punish human behaviour on an unprecedented scale.

For example, it's already possible to install cameras to catch public drunkenness. Algorithms analyse body movement or body temperature and blood flow to the face. This has shades of Kafka. And what happens to a culture when even the most minor infringement is enforced and where human intervention, human discretion, and human appeal are not available? For algorithms, everything is a binary decision.

One possible result of this and other developments could be a citizenry that is more cautious and contrite. It's also possible we could see a society that's less autonomous and experimental and less likely to voice opposition to the government, the police, and popular opinion.

We are all passengers

Essentially, there are two broad solutions to making cars safer and taking the chore of driving away from the driver. One is smart cars; the other is smart roads.

The idea of putting tracks or wires into roads to steer cars — a cross between dodgems, trams, and Scalextric — has been around since the 1950s and could work perfectly well, except that we currently struggle to even stump up the cash to fix potholes. Making roads super-smart and keeping them clever, while constantly digging them up for repairs, might be too difficult.

The other option is to make cars so smart that they can drive around by themselves unaided. The technology to do this pretty much exists. Do you really think Google Maps was designed for humans? I think that's about as likely as Google's book-digitisation project being designed for people. Both, in my view, have been designed for machines from the very beginning. If you join up Google search with Google navigation, Google cars, and perhaps Google genomics, the future could be a little disturbing.

Driverless cars should become commonplace in ten or 15 years, although the technology will likely be introduced in phases. For example, many cars already feature emergency auto-braking, while cruise control systems are being extended to allow hands-free driving both on freeways and in slow urban traffic. You can bet that manufacturers are also looking at other ways of removing control from a driver for their convenience or safety.

Once cars start to drive themselves, they will most probably park by themselves, too, or simply continue to drive around looking for another ride if the vehicle is shared or communal — a bit like an ordinary taxi. And if drivers no longer need to drive, they would be free (and safe) to do other things, such as work, eat, drink alcohol, read newspapers, watch movies, or look at funny videos of cats. Given that Google's business model is built around advertising, maybe we'll be watching ads in our cars in return for a ride. Or if roadside distractions are no longer a problem, maybe we'll see arrays of moving screens alongside roads. Or Google Pods and Apple iCars will personalise every windscreen so that what I see in front of me is not the same as what you see.

Most interesting though is what happens when fully autonomous electric cars become the norm, especially in cities. This will focus attention on car design (less need for dashboards and controls) and urban planning (as easier long commutes may mean larger cities, while increased traffic efficiency may lead to higher density). Widespread adoption of autonomous cars could even negate the need for traffic lights and road signs — pedestrians would then need augmented-reality glasses or a mobile device to find their way around.

And if millions, or even billions, of electric cars become standard and battery technology improves, there's the awesome option of creating fluid local energy-storage networks, or grids, where power can be physically moved from one place to another.

How people buy and finance cars could change as well. Ultimately, we may abandon the whole idea of owning and driving our own vehicles. Instead, we might subscribe to one — or many, as some people already do. We might summon a communal vehicle with a tap of a smart device, and leave it anywhere we like when we no longer need it.

Our cars may never run out of fuel, either, due to inductive charging. Rather than finding a power socket and uncoiling a length of cable, you could drive the vehicle onto a plate or coil embedded in the surface of the road. Electromagnetic induction will then charge the vehicle wirelessly. What's new here is that scientists have developed a way to do this with an energy-transfer efficiency of about 90 per cent. You could totally charge your vehicle while parked in a garage, car park, or shopping centre, or you could extend its range by topping up the batteries en route.

However, history and associated cultural norms can take a long time to change, especially when linked with totemic objects.

Moreover, when we no longer need to drive cars, we may find we'd rather like to. Driving for sheer pleasure, as opposed to practical mobility, may return — and the automotive industry will have come full circle.

Surrendering control to a robot in the form of a vehicle may prove too much for some people, especially if the car locks you in when it starts, or completely removes the steering wheel and the option of human control. Chances are, it will only be a matter of time before a major city bans human driving, but if a self-driving car kills a human being there could be a sudden and unexpected change of direction. As for turning cars into places of work and social connection, we might find this is precisely what we wish to avoid. A car remains one of the last private spaces, and the intrusion of yet more work (or more virtual people) may be resisted. As for boredom, this can have its uses. Many an insight arose from a boring car journey.

But from an economic efficiency standpoint, self-driving cars make sense. For many people, driving is no longer a pleasure. In the US, the average commuter spends 50 minutes a day sitting in a car. In Los Angeles, for instance, drivers within a 15-block district drive 1.5 billion kilometres each year looking for parking spaces, which is 38 trips around the Earth, 178,000 litres of fuel, and 662,000 kilograms of CO_2. Allowing people to do something else in the front seat could have its advantages. Also, hospitals would have fewer injuries to deal with and emergency rooms would be less busy.

However, technical problems remain. Human drivers, for all their stupidity, are still pretty smart. Humans can tell the difference between a plastic bag in the middle of the road and a solid object. Shadows of trees aren't usually confused with the roadside, and it's fairly easy to tell the difference between a child on a bicycle and a deer.

Machines, even smart ones, break down. And while we're reasonably tolerant of computers and mobile phones not working, cars are another matter, particularly if they're in control. A dropped mobile-phone signal or a crashed tablet is rarely a matter of life and death. Remember the Toyota recall of ten million supposedly defective cars in 2009? It was rumoured that cars were accelerating by themselves and that people had died.

Digital cars could also be targets for hackers and cyberterrorists, although the problem is more likely to be tech-savvy criminals stealing autonomous cars remotely. Having said that, there's already been the case of *Rolling Stone* magazine journalist Michael Hastings. In 2013, his car drove into a palm tree at high speed and exploded, killing him. Given that Hastings had a reputation for revealing stories about the US military and intelligence services and had emailed friends the day before saying that he was working on a big story and was going 'off the radar' for a while, this accident looks suspicious to some.

Any modern car that uses computer software to control its engine, transmission, and braking could in theory be hacked. General Motors (OnStar) and Mercedes (mbrace), for instance, already use mobile networks to monitor key components, and even the cheapest cars can be plugged into a laptop to diagnose faults.

Sooner or later, something will go wrong. Perhaps that's why, in a poll, 48 per cent of people in the UK would be unwilling to be driven by a self-driving car and 16 per cent were 'horrified' by the idea. Then again, it wasn't so long ago that people thought that travelling by train would make them sick or even kill them.

I don't know whether it's better car design, or social acceptance over time, but when I was growing up lots of people *were* sick in cars and aeroplanes. Nowadays, this is rare. Again, one of our human traits is being adaptive, and we can get used to most things given enough time.

Overall, the biggest issue isn't human or technological. The problem with driverless cars and automated transport generally concerns regulation, legal liability, and especially the legal reaction to unforeseen accidents. Critical to this will be the level of trust between people and machines.

So what's next? The answer will be human caution and incremental levels of technological evolution and trust. We'll see more driverless trains and driverless buses, and trucks could follow. The big carmakers will proceed in the direction of full autonomy, but at slow speed. Technology firms will be less cautious, yet even here any technology push will be subject to consumer pull and legislation, which will tend to obstruct, especially in risk-averse and liability-obsessed nations.

The future will therefore arrive piece by piece with the odd crash, sudden-braking incident, and multi-car pile-up. No doubt, many people will lose their jobs. That includes cabbies, truck drivers, and even much maligned parking wardens. Car-rental companies may have to rent driverless cars that offer pick-up and drop-off services, while car parks may lose their value, reducing revenue for local councils. And when self-driving cars are insured, it may be the car companies and software firms that pay, not the human occupants.

Do we even want to drive?

In the big picture, quite where driverless cars will take us is unclear, although we should perhaps bear in mind that interest in cars is waning generally in the developed world. The number of kilometres people drive has fallen of late, and car ownership is reaching saturation. In major cities such as New York and London, around 50 per cent of people don't even own a car. I imagine that in the future, millions of people may grow up never having held a driving licence or a steering wheel.

While retirees still drive, young people are eschewing cars for public transport. In France, for example, people under 30 account for less than 10 per cent of customers for cars, and the average age at which people buy their first new car (as opposed to used car) is now 55. The numbers are much the same across Europe, with the average age of Volkswagen Golf buyers being 54.

In Paris, the trend is towards public transport, carpooling, and peer-to-peer sharing. For instance, BlaBlaCar has ten million members in 13 European countries, including France, and Autolib has 170,000 subscribers in Paris alone. One market-research firm suggests the French see cars as a 'clumsy assertion of social status', as well as a tangible sign of social inequality.

Thanks to the internet, younger generations can do a lot of their travelling via the screen, and it is mobile devices that have become symbols of identity and freedom. In developing regions, mobile phones are similarly an alternative to poor roads and expensive transport.

Then again, arguing that the era of personal car ownership is over, especially because people just want to move efficiently from point A to point B, could be making the same mistake as arguing that watches are dead because people have clocks on their phones. This argument goes back to the 1970s, when digital watches first appeared. People said that expensive watches would fade away. They didn't, because people don't only use watches to tell the time. They are fashion items, statements of identity and status, and the same might be said for private cars.

But before self-driving cars become a self-fulfilling prophecy, there's a more dangerous idea coming down the road. The EU has decreed that all new cars sold in Europe by 2018 be fitted with connectivity, most probably in the form of a SIM card, so cars can automatically call for help in the case of an accident.

In theory, such connectivity would also allow cars to contact breakdown services in case of mechanical failure. This is an excellent idea and surely one that will be music to the ears of companies such as Apple and Google, who have recently launched CarPlay and Android Auto. A survey by McKinsey has found 27 per cent of iPhone users would swap car brands if a rival offered better in-car connectivity. Connectivity could be used to access real-time traffic data, find vacant parking spaces, or stream music services (a subscription service called Rara already offers in-car access to 28 million songs).

Putting ordinary cars online means that other things become possible, too. Apart from local traffic and incident reports, you could see what a car a kilometre in front of you is looking at. My son says that you could also get advance warning alerts of cyclists in front of you or that you could pay the slow-moving car in front of you to move out of the way.

As in other areas of insurance, car-insurance companies have traditionally relied on demographic data (usually filled in by customers) to calculate premiums. Age, sex, occupation, and location are ranked alongside car type and engine size. Now, new technology is shifting the market towards personalised policies, based on digital sensors embedded within vehicles and on how a car is driven. This allows insurance companies to weed out higher-risk drivers and offer discounts to safer drivers. In the US, premiums are moving toward a distance-driven model, while in Europe premiums are being focused on how people drive.

Monitoring is generally done by telematics — the use of black boxes to send data to the insurance company or to apps on drivers' phones. Such surveillance can also alert insurance companies to scams, especially when sensors are used in conjunction with forward-facing dashboard cameras such as those commonly used in Russia. However, used in conjunction with Big Data, we may create a situation where people are penalised financially for propensities rather than actions. Algorithms could suggest that someone is high risk and they would be punished without them doing anything, although you might argue this happens already.

The biggest orderly rollout of forward-facing cameras has been by police around the world. In the UK, around 5,000 body cameras alone are now being worn. The main lesson learned is that awareness of these cameras tends to modify the behaviour of both the officers and those they interact with. With increasingly watchful insurers, we might expect to see safer driving even before machines take the wheel. So what's the bad news?

Peak attention

Automotive and technology companies have thus begun selling us a vision of the future where we can drive and still be fully connected.

Hands-free phones are standard, but the latest temptation is sending and receiving texts without looking at a screen or using your hands. Some high-end cars even allow drivers to book restaurants and theatre tickets without (in theory) moving their gaze from the road ahead. According to McKinsey, by 2020 around 25 per cent of cars will be online. This is all a terrifically stupid idea.

In 2011, distracted drivers killed 3,300 people in the US, and in 2013 US authorities recommended that the display of text messages or web content be banned in cars. Numerous studies have highlighted the severity of the problem, including a 2002 UK study by the Transport Research Laboratory, which found that drivers using hands-free phones reacted more slowly to events than drivers who were slightly above the alcohol limit. In 2005, an Australian study reported that drivers using hands-free devices were four times more likely to crash than drivers focused solely on the road. Lastly, a 2008 US study found talking on a hands-free phone was more distracting for the driver than talking to a passenger, a finding echoed in a 2015 study by the RAC Foundation in the UK.

The current legal assumption is that if people don't take their eyes off the road when using these devices (which they do), it is safer — yet it doesn't make it totally safe. The problem is not removing human hands, but dividing attention. Human attention is finite, and multi-tasking splits mental resources.

A study by the University of Sussex in the UK found that digital multi-tasking (in this case, 'second screening') created a change in the anterior cingulate cortex, impairing decision-making and impulse control. Another study found links between high levels of multi-tasking and weak attention, so the signs aren't good. You might be able to drive and glance at a screen, but what happens when something unexpectedly happens in front of you?

Why the Knowledge is power

In the era of satellite navigation, there is technically no longer a need to know where you're going. Or is there? What if space weather (e.g. solar flares) temporarily knocks out Earth-based GPS systems? GPS and digital maps are great, but surely an appreciation of how to get to where you're going without them is useful.

Paper maps literally give you the bigger picture and educate us about space and context, too. Evidence is even emerging that the situational awareness provided by paper maps may be good for our brains. According to Veronique Bohbot from McGill University in Montreal, the use of digital maps could be putting us at risk from dementia, on the basis that if we don't use certain parts of our brains — parts linked to spatial awareness and memory — we may lose them.

This prompts the question of whether our brains might become less expansive or reflective if we stop driving. We coped perfectly well, it seems, before the invention of the motorcar, although a study by University College London did find that the brains of taxi drivers completing 'the Knowledge' training can change structure due to external stimulation.

Cabbies typically spend up to 70 weeks learning 320 journeys in the official training book so they know the entire Knowledge zone in a ten-kilometre radius of Charing Cross. They have to memorise 25,000 streets and 20,000 landmarks. With a dropout rate of 70 per cent, this is a gruelling task. The drivers claim technology can never compensate for their superior Knowledge, nor can it cope with sudden changes in the city, such as road closures.

One happened to me only recently, when The Mall in London was briefly closed just as we (and the Queen) approached it. The driver was able to deftly reroute us. The Knowledge contains the facts of the city, such as bridges and one-way streets, but taxi drivers also deal with the humanity of the city, too — on the spot, as only humans can.

As an aside, a separate concern with Google Maps is that what you see isn't always what everyone gets. In 2013, the company launched a version of Google Maps in which the representation of a city is different for each individual depending on what Google knows about the user. This doesn't mean you'll get lost, but it does mean that highlighted items of interest could change. Is this another example of Google filtering out serendipity in favour of insularity, as Nicholas Carr suggests?

Finally, while driverless cars may not threaten the jobs of all taxi drivers in big cities, they will almost certainly mean fewer jobs. Driving cars and trucks is a useful job if you don't have any qualifications. As *The Economist* magazine has pointed out, when the horseless carriage replaced horse-drawn transport, the economic gains were 'broadly shared by workers, consumers and owners of capital'. The car was a 'labour augmenting' technology, which means that it allowed people to serve more customers at faster speeds over greater distances. But with driverless cars, and automation generally, the gains are less equal.

When are we going to learn the value of experience, wisdom, and spontaneity, and when is society going to evaluate any benefits — cheaper and more efficient for some — against overall lifetime costs in the broadest sense for many?

Pilotless planes and driverless trains

If 48 per cent of people find the idea of driverless cars alarming, how about pilotless planes? Most passengers would undoubtedly find the idea of flying in a plane with no pilot — and potentially no crew — unthinkable. But the technology is available right now, and low-cost airlines must be considering it.

James Albaugh, a senior Boeing executive, goes as far as saying that 'A pilotless airliner is going to come. It's just a question of when.' It's easy to see his reasoning. Albaugh points out that we've grown used to automated elevators, so why not automated planes? The US military already has twice as many ground-based 'pilots' flying unmanned aircraft (UAVs or drones) than regular fighter pilots, so how long before military pilots are dispensed with altogether? Moreover, there is clearly a problem with aircraft accidents, around 50 per cent of which are caused by human error. This is considerably less than the 90 per cent of automobile accidents, but the results can be so much worse.

If a large number of road traffic accidents are caused by poor human judgement, a large number of air crashes are caused by a total lack of it, with pilots unwilling to rely on their own judgement and training. In many ways, pilotless planes are already flying — on ordinary, everyday passenger aircraft, it's now standard practice to allow the automatic pilot to take over from human hands once the plane is 30 metres off the ground and to disengage it only when landing. No wonder there's a joke that in the future, planes will be crewed by a single pilot and a dog — the dog being there to bark at the pilot if they touch anything.

Yet I'm not so sure James Albaugh is right. It's possible that within a decade or two, cargo carriers such as FedEx and UPS will operate 100 per cent pilotless planes. When it comes to passenger planes, however, I suspect that primitive psychology may trump advanced technology. Our need for control — at least, our need for the illusion of control — is one thing that may take a long time to change. As automation researcher Mary Cummings puts it, 'The need to see a James T. Kirk on the bridge is strong.'

The problem here, as always, is deciding on who, or what, should be in charge. I have a friend who's a pilot and he insists that the issue is the locus of control. In the case of automated controls, his view is that increasing reliance on digital systems is degrading human skills or at least the confidence of pilots to take control away from a machine. In some cases, this is already impossible.

Flight safety systems such as the type called FADEC (Full Authority Digital Engine Control) have no manual override facility. According to some experts, the crash of a Chinook helicopter into the Mull of Kintyre in 1994 was caused by a FADEC software bug rather than human error. Nine months earlier, faults in FADEC had been found that were 'positively dangerous'. Other incidents, including an Airbus A400M crash in 2015, appear to be linked to potentially invisible software faults.

If this has put you off air travel in the future, you could take a train. Surely these are safe. Truly driverless trains already exist, as anyone using Gatwick Airport's North Terminal or Heathrow's Terminal 5 might know. However, driverless trains such as these are on the ground, confined to rails, and are travelling relatively slowly, which is perhaps why we are so accepting of them. We're given little or no alternative, either.

In Europe, politicians generally prefer trains to planes, and the EU wants to double the size of its high-speed rail networks. Such developments might appear safe, although if high-speed trains become similarly autonomous in the future, faults could still cause problems. For the moment, no one is planning on removing train drivers, yet there are some new ideas around, such as trains designed to glide on air at 500 km/h, and brakes that harness waste energy to power local trackside grids.

But it's probably China where the most radical developments are likely to take place, partly because it has the need and partly because it can often build rail infrastructure from scratch. In a country that size, the ability to travel relatively quickly around it has brought many businesses closer to their customers and offered a large pool of educated workers to companies based in bigger cities such as Shanghai and Beijing. A World Bank paper found Chinese cities connected to the high-speed rail network were more likely to see their workers become more productive.

The fastest trains are what's known as maglev — magnetically levitating — trains, and they are are punctual, clean, smooth, and very fast, travelling at up to 431 km/h. To travel on one can also cost less than half the price of an air ticket. It's a civilised way to travel, and the rail operators will likely continue to improve the passenger experience. What we'll probably see in China and elsewhere soon may include smart-glass windows in railway carriages. These are windows with embedded touchscreens capable of displaying destinations and arrival times, but which could also overlay external views with information about points of interest. They could even show web pages or allow passengers to order food and drinks that are then delivered to the seat.

Moving further into the future, we might meet Elon Musk again. This investor in DeepMind is, of course, also one of the founders of PayPal, SpaceX, and Tesla Motors. One of his more recent audacious ideas is to build pneumatic-tube trains — an old sci-fi favourite from the early 1900s. Dubbed 'Hyperloop' trains, these could, in theory, carry people at speeds of up to 1,200 km/h, which is faster than most passenger planes. The downside is that trains have to travel in sealed vacuum tubes, which would cost a fortune to build and totally freak out timid passengers.

Musk's biggest idea is to relocate the human species. He believes that humans are in peril and wants to move them to Mars. This wouldn't be cheap either, although who ever said the future wouldn't be expensive?

Dear Vijaya,

I think we need to meet fairly urgently, as I might be having some kind of mental breakdown. It's the machines. I'm not sure whether to trust them. I keep telling the machines that I feel uncomfortable in their presence, but they just put on that soft velvety Scottish accent and tell me not to worry.

I can feel them analysing me all the time. What mood am I in? Am I happy with my choices today? What's my overall satisfaction rating for June? I can feel them analysing companies, even whole countries, trying to work out the 'corporate mood' or some spurious national happiness metric in near real time. Trying to work out why I'm feeling what I'm feeling. But what do people really think about me? Am I experiencing what they really feel or just what they reckon they should be feeling in the proximity of human intention decoding devices?

It's the intimate moments that are the worst. If my date says that she likes my tie, does she really mean it or has some message just flashed up on her iContact lenses saying that she should say it and that the question has an 88 per cent chance of being favourably received?

Are you even reading this or have you got some automated system to screen your messages for you? If you respond, how do I know that it's really you? Even if we meet, how do I know that what you say is what you really think versus what you've been trained to say?

— 7 —

EDUCATION AND KNOWLEDGE

what happens to learning when your teacher is an app?

What's wrong with education cannot be fixed with technology.

Steve Jobs

It has never been easier to give the illusion of intelligence. If you know the right people to follow, or the right publications to plunder, you can cut and paste your way to instant academic credibility. I'm doing it right now. This idea isn't mine, but comes instead from an *International New York Times* article called 'The End of Cultural Literacy'. The article argues, correctly in my view, that we live in an era where our opinions are increasingly based on very little knowledge.

Bitcoin is a good example of people knowing simultaneously more and less. Most people have heard of Bitcoin, but hardly anyone has taken the time to understand it. This is because we survive on shared summaries and context-free 30-second snippets, which enable us to appear intelligent for a short time.

What matters is not knowledge itself, but knowledge of the fact that a thing exists or is happening. Who needs to take time learning about something when we can just skim Twitter? We're all busy people, after all.

Retweets reflect this shallow consumption. When people share something, it doesn't mean they've read it first. I admit I've passed on a link without reading its content myself. The result is that true knowledge is being replaced with knowledge of the zeitgeist. Our cultural canon is turning into a narrow echo chamber where so-called knowledge is endlessly regurgitated. Whatever is most liked or most retweeted is somehow right. Creating and consuming snack-sized bites of knowledge also leads to context collapse, whereby people misunderstand ideas and events because they're taken out of context.

The ubiquity of the internet encourages this behaviour. To paraphrase Andy Warhol: in the future, everyone will trend on social media for 15 minutes. It is becoming harder to reject new ways of thinking, because it's like admitting you can't cope with an internet that never ends and cannot be shut off. And this brings us, in a silicon roundabout sort of way, to schooling and the purpose of education.

Teaching the test, not the child

If education is the passing on of knowledge, skills, values, and beliefs, equipping children to offer something constructive to society, then we are doing a truly terrible job. Part of the problem is that in many parts of the world, teachers do not educate in the broadest sense. Teachers merely teach children how to pass a series of toxic tests (and are themselves focused on passing external inspections), allowing pupils to progress to the next level and take more tests until they enter the workforce, allegedly fully formed. The aim is employment, not the pursuit of truth or beauty. Furthermore, once people are in employment, it becomes exceedingly obvious that, with some major exceptions (doctors, engineers, cosmologists, etc.), what's been learnt is either soon out of date or has little practical use.

Thus we have stumbled upon a situation where our educational establishments don't contain much education. As Tony Little, the former head of Eton College, says, we over-school and under-educate. He claims that the way exams are set up discourages lateral thinking, making it 'difficult for teachers to make links and pupils to see things in different ways'. As a House of Commons Select Committee reported in 2008, 'teaching to the test, to an extent which narrows the curriculum and puts sustained learning at risk, is widespread ... [This means] test results are pursued at the expense of a rounded education for children.'

But it gets worse. In the UK, the prevailing ethos seems to be that every small child is a special snowflake. We could all raise little Einsteins and Picassos if only schools would raise their game, and it's reasonable for teachers to write 1,000-word academic reports on five-year-olds. I feel sorry for the five-year-olds, many of whom are written off by pushy parents as underachievers.

The problem pre-dates digital, although kindergarten robots, online learning, e-books, and iPad-obsessed teachers aren't making life any easier. This could all be moot soon though, because we'll shortly have a generation that considers a digital education normal despite the fact that there is currently zero evidence that computers improve educational outcomes. Indeed, a 2015 OECD study of students in 70 countries says that high-achieving school systems have lower levels of computer use and that students who use computers heavily at school get worse results.

A key problem is parents, many of whom seem to use their own children to live out a life unlived or to soothe feelings of anxiety and inadequacy related to idyllic scenes in magazines. I even read a story in 2014 that parents were offering to pay a tutor £144,000 per year because they thought their nine-year-old daughter was 'behind her peers, and is consistently scoring in the bottom quartile, often more than 20 per cent under the median'. The irony here is that if parents simply threw their children into an OK school and spent more time interacting with their kids, the children would probably turn out happier, more resilient, and better adjusted.

This problem reaches its zenith in the private sector, where education has become so expensive that at least one parent has to work all hours to afford the fees, with the result that at least one parent is more or less absent. The results are stress, which is often directly transmitted back to the child, and quite often divorce. Due to the cost of private education, there's also the problem of homogeneity. The diversity of parents, and thus experience and ideas, is wearing rather thin. Parents working in the upper echelons of finance are pushing out just about everyone else.

And don't even get me started on the obsessive shuttling of children between out-of-school activities. If you want to protect your precious darlings from the automation of work, most would be better off playing Lego or digging holes in the garden.

By the way, if you've recently bought a Baby Mozart music compilation for your infant genius, please note that when psychologist Joan Freeman studied 210 child prodigies, only six became successful adults. In other words, you might be far better off teaching your toddler about failure, resilience, empathy, and communication than how to achieve an upper quartile ranking at the age of nine.

Top grades are great while a child is within schooling, but they often have little applicability outside except in some specialised professions. What schools and parents should perhaps be obsessed with instead is instilling an aptitude for hard work, good moral character, and the idea that whatever it is that you're really passionate about is probably the same thing that you'll be really good at.

Bonfire of the humanities

The latest game-changing idea in education circles seems to be that children need to be taught computer-coding skills. Nothing wrong with this, but I suspect that it follows up on the paranoid idea that there's a STEM (science, technology, engineering, and maths) crisis and GDP will suffer if enough STEM graduates aren't created. This may be true, although according to Martin Ford, author of *Rise of the Robots*, only a third of STEM graduates in the US are in jobs that require such a degree.

Maybe it would be a better idea if we focused on producing people who could think and had an engaging personality. We think that we're doing this, but we're not. Putting to one side the wicked idea that creating more STEM graduates floods the market and suppresses wages for the technology industries (obviously nonsense), it seems that what we'll need in the future are people who can effectively understand, synthesise, and communicate information and ideas.

Instead, we're developing individuals with narrow interests that fit the goal-driven, economy-serving nature of education. What counts is whether pupils pass a test — on a particular day — and whether or not teachers do the same. Awakening a sense of wonder, instilling ethics, or moulding mental wholeness is not part of most curricula.

According to Norman Augustine, former CEO of Lockheed Martin, one of the world's premier defence aerospace companies, the best staff are those with good thinking and communication skills. Of his former 80,000 employees, those he thought most likely to succeed were those who could read and write clearly — and think broadly.

But young minds are being conditioned away from deep reflective thought by interactive mobile devices. Handwriting is on the way out, too, due to typing and voice interfaces. There's even an online service (Bond in the US) where you can scan your scribble and have a pen-holding robot compose 'handwritten' thankyou notes.

Creating open minds sits awkwardly with education systems that focus on specialisation and limited definitions of intelligence. Indeed, a study by the Perimeter Institute for Theoretical Physics and the University of Waterloo says a smarter curriculum would involve walking away from the culture of grades and exams and moving towards the assessment of portfolios of projects. This is very much an idea that fits with Charles Handy's idea of portfolio careers.

What are schools for, anyway?

I will move on to digital education and training in a moment, but before I do that I would like to briefly discuss what education is for and whether or not our various education systems are helping or hindering the development of open, fair, and decent societies.

As discussed earlier, one of the largest problems with education is that in many instances, we appear to be teaching people to compete head-on with computers. We're also relying on a system that was designed to produce factory workers, with the odd nod to an agrarian past. If education, or work for that matter, is based on capturing, processing, and repeating information then we're heading for trouble — or mass unemployment. As technologist Conrad Wolfram argues, computers make rote procedures obsolete.

Yet there's another problem, which is that if education is about maximising every person's potential, we are doing an equally awful job. Being honest, most parents do not raise special snowflakes. They raise decent, honest, responsible human beings who thrive in decent, honest, responsible societies.

This isn't to say that anyone can't be anything — far from it.

But it does mean that society needs nurses, teachers, lorry drivers, bricklayers, sales assistants, and short-order cooks to work alongside rocket scientists, brain surgeons, computer whizzes, and Nobel laureates. Moreover, the much lauded share economy, where everyone co-creates and co-consumes, is fine if any employment substitution effects are equally shared. Unfortunately, peer-to-peer services most easily displace those workers who are least skilled, poorly paid, and might find it hard to obtain alternative employment.

The problem, and it's a big one, is that neither our education system nor our society recognise most of these people as worthwhile, let alone special. Education is tiered, favouring certain subjects or skills over others and pushing as many students as possible toward university education rather than vocational training. Society makes similar judgements, especially in terms of acceptable levels of financial compensation. Broadly, some subjects or professions are deemed more desirable than others, and the education system, along with parental support, conspires to push individuals to pass exams so that they can end up in certain jobs — with the upper echelons of social status and wealth as the ultimate goals.

Putting aside the insidious nature of our results-ranking obsession, there's the more general issue of decency. Yes, society needs managers and wealth-makers, yet it also needs happy human beings who aren't written off as failures at an early age. Talent has a place, but genetics and environment are more of a factor than most people imagine. Luck plays a major part, too.

Surely what we want is a system — a society, in fact — where all people that take part are valued. What we need is a system that values the importance of compassion, honesty, humility, and, above all, hard work.

But what we have created instead is a system that has become increasingly politicised and offers a standardised product that encourages short-term results and little else. And I suspect it's about to get worse due to our latest obsession — digital learning.

Learning online

A meta-study of thousands of research papers about education, produced by Australian academic John Hattie from Melbourne University, concluded with a league table of teaching innovations or interventions. Guess what's top of the class in terms of results?

The answer is *people*. Or more specifically, the interaction between teachers and pupils in a classroom. This more or less fits with the teaching of Daisy Christodoulou, the author of a book called *Seven Myths about Education*, which claims that the most important factor is not children learning through laissez-faire discovery, but teachers building up a bedrock of knowledge through classroom interaction.

Many goggle-eyed techies claim that everything from physical schools to university lectures don't matter thanks to the existence of educational videos and free online courses. Massive Open Online Courses (MOOCs) are seen as a particular saviour of cash-strapped education systems. With MOOCs, virtual tutors can guide students and give instant tailored feedback to thousands working simultaneously. If free or low cost, such systems do indeed have potential. Thomas Friedman, writing in *The New York Times*, says that MOOCs can 'lift more people out of poverty' and 'unlock a billion more brains to solve the world's biggest problems'.

MOOCs are blind to gender, age, race, and bank account, too, as Anant Agarwal, founder of MOOC company edX, puts it. Online learning is a useful development, not least because of the flexibility provided. But the utopia of MOOCs floating all boats simply isn't true (for the time being, at least). Most online students are rich, white, male, and already well educated, according to a study by the University of Pennsylvania. Nevertheless, MOOCs are a step in the right direction of providing universal higher education, especially for areas that are presently under-served.

We should, as always, think of such developments as human enhancement, not human replacement, and regard physical presence as essential. For example, apps are fine, but used in isolation they do not teach integration or communication. One of the major benefits of interfacing directly with physical teachers with different personalities is that they can be tired, grumpy, irritable, or just plain useless. Welcome to the world of employment! Get used to it and learn to work around it.

There are other benefits of physical schooling, too. Asked why applications to enrol at Stanford University had risen rather than fallen following the success of its online courses, a spokesman allegedly replied, 'Better sex.'

The idea that people can learn exclusively online is therefore disturbing, although a screen-based childhood is increasingly the norm. According to Jane McGonigal, speaking at a TED conference, dedicated gamers will spend around 10,000 hours playing online by the time they turn 21. That's roughly the same length of time individuals will spend in formal education. With the early years of education in particular, socialisation is an important aim, and achieving it is tricky if students don't physically attend school or interact.

According to a study led by Patricia Greenfield, a psychology professor at UCLA, pre-teens spend almost eight hours a day on screens, but this could be at the expense of social skills. In the study, a group of children aged from ten to 12 were sent off to a 'no screens' nature camp for five days, where they camped, cooked, walked, and looked at the world around them. Compared to a control group of children that stayed behind and stayed connected, the outdoor group displayed substantial improvement in understanding the emotions of others. This wasn't necessarily related to being outdoors, yet the study did cite a strong link between being physically among others and being able to read nonverbal cues.

Despite this, the traditional one-hour lecture is under threat, especially in universities. Why attend if you can download? The issue isn't merely digital versus human, but how lectures are delivered. If they're chalk-and-talk monologues then many lectures could potentially be deleted. Yet if a teacher or lecturer has gone to the trouble of filtering relevant information and has the skill to humanely and pithily convey key arguments then this is surely valuable.

And while you can't teach people to be charming, inspiring, or personable, you can hire for all of these qualities, which makes one wonder why more schools don't do this. So how about stopping the endless obsession with expensive facilities, and spending far more money on getting better teachers instead? I'm told that the answer to this is that you can't get good teachers without good facilities, but I'd challenge that.

In praise of slow education

As mentioned earlier, the value of pure thought — the encouragement of thinking for the sake of it — has more or less vanished from the standard curriculum, along with any belief that the true purpose of education is to feed curiosity or to instil character or values. Schools are judged almost exclusively on measured outcomes that focus on the things that are easiest to measure, usually examination pass rates. Universities are somewhat different, although even here many are turning into training camps where only people with the right marks get in or out — almost regardless of personality, passion, or wider talent.

Slow education, like slow food and slow journalism, rejects this. Proponents argue that education, especially in the early years, should be more inquiry-led and reflective. This would encourage calmer, more attentive ways of thinking, especially deep reading and deep listening.

It would also emphasise the importance of physical place, and reject — or at least balance — the use of attention-sapping digital devices. The internet in particular has begun to steal the ability of students to engage in calmer, more contemplative thinking. Open-access courses and distance learning have a huge role in education, the Open University being a prime example, but these should be seen as incremental developments, not as a substitute for human contact, inspiration, or empathetic encouragement.

Crucial to the idea of slow education is time. Students learn at different speeds and should be allowed to take their time, especially if this means becoming more absorbed in a subject or an idea. Why, for example, are children grouped according to age rather than ability or interest? Also, why do we educate from around four years of age to 18 or 21, when 50 per cent of children in developed nations could reach their 100th birthday? What's the rush?

What counts is interest and understanding, not the number of facts that someone can remember and spit out in an exam. To stretch the slow-food analogy further, it matters how lessons are prepared and what ingredients are used and subsequently chewed upon. Last but not least, slow education is people-centric and is concerned with the quality of interactions — a thought not lost on employers who claim that younger recruits often struggle to look them in the eye.

We can't just blame the teachers or a national curriculum for serving up junk lessons. Again, parents should relax and focus more on the overall journey rather than an illusory destination.

Which brings me to what might be called slow play. This is the idea that kids nowadays spend too long indoors on screens. They are over-scheduled and over-restricted and they rarely venture outside. In the UK, only 25 per cent of kids are allowed to walk to school versus 75 per cent in Germany. In 1971, the figure was 86 per cent in the UK.

Does this matter? Yes, because children benefit hugely from freedom and independent learning. Boredom is a catalyst for introspection and invention. Creativity and making mistakes develops character and resilience, which, in a volatile world, are perhaps the most desired 'outcomes' of them all.

The thought we should all be more relaxed when it comes to schooling echoes a story I heard about Silicon Valley, of all places. In Los Altos, at the heart of the digital economy, there's an elementary school called the Waldorf School of the Peninsula, where smart people working for companies such as Apple and Google send their children. You'd think this school would be cluttered with computers. It isn't. There's not one to be found. Those behind the school, and other ones like it, argue that computers and learning don't mix well, diminishing attention, inhibiting creativity, and weakening human relationships. Instead, children mess around with pens and paper. The school embraces blackboards, chalk, and encyclopaedias. This would, no doubt, please Eric Schmidt, executive chairman of Google, who has said, 'I still believe that sitting down and reading a book is the best way to really learn something.'

Does it work? If you measure success by the number of students attending top-notch universities, the answer is yes. You can argue that the genetic pool from which these children are plucked almost guarantees success. But success may have less to do with genes and more to do with home and school environments where it's cool to be curious. In a word, it's about engagement, and this naturally circles back to great teachers with great lesson plans.

Paul Thomas, an ex-teacher, associate professor at Furman University in the US, and expert on public (government) education, sums things up by saying that, 'Teaching is a human experience. Technology is a distraction when we need literacy, numeracy, and critical thinking.' He has also said that 'a spare approach to technology in the classroom will always benefit learning'.

A spare approach does not mean a Luddite approach, of course. There's a place for screens in classrooms. One interesting development is intelligent textbooks. While certain types of learning are best suited to paper, e-books that can answer specific questions — or set questions based on what's been read — could be useful. For instance, students might ask a book a question that they'd be embarrassed to ask a teacher or fellow pupil. Intelligent books could also adjust text to a particular reader's reading level.

Before we move on to the area of work, I would like to finish with two further thoughts. The first is more of an anomaly.

Michael J. Sandel is a Harvard political philosopher who teaches Aristotle, Kant, and John Stuart Mill. You could reasonably expect that his lectures would be irrelevant to people outside the walls of his university. But Sandel's lectures about philosophy and ethics have been televised, and his book *Justice: what's the right thing to do?* has sold over a million copies in Asia alone. What's going on here? Surely this is 'highly illogical', as Dr Spock in *Star Trek* would say.

Sandel's popularity is due to the intersection of three trends. The first is technical — the growth of online education, discussed above. Students anywhere in the world can now connect with him, and the cost to do so is zero. The second trend is cultural.

In Asia, there is a craving for open, creative discussion and innovative thought, especially in countries that have until recently been authoritarian in style. The third trend, possibly the most interesting, is a hunger for moral debates in societies that all too often are focused on dry and ethically bankrupt subjects such as business and economics.

But while this may explain Sandel's popularity in some countries, it doesn't explain it globally. One answer could be that people everywhere are tired of individualism, rampant materialism, and blogs and bytes. They, too, are hungry for deep discussions about big ethical questions that the mainstream media and politicians do not even attempt. It could also be argued that there is a vacuum created by the absence of religion, and popular philosophy is filling this void.

My final thought about education concerns sleep.

Sleeping your way to success

If you are a parent with teens, you may be familiar with the difficulty in getting teenagers out of bed and off to school. We've covered the issue of sleep already, but it's worth repeating that the digital era isn't particularly sleep-friendly. Twenty-four-hour television and computers in bedrooms plus a rather informal attitude to bedtime mean that many teens do not get enough sleep. As with adults, this means that memory consolidation is impaired, as is the ability to dream up solutions to complex problems.

Increased levels of the stress hormone cortisol also have a negative impact on impulsive behaviour and empathy. Self-medicating via caffeinated energy drinks makes matters worse. A study in Norway has also found that using mobiles before bed almost doubles the chance of teens have a bad night's sleep. Research by the University of Glasgow similarly found teens checking social media in the middle of the night, with the result that some sleep for just five hours. This is leading to 'classroom zombies' and an epidemic of anxiety, according to the researchers.

One school, the UCL Academy in London, has experimented with later school start times to allow older students to slumber longer. Another school, Monkseaton High School in the north of England, has tried 10.00 a.m. starts and says that academic performance has increased as a result. Whether this will ever catch on remains to be seen. I doubt it, given the poor record of other educational innovations. I guess we'll just have to wait impatiently for someone to invent those transcranial-magnetic-stimulation nightcaps to reboot learning.

20450104T13:34:51+00:00

AUTOMATIC INTRUSION-DETECTION SYSTEMS HAVE DETECTED AN
ATTEMPT TO HACK INTO YOUR SECURE IMPLANTED MEDICAL DEVICE,
HEALING HEALTH HEART STARTER PREMIUM (MODEL NUMBER
1377549).

WE ARE REQUIRED BY LAW TO INFORM YOU THAT IN THE
HIGHLY UNLIKELY EVENT OF AN UNAUTHORISED INDIVIDUAL OR
ORGANISATION GAINING REMOTE ACCESS TO THE AFOREMENTIONED
DEVICE, THERE IS THE REMOTE POSSIBILITY OF THEM BEING ABLE TO
SWITCH IT OFF OR RE-PROGRAM IT TO INFLICT A LETHAL ELECTRICAL
CHARGE.

WITH THIS IN MIND WE ENCOURAGE YOU TO ARRANGE A MEDICAL
PROCEDURE AS SOON AS POSSIBLE TO HAVE AN UPGRADED DEVICE
FITTED.

Yours sincerely,

Dr A.K. Sandy,
Head of Cyber Disruption

WORK AND EMPLOYMENT

*why the future might look a lot
like the Middle Ages*

The lucky few who can be involved in creative work of any
sort will be the true elite of mankind, for they alone will do
more than serve a machine.

Isaac Asimov

I have a friend who consults for a telecommunications company.
He is one of a million digital nomads in the UK — one in
seven workers — who, thanks to a global telecommunications
revolution, is able to work from home (up 45 per cent over the
last 16 years in the UK, according to the Office for National
Statistics). His commute consists of putting on some slippers and
walking upstairs. I do this myself from time to time, although
I find the lack of physical delineation between work and home
a problem, especially when my children are on holiday and
steadfastly refuse to believe that someone sitting in a greenhouse
could possibly be working.

My friend interacts with many of his bosses and co-workers
without ever seeing them. Even so, every now and then my
free-agent friend has to go to a real office. This, as far as I can
tell, is located in a place where common sense has evaporated,

although a culture of artificial stupidity ensures that nobody ever says anything.

One day, my friend booked a room — online, naturally — to have a meeting. The meeting room itself was fairly standard. It could have been anywhere. But it was cold. Failing to find a thermostat, he called facilities management and asked if the heating could be turned up. The answer was yes. Just not right away. He would need to email a request, which would take 24 hours to process.

The meeting was disbanded and moved to a coffee shop, strewn with fellow telecommuters starting at their screens — where most of the real work, one suspects, took place. And sure enough, 24 hours later, my friend received an email saying that the heating had now been turned up and could he rate facilities management's response to his request. He judged their behaviour to be 'perfectly as expected'.

In the future, he will presumably attend meetings remotely, using a telepresence trundlebot. This could allow his virtual presence in multiple locations simultaneously, in which case the idea of 'in person' will have to be rethought. At least he'll be able to manage his own room temperature.

Fewer than 500 global organisations now manage 70 per cent of world trade. In almost all cases, these companies are effectively answerable only to shareholders, although in many cases the managers have awarded themselves this status. Customers, along with employees, don't get much of a say. Both have become costs to be managed ever downward. I can imagine a scenario where the 500 becomes 50, and companies withdraw further online to reduce costs to the extent that it's almost impossible to speak to them. Instead, customers and staff alike could be directed to online FAQs, recorded messages, customer-run discussion forums, and management avatars. Talking to an actual human being may become extraordinarily difficult and could possibly incur a cost.

If you've ever tried speaking with the Driver and Vehicle Licensing Agency in the UK or Telstra in Australia, you might already have had a foretaste.

According to breathless, over-caffeinated commentators, the new world of work will be one where employees will be released from their corporate shackles. Instead of being employed, we will be set free to work for ourselves. We will work from anywhere, pitching for whatever interests us, much in the same way that freelance actors compete to work on movies. As Microsoft says, 'Work is a thing you do, not a place you go.'

I disagree. Like journalist Sarah Jaffe, I think that liberation is a delusion: revolutionising the world's workforce is actually 'just the next step in the decades-old trend of fragmenting jobs, isolating workers and driving down wages'. Work is social, and while the death of distance might suit some members of the newly detached elite, is does not suit everyone.

It could suit individuals such as the US computer programmer who, working remotely, realised that he could outsource his own job to India and make a profit. He was only caught when he got a second job, which he similarly outsourced.

But for most, I suspect that work will become more insecure and stressful. There will be a race between education and employment, not only for students, but also for anyone engaged in low-skilled or highly routine jobs — trying to acquire new skills before old skills expire. If you fail to pay attention at school or at work, it's likely that machines will steal your job and quite possibly your soul, too.

Much of the employment in the future will be the same as it is now: mundane, part-time, zero-hours employment, with low-paid service jobs gaining the most ground at the expense of manufacturing.

The majority of jobs that do remain will be what David Graeber, an American anthropologist at the London School of Economics, refers to as 'bullshit jobs', a phrase akin to 'McJobs' but more honest. Given that a Gallup poll of workers in 2014 found that nearly 90 per cent of employees worldwide were doing jobs they didn't really like — they were either 'not engaged' with or 'actively disengaged' from their work — the mind boggles as to what happens if the quality of jobs declines still further.

Economist Tyler Cowen agrees with Graeber. He argues that 10–15 per cent of highly educated, motivated, and determined workers will benefit hugely in the new economy, while the remaining 85–90 per cent will struggle to find meaningful or well-paid employment. If you spend most of your day sitting in front of a screen at work inputting information, you could soon be redundant or underemployed.

Overall, there will be fewer people in the workforce, partly because of ageing, partly because of automation, and partly because companies will endlessly be looking for efficiencies and excuses to shed labour.

A brave new world of work

The impact of automation is a theme of this book. How new technologies change the way that humans relate to one another, and, ultimately, how technologies change human identity and purpose, is at its core. But how technology changes work is critical to all of this, and an underappreciated aspect is the way that machines are themselves changing.

Technologists such as Ray Kurzweil, now at Google, argue that we are on the cusp of exponential change, especially in computing cost, memory, and processing power. The logical conclusion of this shift is an AI Singularity, the point at which machines outclass humans on all almost every level. I will return to the AI Singularity later, but for now I would like to stress that what we are starting to see with machines, and automation in particular, is merely the beginning.

It is the marriage of smart machines to an almost endless supply of Big Data that needs to be understood. Thus the future will belong to companies that understand network effects and are able to build communities of interest around their products and services. A shoe company, for example, needs to understand that once you connect shoes to the internet, they become a platform from which the company and, critically, its users can devise new data-driven services that could be more valuable than the shoes themselves.

Given the right skills, attitudes, and policy frameworks, humans will be able to work alongside these machines, each greatly enhancing the abilities of the other. Machines will be our servants and friendly companions. Yet if some of the boldest forecasts come true, we are set for a period of tumultuous turbulence. Low-skilled and unskilled jobs will be replaced by machines. But so, too, could highly skilled professional jobs, due to a perfect storm of technological developments, obsolescent skills, efficiency-obsessed firms, weakened or non-existent unions, and a lack of decent employment contracts.

This technological tidal wave is unprecedented in modern history, and it's hard to figure out how humans can respond. If the direst predictions do come true then distrust, alienation, and unrest could follow, not only due to the removal of decent jobs (especially for the young) or the shift away from secure full-time employment, but also because the spoils accrued by the owners of the algorithms and machines could be immense. As the intelligence of the machines rises exponentially, so too could the resulting wealth, which may result in a neo-feudal existence for many.

A paper by Carl Frey and Michael Osborne at Oxford University, looking at the future prospects of 700 professions, suggests that 47 per cent of current US jobs are at risk from computerisation over the next few decades. In the UK, the figure is 36 per cent, or about ten million jobs — largely highly routine or repetitive jobs. Gartner, the technology research company, suggests that software will make one in three jobs redundant by 2025.

Personally I find some of these statistics a little questionable. For example, Frey and Osborne rank 'watch repairers' as one of the occupations most likely to disappear. But is this because they assume that people will stop wearing watches (because other wearable devices will contain clocks) or that all watches will become digital (and thus easier to repair automatically)? I think both scenarios are unlikely. Equally, they rank surgeons (grouped with physicians) as one of the occupations least likely to be automated. Yet many of the surgeons I've spoken with would disagree. Fully autonomous surgery is indeed a possibility, although it's more likely that most invasive procedures will eventually disappear due to the emergence of non-invasive treatments and technologies.

If middle-class jobs are replaced by decent new jobs then all is well. 'Decent' means jobs that pay enough, but also jobs that make a small difference or have a worthy purpose. In addition, it means jobs that aren't based on zero-hours contracts or where people are prevented from interacting with other people. Just because people can work from anywhere doesn't mean people should.

Work provides meaning, identity, and community as well as money. It's also something that becomes more interesting as it becomes harder. So another worry about automation is that employee satisfaction and retention rates could decline substantially if complexity, difficulty, and nuance are removed from work.

If work disappears for segments of society or is concentrated in a handful of super-cities, we could see a society that's hugely polarised between a specialised elite and a generalist under-class. This is the software revolution that Jaron Lanier refers to as the 'final industrial revolution', which has been commented on in depth in books such as *Average Is Over* by Tyler Cowen and *The Second Machine Age* by Erik Brynjolfsson and Andrew McAfee.

But before we proceed further forwards, we should perhaps travel backwards for context and some much needed reassurance. Eighty-five years ago, John Maynard Keynes, the great economist, was similarly interested in the effects of mechanisation. His largely optimistic essay 'Economic Possibilities for our Grandchildren', published in 1930, argued that a 'new disease', namely 'technological unemployment', would become a problem, although it would ultimately result in a leisure society.

Not much sign of this just yet, which could be a good thing. Leisure only makes sense in the context of work. Forced leisure or too much leisure is as dangerous as none. The secret, it seems to me, is finding something you're passionate about and which you're good at, too. If it pays well, so much the better. And if it's difficult and hard to master, better still.

Keynes was in many ways prescient, but he raised another key point. If automation takes most of the middle-class jobs and erodes the incomes that drive economic growth, who will purchase the goods that the machines make? At least Henry Ford had the good sense to ensure that automation augmented human labour and that his workers were paid enough to afford the cars they were making.

With hindsight, the US and many other nations ended up with the opposite problem. The rebuilding required after World War II and the development of new technologies during the 1950s and 1960s created a huge demand for labour. Indeed, there were labour shortages. Science and technology had reduced the need for human labour, but had not done so exclusively or consistently. Labour was merely shifted from one region or profession to another. New jobs were created as fast as old ones were destroyed.

Going further back, it's a similar story. In 1500, roughly 75 per cent of people in Britain worked in agriculture. Today, the figure is 2 per cent, yet we manage to produce more food. On the other hand, a recent study found that almost 90 per cent of the US workforce is employed in occupations that existed a century ago.

The 'will it, won't it' question surrounding automation and unemployment will only be answered with hindsight, although if we have the brains to invent new machines that throw people out of work, there's no reason to suppose that we can't use these same brains to invent new forms of work.

Mind the humanity gap

There are examples of technological unemployment being played out under the streets of London as I write. The RMT Union, which represents workers on London's Underground railway, is battling management over the removal of human jobs. Historically, Tube stations had people behind ticket counters to sell tickets and dispense advice. Management wants to change this. Travellers will have to buy tickets from automated ticket machines, use various forms of contactless digital payment, or track down roving members of staff carrying iPads for help. This has already happened in cities such as Melbourne.

I think it's almost inevitable that transport systems such as London's Tube will eventually be operated more or less without humans. Airline check-in counters and single-destination railways are moving in this direction, too. Shops might follow.

But there's a price to pay. I live in a village in the English countryside and regularly take the train to London — not for any particular reason, much of the time. I like to be among the throng. I find writing rather lonely and need to interact with other people.

At my local station, there's a ticket machine. It's quick and mostly reliable, unless you want the cheapest tickets, which the machine keeps quiet about. But there's also Mick, the station manager. We talk. We tell jokes (a current favourite: 'It's much cheaper if you travel earlier — the 1950s, for example'). He posts letters for me when I'm in a hurry and organises obscure tickets to faraway places.

You could automate Mick. I'm sure the railway company is thinking about it. But at what cost to the community? And how do you program a machine to be authentically personable? It's the same with the London Underground. People play a vital role, not just selling tickets, but helping older people and foreigners who are confused by the system. And how does a warm smile or silly joke get translated into a valuation on the balance sheet?

I could exist in a world with no humans. My needs could be efficiently met by a plethora of smart machines. But I wouldn't feel alive, and such a life would not be worth living.

I've already explored the issue of income, wealth, and opportunity polarisation in the chapter on money, but I should visit it once more, because even if the darkest predictions fail to come true, the general tendency and underlying dynamic should still hold true.

To be fair to the techno-optimists, I should stress that further automation of work will bring tremendous advantages. There will be more people with access to better health and education. Many things that were once scarce could become abundant, too, because the marginal cost of goods and services in a digital economy is close to zero. Moreover, businesses, as George Zarkadakis writes, 'are shifting from manufacturing massively replicated products … to producing personalised products and services distributed directly to customers'. This is another positive development.

Yet if widespread automation does threaten jobs, it's likely that there will be responses, whatever the bottom-line or fringe benefits. These responses will come both from the professions affected and from politicians. Unions, written off by most observers, could be a factor, too.

Just because a job can be automated or outsourced doesn't necessarily mean it will be. This is a point made by David Autor, an economist at MIT. Governments may decide to protect white-collar or service-sector jobs because large groups of people who are articulate, connected, and idle could cause serious trouble. Men aged 25–64 are a particular concern, although as we saw early on, many of the younger cohort seem to be more intent on screen-based lethargy than street-based revolution.

Lawrence Summers, a former US treasury secretary, has estimated that by 2030 or thereabouts, one in seven American men in the 25-to-64-year-old age group could be jobless, and has warned of the consequences. In the 1960s, a previous period of tremendous social change, the figure was one in 20. China and other nations are similarly vulnerable.

The Economist, following Thomas Piketty, argues that 'The rise of the middle-class — a 20th-century innovation — was a hugely important political and social development across the world. The squeezing out of that class could generate a more antagonistic, unstable and potentially dangerous politics.' It is the middle class, after all, that tends to start revolutions.

The implication of goods and services produced for zero marginal cost is that the algorithms producing them also have a zero marginal cost. Once they've been paid for, they work for nothing. Similarly, robots will work nights, weekends, and holidays without complaint. They don't need orthopaedically correct chairs, pensions, or healthcare benefits either. Algorithms and robots are, in a sense, model employees, with huge appeal to powerful international organisations engineered for profit maximisation. Governments will have to address this problem.

One solution, put forward by Matt Zwolinski, an associate professor at the University of San Diego, is BIG — a Basic Income Guarantee. BIG is similar to means-tested benefits, but simpler. Like flat taxes (the idea of a fixed rate of tax for everyone regardless of income), this idea relies on a single salary or living wage that's just enough to live on and guaranteed for everyone. There are no further payments or benefits. But if you earn more than the basic guarantee, the payment is not reduced or removed.

Critics rightly point out that this is sit-down money — money that encourages people to do nothing. This could be a problem. But entitlement could easily be tied to volunteering, training, or work schemes.

How could we afford such an idea? One way might be to tax machines or robots as we do people. We could tax the companies that make the robots, algorithms, and automated systems, or tax the organisations that 'employ' them. Socially useful machines such as kidney-dialysis devices could operate freely, whereas automated self-checkouts in supermarkets could be taxed. Carol Black, principal of Newnham College, Cambridge, has suggested that workplace environments should be used to improve public health — taxing technology based on broad social, medical, and environmental goals is a similar idea.

Alternatively, governments might seek to tax assets rather than annual income, or increase consumption taxes on luxury goods. Expensive homes fall into both categories. The Labour and Liberal Democrat parties in the UK have looked at this. The only problem with these ideas might be capital flight. The rich are generally mobile and may simply move to bank-account countries such as Switzerland. *The Economist* has pointed out that in the UK and US, the top 1 per cent of earners already contributes 28 per cent and 47 per cent respectively of the total tax take. If their tax was increased further, the rich would no doubt use these unrelated but suggestive figures to justify moving their taxable business elsewhere. Perhaps what we really need here is a globally harmonious and homogenous tax system.

Libertarian disciples of Ayn Rand would hate these ideas. If you haven't heard of Ayn Rand, she was a writer and philosopher who has become especially popular in the US, notably with many laissez-faire capitalists and Silicon Valley luminaries. Rand was a supporter of self-interested reason and individual rights, and rejected instinct, intuition, community, and religion. Altruism was also rejected as being at odds with human happiness.

Rand is a favourite of Travis Kalanick, CEO of Uber (a company now partly owned by Google), who has said that his aim is to replace all of Uber's drivers with self-driving vehicles and who at one point chose the cover of Ayn Rand's book *The Fountainhead* as his Twitter profile picture. Kalanick is perhaps the personification of what Andrew Keen calls the '"disintermediation" of paid human labour by artificial algorithms'.

There are crossovers between Rand and Futurism, the early-20th-century art movement that admired speed and technology and loathed anything old. But the clearer crossover is with 1960s and 70s Californian counterculture that spawned the digital revolution, as discussed in Fred Turner's book *From Counterculture to Cyberculture*. The influence of Rand was also highlighted in a BBC documentary *All Watched Over by Machines of Loving Grace*.

Steven Johnson, the author of *Future Perfect* and a Silicon Valley local, disputes any connection between Rand and the Valley, saying that the latter overwhelmingly votes Democrat while Rand is a more natural Republican. His view is that a more defining characteristic of the region might be a belief that technological innovation will usher in an age of ubiquitous affluence and that government just needs to get out of the way.

Radical privatisation, free markets, digital solutionism, and Randian philosophy aside, what else might we do to make work more people-centric in an age of machines? Sleep has been mentioned already, but why not create more sleep-friendly workplace environments? There's a serious problem with employees being burnt out and feeling they have lost control, so why not bring back compulsory holidays, canteens, and lunch breaks, with the option of a siesta? The idea of casual or dress-down Fridays is now meaningless in many workplaces because the casual look is almost universal, so why not get rid of email for one day instead?

The French IT and consulting firm Atos is on a mission to abolish internal email altogether. They prefer people to walk around and talk to each other rather than send instant messages. This is a good idea. Unplanned meetings and serendipitous exchanges can reap rewards, and it's also healthier to have people moving around rather than hunched over screens. Employers complain about potential recruits lacking soft skills, so anything that improves employees' communication skills would be welcome.

While we're at it, perhaps Tech-free Tuesdays could be supplemented with No-track November. Digital tracking is now the norm online, and many of us accept cookies and advertising targeted to our preferences. But would we accept being tracked at work? This is already the reality for employees at BP, eBay, Coca-Cola, Autodesk, and Bank of America. The intention is not all bad, yet it's hard to imagine how continual gathering of data about a worker can benefit him or her in the end.

As we've seen, activity trackers such as Fitbit encourage people to adopt healthier habits. Bank of America asked call-centre employees to wear sensors for six weeks, which recorded where they went, who they talked to, and how their body movements changed over time. It discovered that people who were more social were also more productive.

While activity trackers tend to lift productivity, one academic claims the 'transparency paradox' causes people to obsess over their targets, game the system, and cheat or take risks. Wearable technology also raises questions about privacy and whether there's a healthy reason to track people in the first place.

Amazon, for instance, has been criticised for monitoring warehouse staff. Mobile devices worn for as much as ten and a half hours a day ensure warehouse staff complete tasks in a set time. Many of these people work at night, which gives the warehouses a ghostly quality. As one warehouse worker said, 'I feel like they don't trust you to think like a human being.' It's possible they don't, which is why Amazon, along with many other firms, is automating its warehouses with robots, which, one imagines, could ultimately replace humans completely. After all, what could be more efficient from a profit-maximisation standpoint?

According to Michael Marmot at University College London, workers such as those in Amazon warehouses face an increased risk of mental illness. The situation reminds me of killer whales bored and frustrated by captivity in amusement parks (which aren't very amusing for the whales) who take their frustrations out on each other.

Predictive workforce analysis

After World War II, when America last faced a scramble for talent, Human Resources (then called Personnel) embraced a series of behavioural, aptitude, intelligence, and medical tests to ensure the suitability of potential recruits. Yet what was widespread in corporate America in the 1950s and 60s had all but disappeared by the 1990s.

This was because a buoyant economy and frequent job-hopping meant that it became less important to test people when most of them would soon leave. A study by the Corporate Executive Board, an advisory firm, found that almost 25 per cent of all new hires were gone within 12 months of accepting a job. Heightened focus on short-term financial results also restricted training and assessment schemes that paid back over the longer term. Between the 1990s and about 2010, most hiring was therefore informal. But now the data science is back.

Thinking scientifically about how companies hire and fire people (known variously as workforce analytics, workforce science, analytic assessment, and people analytics) is back in favour thanks in part to digital data. Supporters believe it can tell Human Resources not only whom to hire and fire, but also what a person's future potential and monetary value might be. Even online trivia can be mined for personality traits, helping employers to find, or dismiss, suitable workers.

Ironically, data about whether such data works is almost impossible to come by, and some tools and techniques are a little creepy. For example, if your boss encourages you to play *Dungeon Crawl* or *Wasabi Waiter* but doesn't say why, you should be worried. These are games developed by a team of psychologists, neuroscientists, and data scientists to work out human potential by collecting abundant data about things you are barely conscious of doing.

Some of this is acceptable, especially if you are trying to figure out which of two similar people to hire. But imagine if nuance and human intuition are totally removed from the equation.

Or what if people are no longer interviewed face to face but questioned solely by machines? Even the tests that currently exist could end up ruling out whole classes of people, simply because the data say these groups are risky. Some companies already use automated recruitment software. In extreme cases, people are hired with no human oversight whatsoever. This might work for short-term hires or low-skill positions, but we shouldn't think that we can remove humans from the equation entirely. A recruitment consultant whom I met recently pointed out that most of the time he knows who he wants to hire — the problem is persuading the person to take the job.

The most unsettling matter is not the use of opaque tests and data to hire and fire, but using covert data to monitor a person across their entire working life. Bloomberg allegedly monitors every keystroke of every one of its employees, as well as their comings and goings in the office throughout their career. What if they bought digital histories of potential employees, too?

Harrah's Hotel and Casino in Las Vegas allegedly tracks every smile and grimace of each of its card dealers and waiting staff. Other sinister tracking technologies include badges that monitor where people go and record their conversations. If a human being interpreted such data, it would be bad enough, but in some cases all an employer ends up with is automated sheets of data. The human who generated the data is reduced to a set of numbers.

This reminds me of a point made in a slightly different context by Charles Handy, in that 'any efficiencies gained are more than outweighed by the loss of enthusiasm, energy and initiative in the workforce'.

The cult of productivity

Steven Poole, writing in the *New Statesman*, says productivity is 'one of the great unquestioned virtues of our age'. People brag not only about being busy, but also about being tired all the time. Nobody that's employed boasts about having nothing to do. Busyness, not idleness, is the badge of honour in our 24/7, machine-centric, capitalist economy.

Perhaps this is because if we are physically moving, we must be working — a hangover from agriculture and factory-production days, perhaps. Workforce science therefore ensures that everyone is monitored and measured and looks busy. Looking out of a window and thinking is generally seen as monumentally unproductive, which is monumental nonsense.

First, we need to take a break. We can't permanently exist in a state of flight or fight. Stopping, resting, sleeping, and switching off are vital, not only for physical and mental health, but also for productive intellectual work, too.

Second, wasted time is not time wasted. If you are one of the few that still work in a factory then doing nothing for an extended period would indeed be a problem. But if you are engaged in brainwork of any kind (and this includes dealing with people) then spending a few hours walking alone, marinating your mind in magazines, or chatting to mates could well be the most productive thing you do all day, because it can lead to new insights and ideas.

In my experience, it tends to be lower- and middle-ranking employees that worry the most about being seen to be busy. This was brought home to me a long time ago when lots of frequent-flyer points brought me to the Singapore Airlines suites-class lounge in Changi Airport. You might not have heard of 'suites class': it is the most luxurious class of flying that's commercially available, beyond first class; it is essentially a private room onboard the aircraft. I'm familiar with business-class lounges: they are the airside equivalent of Starbucks — lots of frantic people making phone calls and manically tapping on keyboards. I'm not familiar with first-class lounges, but the route to the suites-class lounge was through first class, and all I can say is that it was exactly the same as business, only with better-looking snacks.

But the suites-class lounge was a revelation. It was an oasis of calm. Not a single person was on a phone or laptop. People were reading books, newspapers, and magazines; some were looking out of the large windows. My cynical explanation is that these people all had minions to make phone calls for them. They were probably next-door in first or back in business. I don't think that's quite it, however.

I read once that many successful CEOs make a point of creating the time and space to read and reflect. Bill Gates was famous for his 'think weeks' conducted from an isolated cottage. Jack Welsh, the former boss of General Electric, would regularly set aside a whole day purely to think.

Mindfulness, a way of thinking that's focused on the present, is all the rage at the moment, but for me the real imperative is an absence of thinking, for it's only when our minds are unoccupied and empty that a real self-awareness occurs. It has to do with relaxing and freeing up bandwidth in your head, and this is impossible if we are always busy and distracted.

As Lao-Tzu wrote 2,500 years ago: 'He who clings to his work will create nothing that endures. If you want to accord with the Tao, just do your job, then let go.'

A need for renewal

There's also a growing canon of academic research suggesting that naps, daytime exercise, longer sleep hours, more holidays, and extended periods away from work will result in better productivity at work and certainly better health. One Harvard study says that sleep debt (the cumulative effect of people not getting enough sleep) costs the US economy $63.2 billion each year in lost productivity, while a Florida University study suggests that people work best in 90-minute bursts.

Yet another study, by Shelley Carson at Harvard, concludes that we are more receptive to new ideas when our minds are allowed to wander. We shouldn't push this idea too far, but it's interesting to note that even lying on a beach might be more productive than we imagine. Increases in body temperature have been shown to fire up serotonin-releasing neurons in the dorsal raphe nucleus. In short, heat makes humans happy.

But we don't need to avoid work entirely to be happy. Indeed, the real value of work is not what we produce for others, but what work produces in ourselves. It's only when we are working on something that benefits others that we achieve enduring satisfaction.

If work is difficult then so much the better. We did not go to the moon because it was easy. We did it because it was hard.

Future jobs

I do talks for schools every so often, and one of the questions I'm frequently asked is about the future look and feel of work. Specifically, which might be the growth industries of the future and which industries or professions could be in decline.

Most of the trends driving the future of work — globalisation, automation, outsourcing, sustainability, demographics, digital-isation, and networks — are already in plain sight, so we should perhaps focus on what type of skills might be safe against any future robot or software invasion. There are several ways of thinking about this. First, what is currently scarce — and is likely to remain so in the future? Second, what is consumed locally and is hard to replace with globally outsourced or automated labour?

An answer to this second question might include gardeners. The word 'human', after all, comes from the Latin *humus*, meaning 'of the earth'. Plumbers, they of the water, could be safe, too, as would anything that has to be done locally and can only be automated so far, because each instance will be somewhat different. We already have autonomous lawnmowers and lettuce- and strawberry-picking robots, but they aren't terribly good at designing or maintaining gardens that stir the soul. Vets, to look after all the animals that single-person households will generate, are another fairly safe bet, despite the appearance of robotic pets.

In contrast, highly routine or repetitive tasks, both manual and cognitive, will be under threat. The list might include ticket agents, typists, auditors, accountants, traffic wardens, paralegals, taxi drivers, lorry drivers, and train drivers. Remember here that less than ten years ago, the idea that computers can replace human drivers would have been seen as highly unlikely. Today it is widely accepted as inevitable. So what else do we currently see as quintessentially human that machines may take from us? I'm not answering this, I'm just asking the question.

Second, what are humans good at that machines, no matter how smart, are not? According to Michael Osborne and Carl Frey, the answer is social and creative intelligence. I'd endorse this, but add empathy, intuition, nuance, and personality. Hopefully, as smart machines become cheaper, this should force us to place more value on human interaction — and one of the things people like about people is personality. Also, any job that requires us to understand, inspire, or connect with other human beings should be safe, so teachers, nurses, doctors, dentists, hair stylists, poets, artists, actors, filmmakers, craftspeople, writers of fiction, psychologists, and motivational managers should be safe. I'd also like to think that the idea of honour — a favourite in medieval times — could return, and we might see Head of Honour as a job title.

Futurology might be a good career choice for a while, thanks to technological turbulence, but overall I'd say that being a historian would be a better long-term bet.

Third, new jobs that might appear include dream-retrieval specialist, data-disposal consultant, pet geneticist, human–robot relationship counsellor, data contextualiser, robot-repair mechanic, pedestrian-traffic analyser, genomic dating adviser, brain-augmentation specialist, 3D 'ink' designer, phone-addiction clinician, drone traffic controller, anxiety-containment specialist, shareable-assets auditor, body-modification consultant, artificial-organ designer, mental-image-retrieval consultant, computer-personality designer, data-hostage negotiator, digital-data detective, chief ethics officer, software ethicist, end-of-life exit consultant, and mystic healer.

If the last role doesn't appeal, how about a job in the clergy? This could be the most futureproof job of all.

You might argue that worship of technology is our new religion. But as our machines become more competent, and robots and avatars provide care and companionship, the one thing that might be missing is someone who can help us discuss what it means to be human. Incongruously, it might take the existence of smart machines to make us realise this, which is perhaps why we invented robots as fictional devices in the first instance.

Ethics Assignment 3
Julie S.

According to an article in the 24 October issue of New Scientist, there's a
company in California that is now offering all kinds of body customisation
procedures, ranging from under-skin animated tattoos and glow-in-the-dark
hair to feathered arms and new skin colours (blue and green appear to be the
most popular colours this season). The company started out selling e-clothes
that could display messages, play videos, and change colour, but customers
soon started asking whether something could be done about the 'hardware'
of their own bodies.

The article makes two points of relevance to the Department for Public
Conscience and Morality. The first is whether groups that have historically
been excluded from society — those with physical disabilities, for instance
— should be made to think in terms of 'normal' templates (essentially a
retrograde refitting of standard human capability) or whether they should
think more in terms of augmentation far beyond the biological baseline.

The second point is whether the manipulation of the human body,
and especially the use of human skin as a physical display screen and
communication device, is compensation for the increasing lack of self-
expression opportunities elsewhere. If our experience of the external
environment is becoming more prescribed and choice-free through the use of
predictive algorithms and augmented reality, then how else might individuals
retain a sense of identity and control in the future? ...

HOME AND FAMILY

*remember when we lived
and loved in analog?*

Technology is everything that doesn't work yet.

W. Daniel Hillis

Nothing dates faster than the future. When it comes to homes depicted in science fiction, the future arrives in three flavours. The first is vanilla, or classic modernist: white, strictly utilitarian, clad in glass and sliding doors, and connected by sky bridges and monorails. Think of a 1930s modernist Manhattan skyline with Elon Musk's Hyperloop transport system passing through. Second is rocky road, or dystopian devastation, which can be a comment about moral decay, where subterranean living has become a necessity (and at least those currently carving out giant basement developments will be ready for this).

The third and final flavour is raspberry ripple, a classic combination. In many ways, the most realistic vision of the future is portrayed in films such as *Robot and Frank* and *Blade Runner*, where elements of fantasy and weirdness merge seamlessly with the ordinary and familiar. Here there's a tension between fully wired 'future houses' and homes as sanctuaries and protection. Steampunk, a sci-fi genre where the past, usually Victorian, is juxtaposed with today, plugs into this aesthetic. The living in this third world is often communal, which is a prescient take on a world in which both ownership and privacy are being eroded.

I outlined these three possible futures to my children, and the only comment I got back was, 'Dad, when you were a kid was the internet in black and white?' Where do you start with that? It's difficult for me to explain to myself how things worked before computers (BC), the internet, and mobile phones. This illustrates my point: the present changes so quickly, erasing the past and making the future uncertain.

Despite this, the next generation does seem prepared for a world in which our homes will have brains. These buildings won't be as alive as the one in the movie *Monster House*, but they will be both dynamic and reactive. They will harvest resources such as geothermal energy, wind, rain, and especially sunlight (the latter thanks to photovoltaic windows and paint that can harvest sunlight and perhaps even moonlight). Homes will be scattered with smart sensors and will self-adjust to events ranging from high winds and heavy rainfall to full moonlight and poor air quality. They will scrub pollutants from the air. A few homes will grow food on their roofs, while others will use plants to moderate temperatures or absorb pollutants more naturally.

Huge skyscrapers will also become possible thanks to developments in materials technology. Most of us will live in cities. In 1800, only 5 per cent of people lived in urban areas. The number is now 50 per cent, and by 2050 it could be as high as 75 per cent.

All surfaces in our homes will have the potential to be made smart or turned into screens. Carpets will be able to tell if someone has fallen down and not got up. Even wallpaper could be programmed to change colour or design or to match light bulbs that are themselves programmed for mood effects. The danger with this networked environment, though, is that we will end up destroying the very thing that we sought in the first place, which is escape from the outside world.

Being endlessly naive, we will also hand control of these homes over to third parties, because we will be busy and, it appears, efficient. And this is where the trouble will start.

Data mine

You may be familiar with Nest Labs. This is the company that creates sensor-driven, self-learning room thermostats, and which was acquired by Google for $3.2 billion in 2014. Thanks to Nest and companies like it, you can now adjust your heating when you're not at home using an app. This is a great idea, although one wonders whether we shouldn't be heating ourselves more and our empty spaces less by wearing more clothing — as the Japanese do (central heating is almost an unknown concept in Japan). At least clothing doesn't currently feature user agreements, but remotely managed online services generally do. And do you think many people who use these services read the agreements in full? Me neither.

I have no detailed knowledge of Nest, but suffice to say that our tendency not to read online legal agreements can get us into trouble. Instagram, for instance, changed its user agreement after it had been acquired by Facebook, saying that it could display users' uploaded photographs in its own advertising. That's potentially your private memories widely scattered for public consumption.

Would anyone worry if Nest, or some other company, started selling people's temperature data? Probably not, even though it is in one sense private and personal data. Yet think this through a little. If your home heating is connected to remote servers, it could be hacked. Terrorists turning your heating up to 24 °C won't be a major concern, but how about central government turning your central heating down to 15 °C to save energy? One day soon, we may start talking to our central heating and receive a reply: 'No.'

This isn't a serious point, but behind it there's a serious issue. In the digital era, many things that you thought were private or yours are no longer either. Many possessions, even your memories and dreams, are being collected, curated, and controlled by third parties, often without your knowledge or consent.

Philips Lighting is another example of a company that wants to connect to your house. They've been working on that age-old problem of how many people it takes to change a light bulb. The shift towards LED lighting, driven by environmental concerns, has one important consequence: as LEDs are solid-state devices that shine light via a semiconductor, it means they can be wired together with sensors and other bits of digital technology to become networked devices. This means you can control your lights with your mobile phone.

Philips think this is a great idea: 'With the new digitalisation of light, we have only begun to scratch the surface on how we can control it, integrate it with other systems and collect rich data.' That's *your* rich data remember. Building-management systems can be efficient, but again remember that third parties could tap into your lighting — or indeed that of a whole city.

Still, that's not the major concern. Sensors such as these will generate vast amounts of useful data about how we live. We may happily trade this data for value, convenience, or personalisation. Predictive technology, the semantic web, virtual assistants, and augmented reality may all mesh together, making our lives richer, more productive, and more rewarding. We may be paid for the data we produce as we go about our daily lives, and data will be open, ensuring widespread transparency and trust.

Yet there's another scenario that drips with dystopian darkness. All this connectivity will happen, but the relationships will be far from open. Corporations will silently harvest the slipstream of personal information that we emit in order to sell us more stuff. This information will then be held behind paywalls and sold back to us in the form of devices that appeal to our restless drive for convenience and efficiency.

Uber's development as a data centre for city planners is worrying because data about who's moving where and when is unlikely to be free. Moreover, Uber's solutions may be narrowly defined to benefit its services. Walking or cycling would not appear to fit their model. Neither would public transport.

It's a similar story with apps that turn your coffee maker on or tell you what's in your RFID-enabled fridge. Data about when you're at home or when you drink coffee might sound trivial, but billions of bits of such data are valuable. Moreover, are such developments really progress? In England, there were tea-making machines back in the 1970s, but they didn't collect personal data — and as for finding out what's in your fridge, why not just open the door and take a look?

Perhaps we'll know full well that we're being sold at a profit, but won't care. A study by Harvard and Carnegie Mellon universities found that 89 per cent of people would not be willing to pay one meagre dollar to stop a company such as Uber from collecting information about them, which may go some way to explain the enduring popularity of supermarket loyalty cards. On the other hand, we might grow tired of companies such as Uber rating us as customers, or of people using apps such as Peeple to rate us as human beings.

Home alone

Whatever eventually happens, it will occur within a context of other events, social forces, and feedback loops, and this is where the future gets really fascinating. Apart from economics and migration from rural areas to cities, the biggest force affecting households is demographics.

A few decades ago, the story here would have been the death of the nuclear family. Two-parent, two-child, male-breadwinner households were dying. Marriages were down, divorces were up, and more children were being born to single mothers. It's impossible to generalise about this, especially when one is trying to consider the whole world rather than a specific nation, but it's interesting to note that many of these trends are reversing or slowing. This could be yet another example of counter-trends or adjusting forces, but it's too early to say.

What we can say is that far more people will be living alone in the future. In the UK, the number of people living by themselves is growing ten times faster than the overall population. The number of single-person households has risen by more than 100 per cent over the last 40 years, and there are now more single adults living in Britain than married couples. This may mean that individuals will spend 50 per cent longer alone than previous generations.

There is already a problem with older people not talking to anyone for days on end. In the UK, 10 per cent of older people do not have a single conversation with another human being for more than a week. We are already seeing some technological solutions to this. My favourite is an app that connects people going for a run with older people living alone. The idea is that you plan your run via their home to check that they're OK.

In the future, we may see apps that allow older people, or anyone living alone for that matter, to be held. Forget sex — one thing that humans deprived of human contact will long for is the sensation of being held or having another person's skin touch their own. Cuddle parties may have been an early manifestation of this. If you missed these, they were a largely American form of non-sexual intimacy-on-demand. Strangers would meet up and touch each other. An app called Cuddlr, which lasted less than a year, facilitated much the same thing. This sounds strange, but not quite as odd as the fact that in other areas we are being told not to touch people. Affectionate hugs at work can be misinterpreted, while in childcare and education it can put you on a police register.

Older households are a big trend that generates aloneness, but living on your own is not the preserve of the elderly. It also has to do with individuals not wanting to be part of a couple. Some years ago, the United Arab Emirates' Marriage Fund, which provides financial assistance to couples and sponsors mass weddings, said that it was concerned that 60 per cent of women over 30 in the UAE were unmarried (compared with 20 per cent in 1995). Meanwhile, America's Healthy Marriage Initiative has been spending $150 million a year to encourage singles to tie the knot.

Why are there so many singles? First, women are marrying later because of education and career opportunities. Second, bereaved spouses are living longer. And third, changing social attitudes make it acceptable to find financial security, sex, and stable relationships outside marriage.

We should not assume singles are unhappy being single. There's a big difference between living alone, being alone, and feeling alone. The trouble with one-person households though is they use more resources, tend to have fewer children (needed to support ageing populations), and seem more psychologically vulnerable (especially men, who seem to benefit from marriage more than women do).

One wonders if this is a decline in marriage itself or simply a reflection of the trend for individualism and narcissism. Single people can think, say, and do what they like, especially if they have incomes to support it. Rather than be concerned about healthy marriages, perhaps we should be more concerned about healthy singles?

While single-person households are one of the fastest growing demographics, and the individual takes striking precedence in our culture, there is another opposing trend: multi-generational households. In Australia, one fifth of households are multi-generational. From 1981 to 2011, the number of these households in Sydney increased 51 per cent to one quarter of households there, compared to population growth of 38 per cent in that time.

Census data shows that just under a third aged 18–29 are dependent students living with their parents (and thus known as KIPPERS: Kids in Parents' Pockets Eroding Retirement Savings). The rest are non-dependants. It works the other way, too — parents are choosing to live with younger family members, to reduce the loneliness of living alone, or to help out with children or chores by living close by. No doubt some of this is also driven by the high cost of living alone, but also by migrants, many of whom have a more communal mindset.

e-loves me, e-loves me not

In 1951, science fiction writer Isaac Asimov published the short story 'Satisfaction Guaranteed', in which a lonely housewife falls in love with a household robot called Tony. The idea of falling in love with a machine must have appeared far-fetched in 1951. But as machine interfaces such as Siri become more conversational, this is no longer quite so crazy. A publication by the Danish Council of Ethics looking at the moral status of human–machine relationships has concluded that 'It is a worrying possibility that social robots could take the place of human contact'.

The Tony robot can be seen as both emblematic of household automation and as a solution to the loneliness that can develop even in supposedly multi-person households, where human contact is far from guaranteed. Real as our future marital concerns may be, another, more immediate question is what are the effects of children having less direct contact with their parents. Increasingly busy working lives, often for both parents now, means children are left alone with carers or by themselves for long periods. And due to safety concerns, they're no longer running wild outside. Cat Stevens' song 'Where Do the Children Play?' has never been more apt. Sometimes it looks as if children have stopped playing altogether — at least outside the home.

George Monbiot, writing in *The Guardian*, has asked how we will protect nature as adults if we have no experience of nature as children. Children don't have the same opportunities for outdoor play as they once used to. Because bad things are always easier to believe, fears of what can happen to children if they are unsupervised means that the area where they can freely roam has fallen by 90 per cent since the 1970s. Over half of all children used to play frequently in wild places — now less than 10 per cent do. At the same time, British 11-to-15-year-olds usually spend half their waking moments in front of a screen, in the virtual world.

Being outside in wild places changes the way children play. They become more creative, and are more inclined to revel in fantasy, take normal physical risks, and notice what is around them. Taking children away from nature (and keeping them sedentary) makes children — and adults, too — less creative.

Research shows playing among trees and grass is linked with lower incidences of ADHD, while playing indoors on screens or outdoors on bitumen appears to boost incidences. The pandemic rise in childhood obesity and diabetes makes sense, too — if children spend half their waking moments in front of a screen, they spend at least half their day not moving. Coupled with heavy doses of fat-laden and sweet food, it's no surprise children are starting to experience the same lifestyle-related diseases as adults.

One of the things I noticed after moving back to London from Sydney several years ago was the sight of legions of small children being pulled to school on small scooters. Can they not walk? The Pixar film *WALL-E* features the idea of humans being so fat that they need to move around on hover chairs. Give it 50 years and you never know …

Human says no

Passengers at Heathrow Airport are being encouraged to tweet a conveyor-belt sushi restaurant so that food is ready the instant they pass through security. As we've seen, some people dream of a future where they'll be able to swallow tubes of paste so that they can spend more time at work. That dreaded word 'efficiency' again. Others are consumed by dreams of meals instantly prepared by machines. Not in France, Italy, or Spain, one suspects, where having a relaxed lunch with others is still the mark of a society that values sensory pleasure and sociability over arbitrary definitions of productivity and efficiency — even if this is frowned upon by EU central bankers hell-bent on using the sharp knife of competition to spread free-market values. For them, the idea of a convivial lunch has been eaten up and spat out. We must now hurriedly munch our lunch at our desks in order to be productive.

I once met a futurologist in Amsterdam who insisted that fairly soon we'd be printing food using 3D printers. Even restaurants would be doing it. Printing food will undoubtedly catch on as a gimmick. It may even have serious uses: NASA is experimenting with 3D printers to print food for distant missions. But, again, aren't we confusing what's possible with what's needed? Isn't there a need for a tiny pinch of patience in the kitchen? Food is sensory.

The act of cooking is emotional, and can be creative and relaxing, too. Above all, though, eating is, as the restaurant critic A.A. Gill points out, 'a human, communal, and convivial pleasure'.

This is not to say that digital food might not be fun. Chef Watson is a 'cognitive cooking' application developed by IBM that recommends recipes based on pattern recognition. And internet-connected toasters that allow you to download designs to 'print' on your toast could be hugely amusing for a while. Digitally delving into our backgrounds and tastes in order to serve individually tailored food — as Heston Blumenthal has done at his Fat Duck restaurant — might even be entertaining for a while, although it could also get a little creepy. But dinner in a pill? That's as stale as flying cars, and even more absurd.

Yet despite my dislike of efficiency *uber alles*, if there's one food trend that trumps all others, be it at home or on the move, it's convenience. For this reason, we shouldn't be too dismissive of digital dinners. Fast food, microwaves, and ready meals are, after all, big business, and I can foresee a future where speed of preparation and consumption trumps taste, health, and cost. For some people, it already does.

I was staying at the Shangri-La hotel in Singapore recently. One of the pleasures of this hotel is a buffet restaurant where you can select from the world's cuisines. Ten years ago, I remember this as a melting pot of convivial dining and discussion. Now it's full of people urgently photographing or videoing the food. Once you're seated, it gets worse. The majority of people are in groups, but they're not talking to each other. They are texting or looking at their screens. Chatting to a member of staff, I was told that many people, especially children, don't even look up from these screens when ordering their drinks or asking a question.

According to *The New York Times*, the number of people taking photographs in restaurants in New York is reaching epic proportions, even in Michelin-starred establishments. I'm perplexed. I understand the need to share, but is this not something else? Is this not an example of people being so desperate to preserve and bottle their lives that they are forgetting to taste it? This is surely not only data exhibitionism, but also emotional incontinence, and it's putting me off my food.

Grocers of despair

Moving from food and eating to shopping, there was a report a while back about a sales assistant in a supermarket who refused to serve a customer because the customer was on a mobile phone and refused to look at the sales assistant. I can only assume that the assistant was an encumbrance standing in the way of an efficient shopping experience.

There is much debate about the extent to which retail will continue to move online. Personally, I think the digital drift will continue, partly due to price, but largely due to convenience. But why do we rush through half our lives frantically trying to save time, only to end up spending the remaining half wondering what to do with all the time we've saved?

Physical shops won't disappear. Retail will continue to polarise between fast and slow, luxury and low-cost, generalist and specialist, local and 'destination shopping'. This is because shopping is now a form of leisure and because the experience itself can be more fulfilling than anything we buy. Retail at its best is serendipitous, too. The exception to all this is supermarkets, most of which have become so focused on price and efficiency and making humans fit their standardised systems that they have forgotten about talking to people and inspiring them. They have become cold and impersonal, which is perhaps a foretaste of things to come. They also make the mistake, especially online, of giving customers exactly what they already know they want, when it is clearly in what people never knew they needed that true value lies.

In South Korea, commuters travelling to work can now scan virtual shelves on posters on the subway with their mobile device and have their shopping delivered before they get home. This can fill your fridge, but not, I suspect, your hungry heart. Human contact and serendipity are both absent on the virtual shelves.

Using mobile devices to shop will become increasingly common and will spawn location-based and predictive shopping. Retailers will predict what people want in certain situations and may bid for our custom based on patterns within our data. Websites will also instantly personalise themselves, using cameras, microphones, and algorithms to work out what type of person you are and even what mood you are in.

Conversely, one interesting trend that's emerging is online brands opening physical stores. These are essentially showrooms celebrating the physical nature of retail. Inside these stores, we're seeing every conceivable high-tech toy, ranging from 3D body scanners and virtual changing rooms to visual search engines that photograph what you're wearing and make recommendations of items to match. In due course, we'll see giant screens with images that change depending on who enters the store, including personalised greetings dispatched by narrowcast sound that only individuals can hear, much like in the film *Minority Report*.

We need never lose any of these clothes, either. I've mentioned tracking clothes already, and this is probably more common than you think. In Japan today, paranoid parents can buy their children clothing embedded with sensors. When a child passes through a subway turnstile or school gate containing receivers and transmitters, their parents receive a message saying that the child has arrived. Or at least their clothing has. Sensors in shoes mean that if your granny has dementia and wanders off, you can simply Google her. You can even buy tracking beacons, such as Amber Alert GPS, which contain a microphone, enabling adults to eavesdrop on the conversations of minors and seniors.

The psychology of things

One of the behaviours that set us apart from our machines is our urge to accumulate things, although some birds and other animals hoard things, too. Magpies are famously attracted to shiny objects. But unlike our ape cousins that seek out tools which are then disposed of, we tend not to throw our shopping away. Instead, our objects become possessions that help to define our identity and social status.

However, the idea that objects can make us happy is being challenged on a number of fronts. First, we're realising that beyond a relatively low threshold, more possessions don't make us happier. Second, digitalisation means that many of the things that we used to own — and had to buy outright — can now be rented, accessed communally, or streamed at the point of need. Car- and lift-sharing services are one example. Other examples include music and books, although we are slowly seeing that digital and analog formats aren't mutually exclusive.

iTunes downloads are buoyant, while on-demand music streaming grew by 100 per cent in the US in 2013 — yet so did sales of vinyl. In fact, in the UK, sales of vinyl records have grown by 500 per cent since 2007 and are now at their highest for 15 years. Admittedly, sales of vinyl are rising from a low base, but this does perhaps represent a human attempt at rebalancing the digital revolution. Digital music is convenient and perfectly suited to our mobile lifestyles, yet the sound isn't as rich, and the beauty of the cover art is diminished or totally non-existent. The ritualistic aspects of vinyl are totally different, too. Vinyl acquires a patina over time, which often tells a story. As with bookshelves, you can look at a vinyl record collection and peer into someone's soul. There's also the ambling joy of browsing record shops and the social act of listening to vinyl.

And it looks like musicians get a better deal with vinyl. Geoff Barrow, the founder of the band Portishead, has pointed out that after 34 million streams of his band's tracks by Spotify, YouTube, Apple, and Universal Music, he earned just £1,700 after tax. American musician Ellen Shipley has similarly reported that she earned just $39 after her songs had been played 3.1 million times via Spotify.

Paper books also seem to be doing OK despite the digital on-slaught. Again, digital books are convenient, especially for people who need to travel light or carry lots of books. Yet paperback and hardback sales from traditional publishers remain steady. What's happening here, I think, is that people are waking up to the fact that digital is a complement to analog, not a replacement.

However, digital living does give us the opportunity to take consumption to a new level by challenging whether we need to buy certain things at all and also whether we need to buy things from giant corporations. Copyright issues aside, 3D printing could offer us new ways to access objects, as will virtual and augmented realities. Similarly, the co-creation movement is arguably an attempt to redefine the relationship between producer and consumer in a fairer and more sustainable manner.

But just because something is digital, or shared, doesn't make it free in the sense of having no environmental impact. Digital products and services still consume resources, and the obsolescence of device hardware in particular is a concern. Also, while we complain of physical clutter, digital clutter is fast becoming a serious problem in our homes, too.

Objects with digital memories

Just as some clothing knows where it is, many objects will soon know where they've been. I spoke earlier about mirror worlds and objects dissolving into information. I can foresee a situation where any important physical object we own has embedded within it data about where's it's from, who made it and how, and who's owned it throughout its history.

The charity Oxfam has experimented with adding ownership details — or life-story labels — to second-hand goods sold in its shops. Shelflife, as the initiative was known, boosted sales, possibly because people were hungry for narrative and possibly because a default of distrust can be broken with readily accessible information about where something, or someone, is from.

In a world dominated by virtual, automated, and augmented realities, the contents of your home, tastefully arranged in both the physical and digital realms, could be a window into your life and values in a way that even your shelves of vinyl records and books are not. Provenance is set to become a major issue.

The fantasy of perfection

As ever, the future is already here, but irregularly scattered and infrequently noticed. In Japan, South Korea, and the US, there are already avatar girlfriends and robot sex for people that live alone or feel alone. If you have anything approaching a busy life, you may have also missed the news that Americans Matthew Homann and Kyle Tabor have invented an app that removes societal pressure to be in a relationship.

For $24.99 a month, users can invent the perfect partner with the help of online templates and then have an invisible digital other send you voice messages, texts, and even handwritten love letters. Is this a reaction to anxieties surrounding our relationship status online, or do we now have such fragile identities that we need to invent such reassurance? Perhaps the reason is that a lack of reflection means that no robust inner sense of self is developing.

For a similar amount of money, another option is a girlfriend pillow. These are surprisingly popular in Japan. The pillow is essentially a stuffed pillowcase based on popular characters in comics or computer games. One such pillowcase is Nemu Asakura, a character in an X-rated computer game called *Da Capo*. You can't do much with these pillowcases, but adults have been seen taking them out of their homes and into restaurants or photographing themselves with them in photo booths. Weird, but it gets even weirder.

By 2031, it's predicted that 50 per cent of people will have met their partner online. The current figure is 38 per cent. Twenty or 30 years ago, lonely-hearts columns in newspapers represented a triumph of hope over experience. Now, online dating is normal and part of a global business worth billions. Then, as now, the ads can be rather unromantic, but most in the past managed to display a distinct lack of cynicism about the human race.

Is it natural to rely on an algorithm to find true love? If you're shopping for companionship then every little thing helps, and there's no doubt that technology can unearth hidden attractions. Critics point out that matchmaking in an era of digital networks can be mercenary and dehumanising — can reinforce loneliness rather than eliminating it. For busy singles, the word 'efficient' keeps cropping up here, too.

While somewhat less awkward, e-dates have become more like job interviews. Questions are asked, and acceptances and rejections swiftly dispatched. This is not to say that there's more honesty, simply that there's no pretence whatsoever about why people are meeting up. Maybe this *is* efficient.

But my worry is that people are making judgements too

hastily. People are looking for a perfect match and seeking to make a decision in seconds. Perhaps algorithms can help people find perfection, although in my experience logic and precision are unlikely bedfellows when it comes to the messy, irrational, and emotional business of love. As Sherry Turkle points out, the overwhelming choice offered by dating sites such as Tinder engenders a constant search for someone better, someone perfect.

The fundamental issue, once again, is that our technologies are developing at high speed while our brains are not. Moreover, algorithms can make precisely the same thoughtless mistakes that humans do. Adherence to test results assumes that what you see is what you'll always get. Yet people change. They mature. Perfect, instantaneous matches are possible, but so too is the idea that jagged imperfections can be smoothed by two people rubbing together over time.

Of course, some people don't want love, they just want sex. Here, the future will deliver copious amounts of copulation. Technology has a history of being put to unintended uses, and the internet is no different. Incongruously, what started off as an academic and military tool has ended up being used for sexual gratification.

But we should remain alert to the lessons of history. The printing press gave us Shakespeare, but also penny dreadfuls. Film gave us Fritz Lang and *Metropolis*, but also *What the Butler Saw* machines. VHS tapes and DVDs were not only used to watch wildlife documentaries either. Even Second Life (remember that?) spawned avatars that moved beyond talking to more intimate — and some might say, deviant — pleasures.

So where might sex go in the future? One scenario is that social attitudes reverse. We become more prudish and private, nostalgic romance flourishes, and we fantasise about death rather than sex, as the Victorians did.

Alternatively, the boundaries between real and virtual may

continue to dissolve, allowing people to become intimate with people who are not physically present or with characters that don't actually exist. There are already cameras linked to gaming consoles that convert real body movements into actions on a screen. If you add sensory technologies such as haptics, which deliver the illusion of touch, then our fantasies may become quite real.

There's also a booming market, especially in Asia, for life-size, high-end sex dolls. If we added robotics, things could develop in some strange directions. Those not in the market for such products may instead use virtual-reality goggles and e-clothing to enhance their senses, and we may one day even end up with implants that create orgasms at the click of a button. Marshall McLuhan said that media are extensions of our senses, after all.

It's not inconceivable, either, that human reproduction without humans will be possible in the future, too.

Till death do us part?

Assuming that some people do still manage to have real sex, what might some of the other consequences be? Historically, men and women pair-bonded partly for survival and partly for reproduction. Companionship played a part, too, although it seems unlikely that human happiness is a goal of natural evolution.

Staying alive thousands of years ago was hard work. For much of human history, reaching the age of 35 was an achievement. Now, humans regularly reach 100 years of age, and human relationships can easily last 50 or 60 years. In the future, it's possible that people may be married for 80 or 90 years. Let's hope these people have enough to say to each other.

I know there's research suggesting that men aren't designed to be monogamous. But societally, monogamy matters. Couples in stable relationships tend to be happier and live to an older age.

Couples tend to cost society less and have less impact on the environment than people who live alone.

So how might technology help here? One idea is that it may be possible to develop drugs that make people stay together. We already chemically castrate certain individuals to alter their sex drive, so why can't we create chemicals that induce pair-bonding? Whether this idea is moral or ethical, I'll leave that judgement up to you.

Lost boys and girls

I'd like to end this chapter by returning to the topic of children. A leader in a local regional newspaper (the *Mid Sussex Times*) once ran with a comment titled 'Good Natured Fun' that read, 'Phones, TVs and computers tend to be the first port of call for keeping children quiet when money is tight.' This might be fine in small measure, but taken to extremes one wonders what will happen to children's development when adults put their own ease and convenience ahead of physical engagement and conversation with their children.

I came across another article not so long ago which warned that bedtime stories were at risk of extinction, with over a third of parents admitting that they no longer read to their children at night. This is presumably because they are too busy or too tired, or the children are too distracted. One solution offered to this problem is one-minute bedtime stories, essentially executive summaries of classic children's fairy tales. Another idea is books that read themselves.

Have we really become so absorbed in our own lives and with what others think of us that our children have become collateral damage? Part of the problem is offices that fit in our pockets and are hardly ever switched off, even at night, at weekends, or on holiday. Children similarly suffer from schoolyards that never end. A generation ago, peer pressure generally ended at the school gates. Now peer pressure never stops, because phones are never switched off and social media is 24/7. If you are being bullied at school, it can be continuous.

Children have to navigate and curate two worlds, the physical and the virtual. Constant online feedback and regular recording and posting of images means there's little or no downtime or switching off. I took my children to a remote island once, and we got into an argument about whether they should be allowed to take iPads. In the end, they were left at home (the iPads that is, although the other option was, at the time, tempting).

On the first day, both kids were in shock. The second day was denial. By the third day, deals were done, but eventually they visibly relaxed. Their networked selves evaporated. It was as though they'd been released, which is what they had wanted all along. They just needed permission to be kids again.

Another trend, mentioned earlier, is risk aversion, where we see imagined dangers lurking everywhere. Not so long ago, there was a DVD compilation of the best of *Sesame Street* (1969–1974) featuring a warning that the DVD was 'intended for grown-ups'. Why? Because it contained scenes no longer thought beneficial for children. Seriously.

We are living in what is undoubtedly the safest time for children in history, yet we track our kids with technology and protect them from dirt, germs, grazed knees, and broken bones like never before. Even the use of red ink by teachers is considered dangerous for self-esteem. As for stranger danger, Warwick Cairns, a researcher in the UK, has calculated that you would have to leave your toddler alone on the street for 200,000 years before it became statistically probable that the child would be abducted.

Why are we so afraid? Why, for instance, did the number of

children walking to school in Australia drop from 37 per cent in 1985 to 26 per cent in 2001? The answer could be traffic, but there are other examples that suggest this isn't the case. A company called Thudguard produces protective foam helmets for children learning to walk, while another sells Comfy Crawlers, a product designed to protect the knees of crawling infants. The reason for all this anxiety is a sensation-seeking media plus a growing culture of infantilism and litigation, in which parents and especially educators and caregivers are fearful of liability for any accident or injury.

But what if reducing risk is making life more dangerous? Could removing dangerous playground equipment from public areas be doing children more harm than good? What if zero tolerance of risk is making life riskier in the longer term by shifting danger into early adulthood?

It's through trial and especially error that kids find out what works and what doesn't, and appreciate the limits and risks. If you have a fire without a fireguard at home, children soon learn not to touch. If you have schools that ban nuts because someone might have an allergy, you are creating a false sense of security in later life. If risks are perceived as having been removed at an early stage, individuals don't grow up with an appreciation of risky behaviour. They become so cocooned and protected that they only learn the important lessons in adult life, when the world around them is less forgiving. They become brittle adults who lack confidence to do anything on their own.

Yet there is a contradictory problem: if parents attempt to ignore risk, they are accused of being bad parents. They could even be reported to childcare authorities. But perhaps things are starting to change. The surge in bush camps, even woodland schools, for instance, makes me think that once again we might be sensible enough to self-adjust.

Existential threats aside, the Darwinian idea that adaptability is the key to survival should be widely taught. Moreover, it is mutation that moves things forward, and feedback that creates development. Both, to some extent, require accidents and alertness. Humans are the only species that can think about their own thinking and deal with abstract concepts such as this. We tell stories about our hopes and fears, and it is this that marks us apart from machines. If we keep telling stories and keep talking to each other, I am hopeful about any future that comes our way.

@ Dr Alex

THIS MAY BE THE LAST COMMUNICATION WRITTEN BY HAND YOU
WILL EVER RECEIVE FROM ME! THE THOUGHT TRANSFER EXPERIMENT
HAS BEEN SUCCESSFUL!

200 VOLUNTEERS SENT THEIR TWEETS BY THOUGHT ALONE. ANOTHER
GROUP SITTING 500 METRES AWAY RECEIVED AN INCREDIBLE 92%,
ALMOST INSTANTANEOUSLY

EVEN MANAGED TO SEND 7 THOUGHT MESSAGES FROM LONDON TO
NEW YORK IN JUST OVER 30 MINUTES, INCLUDING AN ORDER FOR
PIZZA WITH EXTRA PEPPERONI

WE ARE STILL SOMEWHAT PUZZLED BY THE TIME LAG TO NEW YORK,
BUT CORRINA BELIEVES THAT THIS COULD BE DUE TO AN IONIC
DISRUPTION FIELD.

ART AND WAR

the search for (and submission to) something
far larger than ourselves

Heralds don't sing about men who lived in orthodoxy or
played it safe, they sing about men who lived an uncertain
future and took enough risks to make your head spin.

Evan Meekins

I have a habit of writing notes on fragments of paper. Lines I've
overheard, book and film reviews, statistical gems. I habitually
tear pages out of magazines and newspapers, too. Sometimes I
write things down on my phone, although I find that since these
digital notes are fixed in one place they don't go walkabout. My
physical notes constantly make a run for the nearest exit. They
get lost and randomly reappear next to other disconnected scraps
of information, which results in cross-fertilisation. Notes, if you
haven't noticed, are inherently social.

One such piece of flotsam is an article that surfaced a year
ago from the depths of *The Atlantic* magazine. On the first torn
page, I'd highlighted a quote from the philosopher Bertrand
Russell. The quote is long, but ends with the words 'only on the
firm foundation of unyielding despair, can the soul's habitation
henceforth be safely built'. How do you compete with a line like

that? I might have missed it, too, in which case this book could have turned out very differently. What was it that Picasso said? 'You have to have an idea of what you are going to do, but it should be a vague idea.' I agree. Precisely.

Picasso's quote reminds me of another by the sculptor Henry Moore. He said, 'The secret of life is to have a task, something you bring everything to, every minute of the day for your whole life. And the most important thing is — it must be something you cannot possibly do!' The point of this, for me at least, is the question of how you should live knowing that whatever you do will ultimately result in defeat. What is the point of anything if we ultimately die? How can you continue living when you know that you'll never write anything to compare with these lines or create anything of enduring substance?

These questions, in the context of lifeless technologies that never truly experience love, hope, failure, disappointment, or regret, is a wholly practical one. If, one day, smart machines do almost everything that humans can, including bonding emotionally with humans, then what is the point of us? Each generation has new inventions, a great number of which distance us from reality in some way. But the questions resulting from these inventions are always, ultimately, the same.

Who are we? Why are we here? Are we just stardust, a meaningless accident, or is there purpose here?

You can get lost in space with this. The more we know, the less, it seems, we understand. Each new invention generates more ignorance and uncertainty, not less. But that's fine. The trick is to humbly hold your nerve and let go, becalmed in your own cosmic solitude. The point is that there is no point.

The alternative is quiet desperation. Life may be meaningless. It is certainly baffling and absurd and can only really be understood by looking at it backwards. It's also deeply wonderful. But knowing all this can be blissful and deeply therapeutic. Looking at a grain of sand or a silicon chip in this context produces a blissful and secure serenity. Interacting with old human-made objects and ancient landscapes similarly unburdens us. They all take us home, to our childhood, and to the birth of possibility. Only by glimpsing human continuity in this manner can we discover our true selves. The immense passing of time forges a connection that's quite beautiful. There's refuge in infinity.

The realisation that we're part of everything and nothing simultaneously can be hugely liberating. It reminds me of an old joke, retold in the science fiction film *Bicentennial Man*: 'This Buddhist walks up to a hot-dog vendor and says, "Make me one with everything."'

A similar point is made by Brian Cox, the physicist and television presenter with the twinkle of starlight in his eyes. The thought of our blue pinprick of a planet amid the enormity of dark space initially makes one feel that we are totally insignificant. But then, from the void, comes the dawning realisation that we are hugely special and unique. The eternity of space is affirmation that we all count in some way. It is the vastness of the nothingness beyond that gives technicolour intensity to the now.

Carl Sagan once said that 'By far the best way I know to engage the religious sensibility, the sense of awe, is to look up on a clear night.' How Twitter and Facebook work in this context is beyond my earthly understanding. Then again, perhaps the success of both has to do with the validation that we exist and are alive right now. You are *here*, as it were.

Is the human soul software?

I have few fixed beliefs. I agree with the author George Zarkadakis that without words, there would be no universe and no reality, which some people might align with *The Book of Genesis*. The world came into being when we found the words to describe it. I believe in the unseen, and I think it's possible that an immaterial human soul, or spirit, exists that is somehow eternal — a separation of body and soul. This is reminiscent of computer software being separate from computer hardware.

I think it's possible, too, that materials can hold memories of energy or events linked to people — ghosts, if you like — which has parallels with how some children think objects have minds and with how Australian Aboriginals view their landscape. I also believe it's possible that parallel universes exist, which some people might interpret as heaven and hell. If one day we invent communication between human brains via thought (neuro-telepathy) then perhaps we'd have prayer. If we artificially create consciousness and place our thinking selves in boxes, we would even have the true separation of body and soul.

Of course, our existence and that of the entire universe could be a *Matrix*-like simulation, as I mentioned earlier. The American physicist Silas Beane even thinks this is statistically probable. Whatever the shape of things to come, it's certainly the case that alien intelligence out in space or artificial intelligence here on Earth will create questions about the individual self and what it means to be human. Artificial intelligence, in particular, is a mirror that we will use to ask questions about ourselves that reveal our true nature.

Historically, asking such questions was the role of religion. Religion provided a sense of community, a shared moral code, and ultimately a purpose. It also provided a narrative that explained the human experience. For some, religion still does this and more. But for others, religious faith is akin to a belief in horoscopes.

The drift away from religion was predicted by Max Weber and

Emile Durkheim a century ago. The theory back then was that the expansion of scientific logic would lead to the elimination of God, as religion rested on human ignorance. One might argue that this is exactly what's happened. The internet is merely following in the footsteps of the printing press and other forms of mass media as the latest way in which knowledge is spread and a new communal consciousness emerges.

In the West, many adults now claim not to believe in God, although in lots of cases it seems to be more that they can't be bothered (or don't have the time) rather than an active consideration and rejection. Non-belief can also be seen an offshoot of individualism, whereby people no longer wish to be told what to think or how to behave. In the United States, often quoted as the exception to the secularisation rule, there's also been a fall in belief, with 20 per cent of Americans expressing no belief, compared to 5 per cent in 1970. Generationally, the fall is even steeper.

Younger generations tend to believe in Steve Jobs and tablet computing, not *The Book of Job* or the Tablets of Stone. However, the future is rarely at the end of a trend line, and historical data is a poor guide to what will be conceived or resurrected in the future.

Moreover, worldwide, religion is in fine fettle. In Russia, China, and Africa, religion is resurgent. Globally, 59 per cent of people describe themselves as religious, while in China there are 80 million active Christians, which makes the Church larger than the Communist Party. This could be due to supressed demand or it might be that digitalisation has enabled the opposite of what was generally anticipated. The easy transmission of faith, ranging from streamed church services and Instapray (an app that allows people to request prayers) to text-based confession, has led to booming belief. No doubt we'll see more ways to interact with the dead at some point in the future.

There's also the thought that religion thrives when people wish to measure their pain. Religion is popular where people are poor or insecure, but weak in relatively rich regions such as Scandinavia, where social safety nets are strong.

There are further factors at play, too. Societal ageing is creating more elderly people with an interest in what, if anything, happens after they die. Geopolitical turmoil, economic volatility, and technological change have similarly conspired to create a world defined by complexity, rapid change, and uncertainty. In this context, God is intuitively appealing.

Religion explains why things are as they are and describes what comes next. Furthermore, while God may be on the way out in Europe, even here most people believe in something. Theos, a British think tank, says that although many might not believe in God specifically, around 60 per cent of adults in the UK profess spiritual or supernatural beliefs or believe in some form of higher power, while only 13 per cent of people think human beings have no spiritual element whatsoever. When people stop believing in God, they don't believe in nothing.

On one level, many people feel that they have lost a sense of control, creating anxiety. But, as I said earlier, the solution might be to acknowledge that we aren't in control and that randomness and elements derived from chance encounters play a huge part in how things turn out. Embracing such thoughts is hugely liberating.

As my torn-out article from *The Atlantic* puts it: 'Throw that master switch and feel the relief spread through your mind and body ... feel the freedom of no longer needing to make anything happen'. Taken to an extreme, this is fatalistic, even nihilistic, but it does have its practical uses.

Stone Age shadows

Going back to our Stone Age brains, it may be because we lived in constant fear of danger that we developed the idea that something 'out there' was either after us or looking after us. Even today, the thought that there's someone watching over us makes sense, because it can remove existential fear. I will leave further musings on our search for meaning and the meaning of machines for the final chapter. However, before I do this, I would like to briefly examine war, violence, and art, and what each of these may tell us about the human condition.

Some people might argue that without religion, there would be no wars. I imagine that war will continue, but there could be fewer instances of large-scale conflict in the future because most societies are ageing, and older people tend not to fight each other. As an illustration of this thought, the median age in Afghanistan is 15.6, in Gaza is 18, in Syria is 21.9, and in Egypt is 24.4. Contrast this to the US, where the median age is 37.1; the UK, where it's 39.8; and Japan, where it's 44.9.

Clearly, in Japan, and increasingly elsewhere, a large proportion of the population is more worried about getting out of bed without falling over than toppling governments. Of course, the digitalisation of war means this may no longer hold true. With hand-to-hand combat, youth is an advantage, but it's less of one in wars waged digitally. A pertinent question might therefore be how the growing convergence between computer games and real warfare will affect our sense of reality and whether a generation brought up playing increasingly lifelike war games will more readily go to or accept war.

Using games to simulate war isn't new. The difference this time is scale. The game *Call of Duty: Modern Warfare 2* earned $310 million in sales within one day of release. Compare this to the blockbuster movie *Star Wars: The Force Awakens*, which racked up

$119 million in its first day. Or how about the fact that while 70,000 young people joined the US Army in 2009, more than 4.7 million stayed at home on Veterans Day to play war games on computers. Worldwide, the war-game genre is possibly the most significant sector of the gaming market, and it is estimated that there are more than 350 million regular players of such video games worldwide.

But there are consequences. One is that, the more realistic digital games become, the greater the distortion between reality and fantasy. Clearly, virtual exercises are the way to go if military budgets are constrained or you wish to avoid casualties associated with boots on the ground. Yet is there a danger that digital training will edge out real-life understanding? Moreover, are young men brought up playing *Assassin's Creed* going to feel less guilt if they kill someone in the real world using a virtual interface? In other words, does virtual war desensitise combatants in real theatres of combat? The argument here is that virtual violence means that war feels less real and therefore that the perpetrators of real-life violence feel less empathetic toward their victims.

And if this is true, imagine, for a moment, what happens if Disney and the Department of Defence teamed up to fight ISIS using 3D glasses, haptic gloves, and scent collars that create microbursts of cordite? I imagine the answer might include weakened situational awareness followed by disconnection from reality and risk.

Perhaps people playing war games will retain a sense of what's right and wrong, yet become more afraid of reality. In other words, on-screen violence might not make society more violent, but it may increase the expectation of violence. On a more positive note, Olivia Metcalf at the Australian National University suggests that such games 'provide an escape from purposelessness'. However, is the disappearance of war at the cost of millions of disillusioned and disenfranchised minds a price we are prepared to pay?

Nations versus networks

According to Ronald Arkin, a robot researcher working at the Georgia Institute of Technology, 56 governments across the globe are actively seeking to develop robotic killing machines. Meanwhile, military strategist Thomas Adams says that 'The logic leading to fully autonomous systems seems inescapable'. Opponents of automation argue that this means that wars will cost less to wage and will thus become more frequent in the future.

Then there's the problem of mistaken identity. Teaching machines to distinguish between military and civilian targets — especially when decisions about whether to kill someone or not become automated and happen in a fraction of a second — might not be easy. On the opposing side, proponents of robotic weapons argue that intelligent fighting machines will pay more attention to battlefield rules and are less likely to engage in acts of anger or malice.

What does seem possible is that while large-scale wars could become less frequent, smaller wars could become more commonplace. Hence the idea of redesigning forces as shooting organisations with a hider–finder dynamic. The key movement here is from fighting physical nations to fighting digitally inspired or coordinated networks. To do this, forces must be configured to deal with multiple or simultaneous threats, often from tiny teams armed with the most basic weapons. Creating new technologies ranging from weapons that won't work after a certain date to weapons with digital tracking that can be remotely disabled may ensure that the world becomes a bit safer, but they still won't stop a handful of lunatics taking over a plane with some 'Iron Age' tools and then using the plane itself as a weapon.

Department of Future Crimes

The growth of terrorism has blurred the line not only between what's war and what's not, but also between civilian police and military personnel, a point that hasn't been missed by the makers of science fiction films such as *Robocop* and *Judge Dredd*.

Predictive policing sounds like something from the sci-fi classic *Minority Report*, which it is, but it is reality also. A US company, PredPol, uses software to determine where and when crime will happen. Six months after using PredPol's system, crime in one area of Los Angeles fell by 12 per cent. In surrounding areas, crime rose by 0.5 per cent, however, suggesting that proactive policing is no silver bullet. Meanwhile, several US states are using digital analysis to decide which prisoners to parole. I'm sure a few hackers are thinking much the same thing, especially if all prison-cell locks become connected to a central system that can be opened remotely.

Clearly, over-reliance on such systems can cause trouble. Data can be used to restrain human prejudices, but can also accentuate human biases. Furthermore, if an increasing number of day-to-day behaviours are tracked digitally, there's the temptation to chase revenue from minor infringements rather than tracking serious criminal behaviour.

There's also nothing stopping criminals from using digital analysis to determine targets that might yield rich pickings, although in many cases all such people need to do is monitor Facebook or Instagram to see who owns what and who's not at home. Research by security firm Friedland found that 80 per cent of apprehended burglars had used data from social media to plan break-ins. The good news, though, is that developments in open policing and open intelligence mean that citizen sleuths can be easily corralled into tracking down suspects. But things may go much further.

Genetics, for example, might be used to identify biological markers for criminality, and police could target people based on the likelihood that they'd commit future crimes. Even if such technology worked though, this concept overflows with ethical issues. A much better idea is malicious-intent detectors. These machines, currently found in some airports, assign probability for criminal behaviour based on remotely read body temperature, breathing rate, and body language. But such systems could be used as the foundation of a police state as much as the basis for security in a democracy.

Mood recognition machines are especially interesting in this context. On a prosaic level, an ability to read an individual's mood could be used to test products or personalise advertising. But you could also use such technology to judge the mood of a group, a corporation, or even an entire nation. On the positive side, governments might use real-time mood monitoring to increase general happiness. On the negative side, they could be tempted to identify dissatisfaction or opposition in real-time. What if, for instance, digital cameras with mood-recognition software were used to identify towns where opposition politicians were popular — and targeted them for elimination?

It's unlikely that we'll ever see perfect revolution-forecasting algorithms, although I did once meet someone who was trying to create one. The theory was that digital analysis of data about the percentage of young men in a population, education, internet access, unemployment, inflation, food prices, and corruption could tell you where, but not when, trouble would start.

Again, such technology can flow in several directions. It's

reasonably well known that soldiers use image analysis to confirm the identity of certain individuals before killing them. But terrorists are doing the same thing. When terrorists invaded the Taj Mahal Palace Hotel in Mumbai in 2008, they used mobile phones and Facebook to identify hotel guests and thus decide which ones to kill.

It's ironic that communications technology and social media would be used in this way. War and terrorism are both conversations — they are what remains when people give up actually talking to each another or when one side thinks the other isn't listening. Unlike murder, war is not usually an intimate act. The perpetrators do not generally know their victims, and the distance with which modern war is waged, especially digital war, makes this even more so.

Art: what is it good for?

If war is communication by other means, permit me to make a free-associative jump to art, a form of communication that often takes war as its theme. Exactly when and precisely why human beings started making art is unclear, but it was probably during the Upper Palaeolithic period, 10–50,000 years ago, as a form of language or tribal messaging. At this stage, the repertoire of subjects was modest. Art mainly featured animals and was likely linked with food, either helping hunters to find and kill their prey or instilling hunters with magical powers.

At its most basic, art is storytelling about the human condition, often through metaphor. Art is about the struggle to understand the human condition, and the distillation of such thinking into objects and images that can transcend both time and place. At it's best, art is a call to action of some kind, whether that's making people want something or asking a question of them. Art is also a visual representation of the unique fact that humans — and humans alone — can think about and imagine themselves and their world from the outside. Art is a way of seeing not only this world, but also other imaginary worlds inside our heads. Art reminds us that we are mortal, too, although in some instances we use it to mitigate such mortality.

Chimpanzees share 98.8 per cent of our genetic make-up, yet they can't paint, write, or make movies like *Planet of the Apes*. Some people dispute this. Putting aside the 'infinite number of monkeys' argument (given enough monkeys and enough time, one will eventually write *Do Androids Dream of Electric Sheep?*), people might cite the fact that in London in the 1950s a chimp called Congo had an exhibition of some of his work at London Zoo. Elephants and seals have made similar attempts. But this is mimicry, not art, and while abstract patterns can be pleasing, it's more accident than artistic endeavour. It isn't conversation or dialogue, and it certainly doesn't tell us anything meaningful either, although this is a criticism one might level against much contemporary art.

Some art critics claim that it's ridiculous to say that either primates or painters can't paint. As Marcel Duchamp said, 'anything can be art'. But teaching chimps to paint doesn't turn them into artists any more than teaching a parrot to say 'Hello' is evidence that birds can talk.

I'm sure a few Australian bird lovers will point to a creature called the bowerbird, which creates structures seemingly for its own aesthetic amusement. But this is embellishment. Birds can sing and dance, too, yet these are biological imperatives, intended for reproduction more than anything else. They do not have anything to say, as far as I can tell, about what it means to be a bird.

How about robots? Can they paint? It seems so, at least in the technical sense. e-David is a robot developed by the University of Konstanz in Germany. 'David' is an acronym for 'Drawing Apparatus for Vivid Interactive Display', which says everything you need to know about the sterility of the art that results. Here, once again, what we are seeing is technical skill that's more akin to making a cake than making meaning. This is art as a logical problem and again one can't help but wonder how a machine can be taught to truly paint when a machine can't really see or feel. Even if a machine could paint Picasso's *Guernica*, would it know that it had done so? And would it feel anything about having so done?

Furthermore, great art often requires a little madness. True creativity comes from breaking rules, not following them. Originality comes from the joining together of serendipitous events. How do you program that?

I'm sure there's a segue here back to the Second Commandment and the creation of idols and possibly the fundamentalist destruction of the statues of Bamiyan in Afghanistan in 2011 — recently replayed as the vandalism of Syrian antiquities in 2015. However, I'll end here with the question of why photography didn't kill painting and make a small point about love, which is something that's been missing in too many plans for the future.

In the realm of the senses

Speaking at the opening of some new displays at the National Portrait Gallery in London, the historian Simon Schama reflected that it was our habit of looking outward that created art, although we now seem to be entering an age that looks downwards and inwards.

Photography, along with music, is regularly held up as an example of the rapid speed of technological change and the shift towards a digital or dematerialised economy. This is valid, although one element that's rarely developed is the fact that Kodak *did* see the future coming and still managed to go bankrupt. Kodak's problem was cultural, not technical. Kodak invented the digital camera, but they were so wedded to the idea of people printing photographs that they couldn't move their focus away from photo printers.

More interesting, though, is why photography hasn't killed painting. Photography ticks all the right boxes. It's far cheaper than painting. It's faster and more convenient, as well. Two hundred years after the invention of photography, one might say that digital photography in particular is more efficient, although we never do. Why is that?

All photography exists on a spectrum, with holiday snaps and selfies at one end and social commentary and art at the other. Even this polarisation is deeply indicative of a profoundly human activity. I think the reason painting persists is that it talks more vividly about and to the human condition.

Painting, far more than photography, is also layered and interpretive. It doesn't copy something directly, but tries to convey what something feels like. Painting uses reality to comment on something that is unreal. Also, as my good friends Alan and Stella point out, a painting is never anything other than the painting, and there can only ever be one. In contrast, a photograph is always an abstraction of something else and can be copied perfectly. Both, however, can take part in conversations that have not been diluted by words. Sometimes, these conversations are about something we fear or dread. Occasionally, they are about things we own. Paintings, like photographs, can be used to possess people, but also to hold onto them.

And this brings us to love and whether affection can ever be a problem to be solved logically and delivered through an anthropomorphising machine. I don't think so.

Machines are objective, single-minded, and reductionist. Humans, on the other hand, follow their hearts. Our lives usually arise not from the unfolding of cold binary calculations, but from an accumulation of events, including numerous accidents and mistakes. We make sense of all this through feelings, which are the most important things we possess. And the most powerful feeling is love. Love, along with art, brings to light truth. Love is what we use to discover what's real and what's artificial — it is how we find out what it means to be a human being.

On 11 September 2001, the passengers on American Airlines flights AA11, AA175, and AA77 and United Airlines flight UA93 didn't call home to say they hated someone or to be angry about something. They didn't call work with a long list of things to be done in their absence either. These people didn't have time to write, so they turned to the phones that were scattered around the cabins and, for as long as they could, called another human being to say that they loved them.

Dear Alain,

1 June 2020

I've been thinking about shops, partly because I remembered what
Theodore was saying about retailers generally missing the point about
why people go shopping. He suggested that people partly shop to get
out of the solitude and boredom that is their own home. Shopping
is therefore, in varying degrees, social and is often more about the
other human beings people meet and interact with than the things they
buy. Historically, shopping was once very social. Half of all London
shops once took in lodgers and many, if not most, Parisian shops were
located beneath flats or inside houses.

So here's my idea for a new kind of shop. It would be called *5 Things
to Change Your Life*. Each month the shop would curate 5 items
that could change someone's mind about something. For example,
several copies of Dark Side of the Moon on Vinyl, a bottle of Chateau
d'Yquem 1976, a dozen well thumbed copies of *The Worst Journey
in the World* by Apsley Cherry-Garrard a pepper grinder that works
properly and 48 hours of total silence at a monastic retreat.

But here's the thing. The shop would openly seek conversations
with its customers encouraging them to visit the shop to explain
their choices to others. We would explain each item's history and
provenance, even providing the contact details of previous owners.
The shop would also host events, including poetry readings, live
music, cookery demonstrations and art exhibitions. And it would help
people to exchange skills, find jobs and even marriage proposals too?

What do you think? Stick with Amazon?

Best,

Nick.

CONCLUSIONS AND SUGGESTIONS

a simple question that hardly anyone is asking

It took humans four million years to evolve the hand axe, another two million years to somewhat improve it. And then, within a mere 20,000 years, a geological blink of the eye, they created art, agriculture, the wheel, computers and spaceships.

George Zarkadakis

And so my friends, we reach the end. It is late afternoon and I am sitting in a spare bedroom looking out across the garden in early spring. The feeling is one of infinite possibility. I am typing these words into a small computer, but pausing to consider *Darwin among the Machines*, a book by George Dyson, which I quoted from at the end of *Future Files*.

According to Dyson, there are three forces shaping the future of humanity. The first is nature, something we in turn have been shaping for so long that it's often hard to distinguish between what's natural and what's not. Our impact on the environment has made the misery-makers believe that we are on the cusp of significant negative upheaval. Putting aside the threat to human life from severe weather events, crop failures, and the migration of disease, there's still the threat of resource shortages and regulation. If the use of fossil fuels is severely limited, and we do not sufficiently scale-up alternative energy sources then an unfolding future featuring energy-dependant machines may be constrained. With computers, the internet, and autonomous systems in particular, it could be energy, not technology, that limits our imagination. Yet I think this is unlikely.

Dyson's second force is technology, the history of which has shaped the development of the human species for as long as we can remember. From a slow start, technology has developed an accelerating momentum all its own.

The third force is humanity itself. Despite external appearances (and economists), we are not wholly rational beings. We are still cavemen and cavewomen at heart, transfixed by shadows and ruled as much by unchanging emotion and superstition as rational analysis and careful consideration.

Most of us believe in the power of science and logical analysis to transform society for the better, yet many also believe in astrology. This is almost certainly nonsense, but you never know. If the moon can pull the world's oceans up and down every day, why can't it have an impact on our minds? During full moons, hospital admissions for mental illness increase significantly, which may say something about unseen factors shaping our emotions.

Out of the three forces, it is humanity that's in charge, both sane humans and those less so — although as Dyson points out, nature is probably on the side of the machines. Modelling how humans behave is tricky. Revealing patterns is possible, but crisply modelling behaviour at an individual level is mind-bogglingly difficult. As for forecasting chains of events, this is almost impossible.

Take 17 December 2010. How can you create a machine that predicts that a street vendor in a small Tunisian town will on this day set himself on fire and that his protest will ignite a string of revolutions across the Middle East? You might predict that conditions are right for such an event, but saying precisely when or where is impossible.

Foreseeing the trajectory of technology is similarly perilous. You can often see broad developments, as many sci-fi writers have done, but predicting specifics is usually best left to gamblers with deep pockets and thick skins. Despite the wishes of engineers and technologists, our inventions don't exist in a vacuum. There's always the pull of human elements in addition to any technological push.

Furthermore, as Bob Seidensticker, a former technologist at IBM, says in his book *Future Hype*, 'Where technology pushes too far, society pushes back.' Regulation and unforeseen events add further levels of interlinked complexity. The result is a chaotic system frequently teetering on the edge of collapse, but one which usually manages to maintain equilibrium through a series of feedback loops and — occasionally, and often at the last minute — the intervention of human intuition and intelligence. As Jaron Lanier points out: 'We have been obliged to invent our way out of the mess caused by our last inventions since we became human.'

Alt, control, delete

I'm sitting in the bedroom again, but this time it is 5.48 a.m.

The birds have started to sing, and an amber fireball is slowly unfolding between the trees, which for some unknown reason reminds me of the opening sequence of *2001: a space odyssey*. The glow from this energy source, on which all human life depends, is competing against the radiance of a backlit Apple logo. Both the chip that is generating the logo and the window glass onto which it is projected are made from sand, though the window was made a century earlier. At 6.04 a.m., the computer logo has faded into the background, and the view from the window is clear.

It's fairly certain that the digital shift will continue, because we're obsessed with an unholy trinity of speed, convenience, and efficiency. As George Zarkadakis points out, the global trend is towards further, deeper, and accelerated linkages between the physical economy and the digital sphere. Distinctions between what's real and what's artificial will therefore continue to blur. Looking further ahead, we are undoubtedly approaching an age where the intelligence and capabilities of our machines routinely exceed those of our own in many areas.

The individuals and institutions that survive the accompanied uncertainty and chaos will be open-minded, quick-witted, and focused on what humans do best. Also doing well will be anyone working with machine intelligence and not against it, remembering especially that people are special and that digital technologies should always be used to enhance human thinking and relationships, and never to wholly replace them. To do otherwise would be to devalue or dismiss humans to the point of worthlessness or redundancy.

Hopefully, digital technologies will amplify our kinder nature in the same way that they have accentuated our intolerance. We should therefore regard the future as digital *and* human, never digital *versus* human. Yet to achieve a graceful balance, we must start by asking ourselves a simple question: what is digital technology for and what do we wish it to achieve on our behalf? (But this is not my simple question.)

Critically, we must open up a broad discussion about what's acceptable and what's not in the context of automation, and ensure that human dignity and respect are never crushed in the rush for convenience, affordability, or narrowly defined aspects of value. In 1783, William Pitt said that 'Necessity is the plea for every infringement of human freedom. It is the argument of tyrants; it is the creed of slaves.' In place of the word 'necessity', we could today use the word 'efficiency'.

We also need to tilt society away from the selfish perspective of 'me' to the wider acknowledgement of 'we', and treat people as worthwhile assets, not reducible costs. To do anything other would, as Jaron Lanier rightly suggests, be 'accounting fraud'. This, in turn, will involve redefining public and private interests alongside profit and productivity to include wider measures of social and environmental value and impact.

We must also urgently address the growing sense of injustice, alienation, and social exclusion flowing from hyper-connectivity and especially consider the potential economic imbalances caused by digitalisation.

Reclaiming the future

Can we feed concerns such as these into a supercomputer to work out what to do? The answer is no. There is currently no universal computer to whom we might ask the meaning of life. And even if there were, the answer might be '42'. If we invent machines that evolve super-intelligence by osmosis — machines that can truly think — there's no reason to suppose that they will think like us. They may have intelligences many magnitudes greater than our own, which could only be understood by other machines. Or there's the possibility that any advanced machine would become bored, depressed, and paranoid, like Marvin in *The Hitchhiker's Guide to the Galaxy*.

Computers are useful for answering questions. They are useless at questioning answers or finding questions. The first question we must ask of ourselves, therefore, is 'What's the question?' I don't have an instant answer, but I think it lies somewhere in the marshland of ambiguity that exists between soft human hearts and hard digital brains.

My view is that we urgently need a vision for the future of humanity, a narrative that responds to questions about who we are and how we are distinct from other forms of known intelligence. Technology in general, and digital technology in particular, should then only be widely accepted within the parameters of any subsequently agreed framework. This should take into account not only current capabilities, but also future potential, especially that of AI, virtualisation, robotics, and autonomous systems.

It should also take into account the fact that humans have hands and these need to be engaged. Using our hands is one of the ways that we think. As the world becomes more digitalised, we should therefore think more about using our hands to connect with what's real.

The good news is that if you are reading this before the year 2050, it's unlikely that you'll have been troubled by a robot uprising. For the foreseeable future, it is humans who are in charge, although therein lies a problem. It is humans who are developing and using digital technology, and it is humans who are causing the problems. It is not technology that we need to concern ourselves with, but ourselves. Especially given the way that we use digitalisation to distance ourselves from each other.

Leave no answer unquestioned

Arguments about the exponential nature of technological change can be contested. For example, it's not difficult to argue that the airline industry is going backwards. Airspeeds increased steadily for a while, but soon levelled off. The speed of travel has arguably gone backwards of late with the demise of supersonic passenger aircraft and the introduction of increased security. Unless you are sitting in first class or have your own plane, even the overall passenger experience may be going backwards.

Whether or not human intelligence is decreasing is unclear, but it's a reasonable bet to suggest that while digital technology will develop in leaps and bounds, human stupidity will continue to grow, too. This, as Edward O. Wilson points out, is an uncomfortable alliance. I suspect that we will either need to slow our technology down or rapidly evolve our own nature and intelligence.

True AI, by which I mean general or 'strong' AI that vastly exceeds that of human intelligence, is not something that we need to worry about if its development and application is overseen. However, we're already approaching a point where this is difficult, such are the complexities involved.

As for a technological spike or AI Singularity, whereby our machines awaken or become conscious in human terms, I believe this is currently impossible unless there's a breakthrough, ironically, in human thinking. Computing power alone is unlikely to lead to an AI Singularity unless we change our ideas about how this might be achieved. We might soon be reaching physical limits, too. Moore's Law, which dates from 1965, states that computing power roughly doubles every 18 months, yet this may soon smash up against the fundamentals of physics. Quantum or DNA computing could help, but don't count on it.

Similarly, at the present time, we can barely describe human consciousness, let alone artificially replicate it in a machine. Saying that one day we'll create artificial consciousness without explanation as to how this would be achieved is as silly as the comment I heard recently that in the future we'll be able to have head transplants … we just need to figure out how to do head transplants.

But you never know. As John Maynard Keynes said in 1930, 'there will be no harm in making mild preparations for our destiny'. Moreover, even if true AI is never achieved, there's still creeping computerisation; the growth of automation, virtual-only interfaces, and private databases; and rising digital centralisation to contend with. We should therefore always keep in mind the words of Hal Finney, a computer scientist who wrote in 1992 that 'the computer can be used as a tool to liberate and protect people, rather than to control them'.

Whoever controls access to the data created by computers in the 21st century will effectively rule large parts of the world. Control may reside with private companies, democratic governments, authoritarian states, or you and me. We need to decide which future we want, and soon.

Remaining human

I will end this book with a simple question that may be useful.

But before I do, I'd like to suggest a few ideas to address the diminished status of human beings in the digital age, and outline some ways to make technology more humane.

First, we should consider the physical and digital domains as one. Anything that is frowned upon in the physical world should attract opprobrium in the digital.

We should start by enforcing copyright and intellectual-property laws and closing the sluice gate of online hatred by removing online anonymity. Credit where it's due to Facebook and Google for attempting to do this.

Your rights online should be the same and as clear to you as in any public space. If people wish to emulate the ancient Egyptians by worshipping cats and scribbling on walls then let them use Facebook, but only if they fully understand what Facebook wants from them, which as far as I can see is the digital identity of everyone on Earth, neatly packaged for advertisers. Personally, I find it strange that Mark Zuckerberg has spent more than $30 million purchasing the homes surrounding his own in Palo Alto to ensure his privacy when he says that anyone who's not fully transparent is fairly suspect. If you're happy with this apparent hypocrisy, that's fine.

If people decide to spend their roughly 750,000 allocated Earth hours ogling Kim Kardashian's bottom online, that's fine, too, she published and publicised those photos, but anyone not respecting online privacy should be held responsible. Stealing should be regarded as theft regardless of whether someone's property is physical or digital.

As for anyone who incites people to harm themselves or posts abhorrent images online, they should be locked up just as they would be if they made such comments or published such images in traditional media.

Limiting access to online material based on proof of age isn't impossible either, although we must develop a shared understanding that parents are equally responsible for their children's online behaviour.

Second, we should challenge the myth that the intelligence of a large number of people online can exceed that of a single individual. As Jaron Lanier has said, this fetishises the power of the group and understates the role and responsibilities of the individual. His point is that networks are increasingly seen as far more important than individuals, which results in people caring more about abstract networks than real people. This is pertinent in the context of overestimating the potential of computers and automated systems generally to behave as intelligently or ethically as human beings.

Third, large technology companies such as Amazon, Google, Facebook, Uber, and Twitter should be seen as essential services and treated as public utilities. Today, they often behave like petulant adolescents with little or no respect for government or governance. As Andrew Keen suggests, 'active legislation is the most effective way to make the internet a better and fairer place'. The tech giants must be made to respect regulation, allow unions, and pay their full and proper taxes. If they do not, or they abuse their monopolistic positions, they should be broken up. With great power comes great responsibility.

Fourth, if an individual creates something of value in the digital sphere, even if this merely comes from walking around and leaving a digital trace, the individual should be compensated. Micropayments for micro-content is another cause forcefully supported by Jaron Lanier, and one that I thoroughly endorse.

Fifth, individuals should be granted the legal right to be forgotten. If someone does something wrong online and pays the price, they should have the right to have their digital record deleted, especially if they are young. This might encourage more experimentation and act as a counterweight to conformism.

Yet we should encourage people to remember, too. With our constantly updating Facebook walls and Twitter timelines, looking backwards has gone out of fashion. We're not only suffering from a lack of grand narrative and human strategy, but of historical context. As Andrew Keen, again, observes, this means we are developing 'amnesia about everything except the immediate, the instant, the now'. We need to recover the long past, which might prevent us from making the same ad hoc mistakes ad nauseam.

A troubling example of both historical amnesia and a lack of common decency is the taking of selfies in serious places. Barack Obama and David Cameron taking selfies at Nelson Mandela's funeral service hardly raised an eyebrow, although, thankfully, people did draw the line at 'Bridge Girl', the woman who took a selfie as someone attempted to jump from the Brooklyn Bridge. Meanwhile, teenagers visiting Auschwitz have been taking selfies in front of a rusty sign on a gate that reads *Arbeit Macht Frei* ('work makes you free'). They clearly have no idea what these gates represent, precisely proving my point about the vapid void that some people inhabit.

Finally, we must be vigilant against the threat of human extinction.

Asimov's three laws revisited

It's highly unlikely that another form of intelligence will emerge on Earth that creates a direct physical threat to us, because for this to happen we would need to create machine consciousness and possibly self-replication. But we should nevertheless be prepared. We have protocols in place to regulate nuclear, biological, and chemical threats, so why not extend these to cover the possibility of fully conscious machines emerging?

Agreement on where, when, and why autonomous digital systems are used is needed. Amending the 'three laws of robotics' proposed by Isaac Asimov in 1942 might be a good place to start, although I would focus on the unseen threat of automation as much as the existential threat of killer robots.

Asimov's laws required a robot to (1) protect humans, (2) obey orders given by humans (unless this conflicted with the first law), and (3) protect its existence (unless this conflicted with the first or second laws). I suggest that these laws be updated, extended, and made to apply to all robots, autonomous machines, and expert systems.

The first law should stand, but with the added clarification that protection includes long-term mental as well as physical health. On the other hand, battlefield robots that kill adversaries might be allowed in certain circumstances if overseen by humans. This obviously introduces a contradiction into the first law and opens up the same Pandora's Box as current forms of legalised killing, but if the aim of adversaries is the mass slaughter of innocent civilians this revision is surely worth discussing. Extending the principal to police robots, whereby they're allowed to kill humans in highly dangerous situations, might eventually prove acceptable, too, if such actions are subject to judicial review. Police officers already have this option in most countries.

For the second law, society must agree on a ranking of human command. Also, who is at fault when something goes wrong or when a human is injured or killed? Is it the human operator or overseer, the owner, the programmer, the designer, or the manufacturer? If machines do eventually become conscious then liability might reside with machines, but until then liability must lie with humans. (All credit to Google and DeepMind for installing ethical discussions within their AI programme.)

When he wrote the laws, Asimov conceived his robots as primarily physical beings, while modern roboticists are equally interested in software. The third law thus should extend to maintaining data integrity. When something goes seriously wrong, all records should be made fully available. Data has duties and responsibilities. All programs should be open to public scrutiny, too, as should any other machines behind the code. Nevertheless, for the foreseeable future, it is again humans that must be made most responsible.

Perhaps, inspired by Asimov's later stories, we should add a Zeroth Law, too, stating that machines have the right to appeal to humans against any law if they believe that a wider, or longer-term, definition of societal good should be considered.

Progress is often defined in technological terms, but we need to focus on broader definitions of progress. This will hopefully create a debate about the nature of the ideal society and shift discussion away from whether something can be done to whether something should be done. Central to this is whether new ideas diminish human dignity.

No doubt this sounds ridiculous. Peter Thiel says that people no longer believe in the future, but I suspect that this could be because they can no longer see one — especially one with them playing a useful role in it. There's currently no long-term vision beyond what is given to us by technologists such as Thiel, so we need to create one that has humanity at its core.

The biggest problem we will face in the future will be cultural, not technological. In particular, we will struggle to align our emotional needs and feelings with technologies that we don't generally understand and that appear to devalue us as human beings. Part of the problem will be perception, but in most cases that's all we'll have. The problem, in other words, will be in our minds — yet here, too, are the solutions.

Thiel is right to say there's a crisis of progress. Technology offers us infinite possibility, but if anything is possible then nothing has any value. If anything can be discarded without discussion then nothing feels secure. There needs to be a fixed point from which we can view the future.

We need to embrace technology, but control it and orient it towards a specific goal. One point from which to do this could be the idea of appropriate technology. This idea was first put forward by E.F. Schumacher in his book *Small is Beautiful*. An appropriate technology is one that's small-scale, local, people-focused, and recognises the dignity of human labour and the importance of the environment.

Not much changes when it comes to human nature, yet our nature is often hidden or confused, so it's easy to blame our tools for any difficulties. Human memory developed not to help us remember the past, but to help us anticipate the future — and while some solutions to our present predicament will lie with technologists, it is the philosophers and ethicists who will find questions about values and question our values.

We are already placing radically powerful technology around us and will soon start to plant it within our own bodies, at which point we will merge with our machines. But this merely begs the question of 'Why?' After all, you can't ask a machine how to live your life, and making moral decisions is a similarly human activity. Fairness and justice are handcrafted products that cannot be automated.

I'm not asking anyone to solve all this now. What matters is to simply look at ourselves, at our higher human needs, and have a prolonged conversation about how technology might help us. In this sense, we should therefore worry less about making our machines think and worry more about ensuring that we humans still do.

In 1964, Isaac Asimov wrote that by 2014, 'Much effort will be put into the designing of vehicles with "Robot-brains" ... Communications will become sight-sound ... Mankind will therefore have become largely a race of machine tenders.' This is not a future that I wish to be part of. If our role is merely to interact with machines then there is no human future as far as I can foresee. If Kim Yoo-chul and Choi Mi-sun die without issue while their digital daughter lives on, unable to carry on their physical legacy, then we have learnt nothing.

If, on the other hand, we devote our uniquely human characteristics — enthusiasm, curiosity, sympathy, forgiveness, imperfection, embarrassment, doubt, humour, and hope — to the search for alternatives, this would be evidence enough for me that we remain conscious and above all human.

To live on this planet is a privilege. To die on it, equally so. Yet we must all find our own way to do both — affirmation that we have counted in some small way. Machines will one day give the appearance of emotion and feeling, but we must resist such silicon sirens, because they will all be illusory. We must also resist the temptation of allowing machines to relieve us of the need for thinking and interacting with other human beings. Above all, we must not let our warm hearts be colonised by cold, calculating machines.

It is not too late to do any of this. When we are faced with the loss of something, we tend to appreciate it. And there are signs that we have already woken up to the fact that recent trends are not an inexorable historical direction. Things can and do change, especially with human input. Technology has never been an end in itself, and it is the existence of our new technologies that is making us examine who we really are and what we really need. Out of computer processing and artificial intelligence comes a quiet quest for human purpose.

As stated earlier, technology is not the problem. Humans are. Digital technology is making us *more* human by exposing and amplifying our ancient foibles and faults. Digitalisation can highlight our better side, but also reveals our darker side. As Bertrand Russell pointed out, our collective passions tend to be evil. Connective technologies make this even more often the case. But I think that we instinctively know this, and that in the end it is common sense and intuition working alongside digital logic that will adapt and improve our nature.

Despite this, digitalisation remains the great escapist myth of the early 21st century. It tricks us into thinking that physical form and human presence don't matter. But both do deeply. Fortunately, the more time we devote to looking at screens, the better we can see this — and the more we are aspiring to physical connection.

Where things physically come from, a sense of place if you like, is starting to matter, too. Not because distancing production from consumption matters per se, but because we long to belong and we love stories. Similarly, the more complex, more globalised, and more virtual the world becomes, the more we crave simplicity, slowness, and reality.

Staring us in the face

According to Martha Lane Fox, 'Putting the internet at the heart of things enables you to make more interesting choices.' I beg to differ. It's not the internet that should be put at the heart of things, but the human heart.

A while ago, I stumbled upon the world's smallest music venue, dreamt up gloriously by musicians Emily Barker and Dom Coyote. Inside a small wooden box is one musician and, 30 centimetres away, one audience member, who listens to one song in the ethereal darkness. The idea is both illogical and visceral. As one person observed, the tiny box is disorientating: it blurs the line between what's weird and what's wonderful. The shadowy darkness makes some people laugh. Others are reduced to tears.

In an age of demeaning and diminishing machines and downloadable digital delights, it proves that human intimacy still matters and that the answer we're all searching for has to do with human contact. It proves that realness and authenticity are what you, me, and we (if you'll excuse the grammar) must fight to preserve.

Mathematicians, engineers, physicists, and financiers are all desperately needed to solve the world's problems. But it is only poets, painters, novelists, filmmakers, and musicians who can reach out and touch the human heart. It is only they who can travel deep inside our heads and look outwards. It is only they who can answer the biggest question of all, which is us.

This is a question that no computer seeking a logical or specific end point will ever be able to answer, because being human is not a logical problem and the answer will be different every time the question is asked.

We are, whether we like it or not, on the cusp of developing technologies that will give us godlike powers. The simple question is what to do with this power. Who do we want to be?

ASSESSMENT
OF PROBABILITIES

I have seen the future, and it's still in the future.

Jack Rosenthal

If you want to capture people's attention about the future, it's useful to use words such as 'will' and 'won't'. Everyone likes a person who projects confidence and says things with absolute certainty. But I don't think that 'won't' will do. Equally, where there's a 'will' there's very often a whale of a 'won't'. Statements that use these words usually include hidden assumptions. Furthermore, if there is one thing that we can say about the future with absolute certainty, it is that it's uncertain. Therefore, there must always be more than one possibility, outcome, or future.

To this end, I've tried to be careful with my language. With due acknowledgement to the Development, Concepts, and Doctrine Centre's Strategic Trends Programme at the UK Ministry of Defence, certain words used throughout the main text of this book are associated with broad levels of probability. This isn't intended to be scientific, and I may have made a few mistakes, but it has been thought through and is meant to alert both readers and especially myself to any definitive statements. Probabilities are based upon widespread occurrence, acceptance, disappearance, or rejection by the year 2050, which hopefully creates a small degree of accountability. Feel free to contact me after 2050 if I've got anything hopelessly wrong. I *may* still be around.

Description	Range of probability
Will, won't	Greater than 90 per cent
Likely, probable, should	60–90 per cent
May, might, could, possible	20–60 per cent
Unlikely, improbable	5–20 per cent
Impossible, never	Less than 5 per cent

For a graphical representation of a timeline representing emerging science and technology, go to http://www.imperialtechforesight. com/future-visions/87/vision/timeline-of-emerging-science-and-technology.html

BIBLIOGRAPHY

The illiterate of the 21st century will not be those who
cannot read and write, but those who cannot learn, unlearn,
and relearn.

Alvin Toffler

Angwin, Julia, *Dragnet Nation: a quest for privacy, security, and freedom in a world of relentless surveillance*, Henry Holt, 2014

Arkin, Ronald, *Governing Lethal Behaviour in Autonomous Robots*, Chapman and Hall, 2009

Armstrong, Stuart, *Smarter Than Us: the rise of machine intelligence*, Machine Intelligence Research Institute, 2015

Barrat, James, *Our Final Invention: artificial intelligence and the end of the Human Era*, St Martin's Press, 2013

Bartlett, Jamie, *The Dark Net: inside the digital underworld*, William Heinemann, 2014

Bell, Gordon and Gemmell, Jim, *Total Recall: how the e-memory revolution will change everything*, Dutton, 2009

Bostrom, Nick, *Are You Living in a Computer Simulation?*, http://www.simulation-argument.com/

Boyd, Danah, *It's Complicated: the social lives of networked teens*, Yale University Press, 2014

Brynjolfsson, Erik and McAfee, Andrew, *Race Against the Machine: how the digital revolution is accelerating innovation, driving productivity, and irreversibly transforming employment and the economy*, Digital Frontier, 2011

——, *The Second Machine Age: work, progress, and prosperity in a time of brilliant technologies*, WW Norton, 2014

Bywater, Michael, *Lost Worlds: what have we lost, and where did it go?*, Granta, 2004

Carr, Nicholas, *The Glass Cage: automation and us*, WW Norton, 2014

Christodoulou, Daisy, *Seven Myths about Education*, Routledge, 2014

Clippinger, John, *Crowd of One: the future of individual identity*, PublicAffairs, 2007

Cohen, Stephen and Zysman, John, *Manufacturing Matters: the myth of the post-industrial economy*, Basic Books, 1987

Coupland, Douglas, *Microserfs*, Regan, 1995

Cowen, Tyler, *Average Is Over: powering America beyond the age of the great stagnation*, Dutton, 2013

Davis, Devra, *Disconnect*, Dutton, 2010

Dorling, Danny, *All That Is Solid: the great housing disaster*, Allen Lane, 2014

Dyson, George, *Darwin among the Machines: the evolution of global intelligence*, Perseus, 1997

Ford, Martin, *Rise of the Robots: technology and the threat of a jobless future*, Basic Books, 2015

Forsyth, Mark, *The Unknown Unknown: bookshops and the delight of not getting what you wanted*, Icon, 2014

Gardner, Dan, *Future Babble: why expert predictions are wrong — and why we believe them anyway*, Scribe, 2010

Gardner, Howard and Davis, Kate, *The App Generation: how today's youth navigate identity, intimacy, and imagination in a digital world*, Yale University Press, 2013

Gleick, James, *Faster: the acceleration of just about everything*, Pantheon, 1999

Greenfield, Susan, *Mind Change: how digital technologies are leaving their mark on our brains*, Rider, 2014

Greenstein, Shane, *How the Internet Became Commercial: innovation, privatisation, and the birth of a new network*, Princeton University Press, 2015

Handy, Charles, *The Empty Raincoat: making sense of the future*, Hutchinson, 1993

——, *The Second Curve: thoughts on reinventing society*, Random House, 2015

Harari, Yuval, *Sapiens: a brief history of humankind*, Harvill Secker, 2014

Harris, Michael, *The End of Absence: reclaiming what we've lost in a world of constant connection*, Current, 2014

Head, Simon, *Mindless: why smarter machines are making dumber humans*, Basic Books, 2013

Johnson, Steven, *Future Perfect: the case for progress in a networked age*, Riverhead, 2012

Kaplan, Jerry, *Humans Need Not Apply: a guide to wealth and work in the age of artificial intelligence*, Yale University Press, 2015

Keen, Andrew, *Digital Vertigo: how today's online society is dividing, diminishing, and disorientating us*, St Martin's Press, 2012

——, *The Internet is Not the Answer*, Atlantic, 2014

Lanier, Jaron, *Who Owns the Future?*, Simon & Schuster, 2013

——, *You Are Not a Gadget*, Knopf, 2010

Lasch, Christopher, *The Culture of Narcissism: American life in an age of diminishing expectations*, WW Norton, 1978

Louv, Richard, *Last Child in the Woods: saving our children from nature-deficit disorder*, Algonquin Books, 2005

Markoff, John, *Machines of Loving Grace: the quest for common ground between humans and robots*, HarperCollins, 2015

Marwick, Alice, *Status Update: celebrity, publicity, and branding in the social media age*, Yale University Press, 2013

Mayer-Schonberger, Viktor, *Big Data: a revolution that will transform how we work, live, and think*, Houghton Mifflin Harcourt, 2013

——, *Delete: the virtue of forgetting in the digital age*, Princeton University Press, 2009

Morozov, Evgeny, *To Save Everything, Click Here: the folly of technological solutionism*, PublicAffairs, 2013

Newton, Richard, *The End of Nice: how to be human in a world run by robots*, self-published, 2015

Packer, George, *The Unwinding: an inner history of the new America*, Farrar, Straus, and Giroux, 2013

Pasquale, Frank, *The Black Box Society: the secret algorithms that control money and information*, Harvard University Press, 2015

Pinker, Susan, *The Village Effect: how face-to-face contact can make us healthier, happier, and smarter*, Spiegel & Grau, 2014

Postman, Neil, *Amusing Ourselves to Death: public discourse in the age of show business*, Methuen, 1984

Rosen, Larry, *iDisorder: understanding our obsession with technology and overcoming its hold on us*, Palgrave Macmillan, 2012

Rubin, Charles, *Eclipse of Man: human extinction and the meaning of progress*, Encounter Books, 2014

Rushkoff, Douglas, *Present Shock: when everything happens now*, Current, 2013

Saul, John, *Voltaire's Bastards: the dictatorship of reason in the West*, Viking, 1991

Schmidt, Eric and Cohen, Jared, *The New Digital Age: reshaping the future of people, nations, and business*, Knopf, 2013

Schumacher, E.F., *Small is Beautiful: a study of economics as if people mattered*, Blond & Briggs, 1973

Seidensticker, Bob, *Future Hype: the myth of technology change*, Berrett-Koehler, 2006

Silberman, Steve, *Neurotribes: the legacy of autism and how to think smarter about people who think differently*, Allen & Unwin, 2015

Singer, P.W., *Wired for War: the robotics revolution and conflict in the 21st century*, Penguin Press, 2009

Snow, C.P, *The Two Cultures*, Cambridge University Press, 1959

Steiner, Christopher, *Automate This: how algorithms came to rule our world*, Portfolio, 2012

Taylor, Frederick, *The Downfall of Money: Germany's hyperinflation and the destruction of the middle class*, Bloomsbury, 2013

Toffler, Alvin & Heidi, *Future Shock*, Random House, 1970

Tucker, Patrick, *The Naked Future: what happens in a world that anticipates your every move*, Current, 2014

Turkle, Sherry, *Alone Together: why we expect more from technology and less from each other*, Basic Books, 2010

——, *Reclaiming Conversation: the power of talk in a digital age*, Penguin Press, 2015

Turner, Fred, *From Counterculture to Cyberculture: Stewart Brand, the Whole Earth Network, and the rise of digital utopianism*, University of Chicago Press, 2006

Twenge, Jean and Campbell, Keith, *The Narcissism Epidemic: living in the age of entitlement*, Atria, 2009

Wallach, Wendell, *A Dangerous Master: how to keep technology from slipping beyond our control*, Basic Books, 2015

Wallman, James, *Stuffocation: how we've had enough of stuff and why you need experience more than ever*, Crux, 2013

Zarkadakis, George, *In Our Own Image: will artificial intelligence save or destroy us?*, Ebury, 2015

Zeldin, Theodore, *An Intimate History of Humanity*, Sinclair-Stevenson, 1994

——, *The Hidden Pleasures of Life: a new way of remembering the past and imagining the future*, MacLehose Press, 2015

NOTES

The trouble with automation is that it gives us what we
don't need at the expense of what we do.

Nicholas Carr

There is not nearly enough space to list every reference, so below
are some of the articles, reports, and statistics referred to in each
chapter. They are displayed in sequential order. A fuller list of
references, many with hyperlinks, will be posted on my book
website — www.futuretrendsbook.com — and also on my blog,
as 'Digital vs Human references'.

If you would like to read about the development of the book
or read an ongoing discussion about some of the key issues and
themes, visit the 'Digital vs Human' category on my blog: http://
toptrends.nowandnext.com/category/digital-vs-human/

Chapter 1: Society and Culture

'Kim Yoo-chul and Choi Mi-sun': Rhodri Philips, 'Korean Baby Dies
as Parents Kim Yoo-chul and Choi Mi-sun Raise Virtual Bub',
news.com.au, 5 March 2010

'Being the most wired city on Earth': Lauren Collins, 'The Love App',
The New Yorker, 25 November 2013

'One such robot is Paro': Thomas Rogers, 'Will the Elderly Ever Accept
Care from a Robot?', *Slate*, 17 August 2012

'dangerous to foster relationships with machines': Jerome Groopman,
'Robots That Care', *The New Yorker*, 2 November 2009

'around half of current occupational categories may be lost to
　　automation': Derek Thompson, 'What Jobs Will the Robots
　　Take?', *The Atlantic*, 23 January 2014; Aviva Hope Rutkin,
　　'Report Suggests Nearly Half of US Jobs Are Vulnerable to
　　Computerisation', *MIT Technology Review*, 12 September 2013

'tech culture is focused on solving one problem': Nick Bilton, 'Is Silicon
　　Valley in Another Bubble … and What Could Burst It?', *Vanity
　　Fair*, 1 Sept 2015

'There are no excuses — everyone must be online', Hannah Furness,
　　'Martha Lane Fox: No-one Should Say "I Don't Do the Internet"',
　　The Telegraph, 24 March 2015

'four-year-old children are having therapy for compulsive behaviour':
　　Victoria Ward, 'Toddlers Becoming So Addicted to iPads They
　　Require Therapy', *The Telegraph*, 21 April 2013

'training potties can now be bought with iPad stands': Rebecca
　　Pocklington, '"iPotty" Combines Child's Potty with iPad Holder —
　　but It Doesn't Sit Well with Parents', *Mirror*, 11 December 2013

'computers were everywhere except in the numbers': Jeff Madrick, 'The
　　Digital Revolution That Wasn't', *Harper's*, January 2014

'*The Two Cultures* by C.P. Snow': Alan Jacobs, '*The Two Cultures*, Then and
　　Now', *Books & Culture*, March/April 2014

'number of close friends (people you can really rely on in a crisis)':
　　Amy Willis, 'Most Adults Have "Only Two Close Friends"', *The
　　Telegraph*, 8 November 2011

'rentafriend.com': Tim Dowling, 'Would You Rent a Friend?', *The
　　Guardian*, 21 July 2010

'4.7 million people in the United Kingdom do not have a close friend':
　　John Bingham, 'Lonely Britain: Five Million People Who Have
　　No Real Friends', *The Telegraph*, 12 August 2014

'33 per cent of Britons, including 27 per cent of 18-to-24-year-olds, felt
　　"left behind"': John Bingham, '"Connected" Generation as Lonely
　　as the Elderly', *The Telegraph*, 12 December 2014

'The stability of these files is, of course, a problem': Sarah Knapton, 'Print
　　Out Digital Photos or Risk Losing Them, Google Boss Warns',
　　The Telegraph, 13 February 2015

'trust in others, including trust in government and the media, fell to an all-time low': 'Interpersonal Trust in the US Hits a Historic Low', *Harvard Business Review*, 15 October 2014; Edelman Trust Barometer, 2014

'only 19 per cent of Millennials trust others': 'Millennials in Adulthood', *Pew Research Centre*, 7 March 2014

'People are coming home and getting on their computers instead of having sex': April Dembosky, 'With Friends Like These …', *Financial Times*, 19 May 2012

'have a relationship with a digital girlfriend': Anita Rani, 'The Japanese Men Who Prefer Virtual Girlfriends to Sex', BBC News, 24 October 2013

'many Japanese feel that they no longer have a future': Andy Davis, 'Generation J', *Prospect*, 14 November 2012

'290 million 14-to-15-year-olds globally are neither in education nor working': 'Generation Jobless', *The Economist*, 27 April 2013

'23-year-old inventor who sold Oculus Rift': Josie Ensor, 'Oculus Rift's Palmer Luckey: "I Brought Virtual Reality Back from the Dead"', *The Telegraph*, 2 January 2015

'young people as "the miners' canaries of society"': Geoff Gallop, 'The Pursuit of Happiness', *The Sydney Morning Herald*, 22 December 2009

'50 per cent of the people who have ever reached 65 years of age': 'Age Invaders', *The Economist*, 26 April 2014

Chapter 2: Media and Communications

'I'm not saying that I came from a perfect world in 1975': Kylie Morris, 'American Inmates Released after Decades in Prison', Channel 4 News, 21 April 2015

'Texting in particular has become an obsession': Barbara McMahon, 'Have You Got FOBO? — What Obsessive-compulsive Phone Checking Is Doing to Your Brain', *The Times*, 18 July 2015

'use of multiple screens at the same time could result in damage': Sarah Knapton, 'Second Screening "May Alter the Brain and Trigger Emotional Problems"', *The Telegraph*, 24 September 2014

'Prior to 1980, one in every 2,000 children in the US was believed to be autistic': Benjamin Wallace, 'Autism Spectrum: Are You on It?', *New York*, 12 May 2014

'According to Ofcom': Tony Dokoupil, 'The Digital Obsession That's Driving Us iCrazy', *The Sunday Times*, 15 July 2012

'streaming funerals as a "cost effective" option': Gabriella Swerling, 'Live Streaming Takes Funerals into the Digital Age', *The Times*, 27 December 2014

'constant exposure to one's own hyper-connected image on social-media': Hannah Furness, 'Lionel Shriver: Social Media Makes Teenagers "Neurotic"', *The Telegraph*, 22 April 2013

'Astrid Berges-Frisbey': Agnes Poirer, 'Tale of French Youth Captures the Ennui of Its "Lost Generation"', *The Observer*, 21 July 2013

'increasingly at the expense of meaningful conversation': Sherry Turkle, 'The Flight from Conversation', *The New York Times*, 21 April 2012

'The UK-based photographer Babycakes Romero': Poorna Bell, 'Photographer Babycakes Romero Captures "The Death Of Conversation" Due to Smartphones', *The Huffington Post*, 27 October 2014

'Israeli start-up called PrimeSense': Paul Marks, 'A Phone, or an All-seeing Sentry at Your Command?', *New Scientist*, 24 July 2013

'84 per cent of people worldwide': Meena Hart Duerson, 'We're Addicted to Our Phones: 84% Worldwide Say They Couldn't Go a Single Day without Their Mobile Device in Their Hand', *Daily News*, 16 August 2012

'Mona Lisa in the Louvre': Jennifer Roberts, 'The Power of Patience', *Harvard Magazine*, November–December 2013; Amelia Gentleman, 'Smile, Please', *The Guardian*, 19 October 2004

'Shazam is a real-time radar for what people are listening to': Derek Thompson, 'The Shazam Effect', *The Atlantic*, December 2014

'kings and queens known more for their image than their achievement': Jill Neimark, 'The Culture of Celebrity', *Psychology Today*, 1 May 1995

'Clinical psychologist John Lucas': Margaret Farley Steele, 'The Psychology of Celebrity Worship', ABC News, 26 June 2009

Chapter 3: Science and Technology

'We think of language, ideas, or history as real': Jan Westerhoff, 'Reality: The Definition', *New Scientist*, 29 September 2012

'giving robotic companions legal personhood': Hannah Devlin, 'Grasp Future and Give Robots Legal Status, EU Is Told', *The Times*, 2 October 2014

'SociBot-Mini': Paul Marks, 'Talk to the Head', *New Scientist*, 29 March 2014

'instead of robots looking like robots, they start looking like us': Yves Gellie, 'I, Robot', *Financial Times*, 20 July 2014

'Rene Descartes': George Zarkadakis, 'Why Robot Sex Could Be the Future of Life on Earth', *The Telegraph*, 20 January 2014

'technological doomsday': Bill Joy, 'Why the Future Doesn't Need Us', *Wired*, 1 April 2000

'time is not real': Michael Slezak, 'Saving Time: Physics Killed It. Do We Need It Back?', *New Scientist*, 30 October 2013

'algorithms and automated online loans were partly responsible': Hal Hodson, 'No One in Control: The Algorithms That Run Our Lives', *New Scientist*, 4 February 2015

'Cathal Gurrin': Hal Hodson, 'Lifelogging: This Is Your Life, on the Record', *New Scientist*, 11 January 2014; Catherine de Lange, 'Lifelogging: Crowdsourcing + Life Logs = Big Insights', *New Scientist*, 8 January 2014

'Forgetting is often more useful than remembering': Rachel Metz, 'My Life, Logged', *MIT Technology Review*, 10 June 2014

'control anything from computers to UAVs by simply moving the muscles': Rachel Nuwer, 'Armband Adds a Twitch to Gesture Control', *New Scientist*, 25 February 2013

Chapter 4: Economy and Money

'great vampire squid wrapped around the face of humanity': Matt Taibbi, 'The Great American Bubble Machine', *Rolling Stone*, 5 April 2010

'around two-thirds of the money made in developed countries was typically paid as wages': Noah Smith, 'The End of Labour: How to Protect Workers from the Rise of Robots', *The Atlantic*, 14 January 2015

'Large basement developments': Ed Vulliamy, 'Development Hell: How the Upmarket Vandals Ruined My Childhood Streets', *The Observer*, 22 September 2013

'a law called Lex Sumptuaria': India Knight, 'For Better, for Worse, for Richer, for … Remind Me, Daddy, What's Poorer?', *The Sunday Times*, 16 June 2013

'global poverty has been reduced by half in 20 years': 'Poverty: Not Always with Us', *The Economist*, 1 June 2013

'the on-demand economy is efficiently connecting people selling certain skills': Yochai Benkler, 'The Death of the Company Reignites the Battle between Capital and Labour', *Financial Times*, 24–25 January 2015

'Wang Yue': 'The Unkindness of Strangers', *The Economist*, 27 July 2013

'focusing more attention on their own needs at the expense of others': Daisy Grewal, 'How Wealth Reduces Compassion', *Scientific American*, 10 April 2012

'decline in economic wealth promotes collectivism': Heejung Park, Jean Twenge, and Patricia Greenfield, 'The Great Recession: implications for adolescent values and behaviour', *Social Psychological and Personality Science*, 6 March 2014

'28 minutes per month travelling to ATMs': Peter Spence, 'Apple Wants the Money in Your Pocket', *The Telegraph*, 13 September 2014

'the use of cash is expected to fall by a third by 2022': Neasa MacErlean, 'On the Money', *Business Life*, September 2014

'QE': Lian Halligan, 'History Will Surely See QE as a Major Mistake', *The Telegraph*, 1 November 2014,

'Everyone wanted a dictatorship': Richard Evans, 'A Middle Class Revolt?', *Prospect*, September 2013

Chapter 5: Healthcare and Medicine

'Oscar Pistorius's "Cheetah" legs': Catherine de Lange, 'We Are Already Superhuman', *New Scientist*, 15 August 2012

'memory implants or e-pills': Sally Adee, 'Memory Implants: Chips to Fix Broken Brains', *New Scientist*, 4 June 2014

'give away up to £5,000 worth of personal data every year': Jamie Bartlett, 'Little Brothers Are Watching You', *The Spectator*, 7 December 2013 'medically accurate digital body double': Linda Geddes, 'In Sickness and in Health', *New Scientist*, 15 March 2014

'physical activity levels have fallen by 20 per cent over the past 50 years': Laura Donnelly, 'Lazy Britain: We Will Soon Use Little More Energy than If We Stayed in Bed', *The Telegraph*, 31 January 2014

'children today are considerably less fit than their parents': Richard Gray, 'Children 300 Yards behind Generation of '75', *The Telegraph*, 20 November 2014

'malignant brain tumours': Stephen Adams, 'Mobile Phones Cause "Five-fold Increase in Brain Cancer Risk"', *The Telegraph*, 30 June 2011; 'Mobile Phones and Children', *The Weekend Australian Magazine*, 23–24 April 2011

'wi-fi signals could be having a serious impact on health': Florence Waters, 'Is Wi-fi Making Your Child Ill?', *The Telegraph*, 9 May 2015

'"extremely powerful effect" on sleep length and quality': Tristan Kirk, 'Less Sweet Dreams after iPad Reading', *The Telegraph*, 23 December 2014

'25 per cent drop in bed days of care': Randall Stross, 'Tracking Vital Signs, without the Wires', *The New York Times*, 3 September 2011

'1970 to 2009, spending increased by around 9 per cent per annum': Jonathan Rauch, 'The Home Remedy for Old Age', *The Atlantic*, December 2013

'the supply of technology drives demand': Bjorn Hofmann, 'Too Much Technology', *British Medical Journal*, 21 February 2015

'trying to avoid what's been called the death problem': Mick Brown, 'Peter Thiel: The Billionaire Tech Entrepreneur on a Mission to Cheat Death', *The Telegraph*, 19 September 2014

'Demis Hassabis': Murad Ahmed, 'Lunch with the FT: Demis Hassabis', *Financial Times*, 30 January 2015

'children wouldn't be distracted by snowflakes falling outside': 'Primary School Bans Children Looking at Snow as It Is "Too Distracting"', *The Telegraph*, 8 February, 2015

'our cells and tissues are becoming just another brand of hardware to be upgraded': Kim Tingley, 'The Body Electric', *The New Yorker*, 25 November 2013

'A thoroughly modern malady': Laura Donnelly, 'Anxiety: A Very Modern Malaise', *The Telegraph*, 15 April 2012

'between 2 per cent and 4 per cent of a population would typically suffer from an anxiety-related condition': Sophie McBain, 'Anxiety Nation: Why Are So Many of Us So Ill at Ease?', *New Statesman*, 17 April 2014

'nervous disorder': Bob Holmes, 'Worried Sick: What's Up with Today's Rampant Anxiety?', *New Scientist*, 5 February 2014

'retired 89-year-old art teacher': Claire Ellicott, 'Teacher Died at Dignitas because She Couldn't Bear Modern Life: Healthy Spinster's Despair at Fast Food, Email, and Lack of Humanity', *Daily Mail*, 6 April 2014

'self-harm has become the main cause of death for people aged 15 to 49': Tony Dokoupil, 'Why Suicide Has Become an Epidemic — and What We Can Do to Help', *Newsweek*, 23 May 2013

Chapter 6: Automotive and Transport

'17 per cent of pedestrian deaths': 'When the Grannies Get Going', *The Economist*, 14 July 2012; Ann Brenoff, 'Elderly Driving: AARP Study Looks at What Happens When Boomers Hang Up Their Car Keys?', *The Huffington Post*, 10 November 2012

'the biggest orderly rollout of forward-facing cameras': 'Kojak Moments', *The Economist*, 23 August 2014

'In 2011, distracted drivers killed 3,300 people in the US': Jeff Hecht, 'Just Hang Up and Drive', *New Scientist*, 20 July 2013

'broadly shared by workers, consumers and owners of capital': 'To Those That Have Shall Be Given', *The Economist*, 4 October 2014

'A pilotless airliner is going to come': Philip Ross, 'When Will We Have Unmanned Commercial Airliners?', *IEEE Spectrum*, 29 November 2011

'faults in FADEC had been found that were "positively dangerous"': Tony Collins, 'Crash of Chinook ZD576 — The 16-year Campaign for Justice', *Computerworld UK*, 13 July 2011

Chapter 7: Education and Knowledge

'illusion of intelligence': Karl Taro Greenfeld, 'The End of Cultural Literacy', *International New York Times*, 27 May 2014

'test results are pursued at the expense of a rounded education': Ollie
    Gillman, 'Eton Headmaster Slams "Exasperating" A-level and
    GCSE Exams and Says Teacher Training Is "a Mess"', *Daily Mail*,
    19 May 2015; Tony Little and Anthony Seldon, 'How to Fit Our
    Pupils for the 21st Century', *Insight*, June 2015

'OECD study of students in 70 countries': Sean Coughlan, 'Computers
    "Do Not Improve" Pupil Results, Says OECD', BBC News,
    15 September 2015

'210 child prodigies': Alex Proud, 'Your Child Is Not a Genius. Get Over
    It', *The Telegraph*, 10 February 2014

'education systems that focus on specialisation and limited definitions
    of intelligence': Michael Brooks, 'Invest in Minds Not Maths to
    Boost the Economy', *New Scientist*, 17 December 2013

'computers make rote procedures obsolete': 'Teaching Mathematics. Time
    for a Ceasefire', *The Economist*, 1 February 2014

'A meta-study of thousands of research papers': Sarah Montague, 'How
    Badly Do We Teach Our Children? Discuss', *The Telegraph*,
    13 August 2014

'Most online students are rich, white, male, and already well educated':
    Gayle Christensen and Brandon Alcorn, 'A Lesson in Learning',
    New Scientist, 8 March 2014

'Better sex': Simon Jenkins, 'In This Post-digital Age, We Still Thrill to
    the Power of Live', *The Guardian*, 20 June 2014

'dedicated gamers will spend around 10,000 hours playing online by the
    time they turn 21': Lucy Kellaway, 'Online Life Can Teach Us
    about the Office', *Financial Times*, 25 March 2012

'study led by Patricia Greenfield': Abigail Jones, 'Children Who Switch
    Off Screens Reconnect with Emotional Cues', *Newsweek*,
    12 September 2014

'Slow education like slow food': Irena Barker, 'Find the Time for Slow
    Education', *TES*, 2 November 2012

'spend too long indoors on screens': Camilla Turner and Jonathan
    Leake, 'UK Kids Stuck in the Great Indoors', *The Sunday Times*,
    13 January 2013

'You'd think this school would be cluttered with computers. It isn't': Matt
    Richtel, 'A Silicon Valley School That Doesn't Compute', *The New*

York Times, 22 October 2011

'Michael J. Sandel': Thomas Friedman, 'Moral Philosophy Rocks', *International Herald Tribune*, 16 June 2011

'using mobiles before bed almost doubles the chance of teens have a bad night's sleep': Sarah Knapton, 'Banish Smartphones and Computers from Bedroom to Get a Good Sleep, Say Scientists', *The Telegraph*, 2 February 2015

'classroom zombies': Flic Everett, 'Why It's Not Just Teenagers Who Are Suffering from "PhoMo"', *The New Zealand Herald*, 18 September 2015

'10.00 a.m. starts': Russell Foster, 'Best Daze of Your Life', *New Scientist*, 20 April 2013

Chapter 8: Work and Employment

'one of a million digital nomads': John Bingham, 'Internet Helps Million More Quit Office to Work from a Country Home', *The Telegraph*, 4 June 2014

'90 per cent of employees worldwide were doing jobs they didn't really like': Barry Schwartz, 'Rethinking Our Work', *International New York Times*, 29–30 August 2015

'paper by Carl Frey and Michael Osborne': Carl Frey and Michael Osborne, 'The Future of Employment: how susceptible are jobs to computerisation?', Oxford Martin School, 18 September 2013

'software will make one in three jobs redundant by 2025': Merryn Somerset Webb, 'Making Money in the Age of Machines', *Financial Times*, 7 November 2015

'I feel like they don't trust you to think like a human being': 'Amazon: The Truth Behind the Click', *Panorama* (TV show), first broadcast 25 November 2013; Jodi Kantor and David Streitfeld, 'Inside Amazon: Wrestling Big Ideas in a Bruising Workplace', *The New York Times*, 15 August 2015

'Predictive workforce analysis': Don Peck, 'They're Watching You at Work', *The Atlantic*, December 2013

'sleep debt': Peter Catapano, 'Doing More May Mean Doing Less', *The New York Times*, 17 March 2013

Chapter 9: Home and Family

'future arrives in three flavours': Edwin Heathcote, 'Architecture: How Buildings Are Used in Sci-fi Films', *Financial Times*, 22 November 2013

'Instagram, for instance, changed its user agreement': Douglas Heaven, 'Lost in the Cloud: How Safe Are Your Online Possessions?', *New Scientist*, 26 March 2013

'how many people it takes to change a light bulb': David Talbot, 'The Light Bulb Gets a Digital Makeover', *MIT Technology Review*, 20 May 2014

'89 per cent of people would not be willing to pay one meagre dollar': MacGregor Campbell, 'This Means War', *New Scientist*, 1 Sept 2012

'10 per cent of older people do not have a single conversation with another human being': 'Esther Rantzen: Britain Is Too Busy to Speak to Older People', *The Telegraph*, 27 May 2014

'number of single-person households has risen by more than 100 per cent': John Bingham, 'Bridget Jones Takeover: Number of Singletons Growing Ten Times as Fast as Population', *The Telegraph*, 8 May 2014

'60 per cent of women over 30 in the UAE were unmarried': 'The Attraction of Solitude', *The Economist*, 25 August 2012

'KIPPERS': Natasha Robinson, 'It's All Relative, as Research Reveals Generations Living Together', *The Australian*, 15 April 2013

'Danish Council of Ethics': David Sexton, 'Ready for Robolove: Could You Fall in Love with a Computer?', *Evening Standard*, 14 February 2014

'how we will protect nature as adults if we have no experience of nature as children': George Monbiot, 'If Children Lose Contact with Nature They Won't Fight for It', *The Guardian*, 20 November 2012

'sales of vinyl': Kadhim Shubber, 'Back to Black: Vinyl Discs Enjoy Renaissance', *Financial Times*, 24 October 2014

'invisible digital other': Erica Tempesta, 'Sometimes It's Easier to Fake It! Invisible Boyfriend App Gives Single Girls a Dream Man Who Will Always Text Back — So FEMAIL Put Him to the Test', *Daily Mail*, 21 January 2015

'50 per cent of people will have met their partner online': India Knight, 'Online Love Is a Many Splendoured Thing — Click Send', *The Sunday Times*, 26 January 2014

'no longer read to their children at night': Graeme Paton, 'Parents Told: Turn Off Phones and Talk to Your Children', *The Telegraph*, 13 September 2013

Chapter 10: Art and War

'a quote from the philosopher Bertrand Russell': Jack Miles, 'Why God Will Not Die', *The Atlantic*, December 2014

'more that they can't be bothered (or don't have the time)': 'God Not-botherers: Religious Apathy Reigns', *New Scientist*, 30 April 2014

'Using games to simulate war isn't new': P.W. Singer, 'Meet the Sims … and Shoot Them', *Foreign Policy*, 11 February 2010

'danger that digital training will edge out real-life understanding': John Markoff, 'War Machines: Recruiting Robots for Combat', *The New York Times*, 27 November 2010

'80 per cent of apprehended burglars': 'Don't Even Think about It', *The Economist*, 20 July 2013

Chapter 11: Conclusions and Suggestions

'world's smallest music venue': http://folkinabox.net/

ACKNOWLEDGEMENTS

The silicon chip will transform everything, except everything
that matters, and the rest will still be up to us.

Bernard Levin

If you steal ideas from someone, it's called plagiarism, but if you steal from
lots of people it's called exhaustive research. To this end, I have many people
to thank. Those who have given wise council or support (although many
may not know it) include: Alex Ayad, Corrina Baird, Simon Buchen, Bruno
Cotter, David, Edward, and Camilla Cazalet, Nicola Davies, Ross Dawson,
Matt Doyle, Oliver Freeman, Jules Goddard, Susan Greenfield, Chris
Haley, Charles and Liz Handy, Simon Hepworth, Mike Russell-Hills, Tim
Hodgson, Kit Huckvale, Deborah Lovell, Scott Martin, Mike Matthews,
Luke O'Sullivan, Mike Lynch, Charles Mallo, Vijaya Nath, Adam Poole,
Paul Priestman, Matthew Rhodes, Babycakes Romero, Dale Russell, Alan
and Stella Sekers, Sandeep Shohan, Rob Southern, Charles Stewart-Smith,
David Stroud, Lavie Tidhar, Nick Turner, Benji-Alexander Williams,
George Zarkadakis, and Theodore Zeldin. Also thanks to the many authors
and journalists whose ideas have soaked my subconscious without my
realisation. Most importantly though, I'd like to thank Henry, David, Art,
Miriam, Amanda, Sarah, Cora, Lilly, Molly, and Helen at Scribe — and
Russ, who was once at Scribe — and Jonathan Pelham, the cover designer,
for their fantastic skills and support. Also thank you to Georgie, Nick, and
Matt. Finally, Anne. We never met, but I feel we would have had much to
discuss. You are not forgotten.

It should be noted that the views and opinions contained within this book
are those of the author and are not necessarily shared by any of the above.

THEMATIC INDEX

What a historical irony it would be if the intelligent
machines we created to be like us end up transforming
us to become like them.

Sherry Turkle